NAZISM 1919–1945

VOLUME 1

THE RISE TO POWER 1919–1934

EXETER STUDIES IN HISTORY
General Editors: Jonathan Barry, Tim Rees and T.P. Wiseman

Other titles in this series include:

Government, Party and People in Nazi Germany
edited by Jeremy Noakes

Nazism 1919–1945 A Documentary Reader
edited by J. Noakes and G. Pridham
Vol. 1: *The Rise to Power 1919–1934*
Vol. 2: *State, Economy and Society 1933–1939*
Vol. 3: *Foreign Policy, War and Racial Extermination*
Vol. 4: *Germany at War: The Home Front 1939–1945* (forthcoming)

Intelligence and International Relations 1900–1945
edited by Christopher Andrew and Jeremy Noakes

The American Constitution:
The First Two Hundred Years 1787–1987
edited by Joseph Smith

The Failure of Political Extremism in Inter-War Britain
edited by Andrew Thorpe

The Last Years of Austria-Hungary:
Essays in Political and Military History 1908–1918
edited by Mark Cornwall

The Origins of NATO
edited by Joseph Smith

The Civilian in War
edited by Jeremy Noakes

Exeter Studies in History

NAZISM 1919–1945

VOLUME 1
THE RISE TO POWER 1919–1934
A Documentary Reader

EDITED BY

J. NOAKES
AND
G. PRIDHAM

UNIVERSITY
of
EXETER
PRESS

First published in 1983 by
University of Exeter Press
Reed Hall, Streatham Drive
Exeter, Devon EX4 4QR
UK

Reprinted 1986, 1987, 1989, 1991
Reprinted with updated bibliography 1994, 1996

British Library Cataloguing in Publication Data
A catalogue record of this book is available
from the British Library

ISBN 0 85989 472 X

Printed in Great Britain
by BPC Wheatons Ltd, Exeter

Table of Contents

Table of Contents

Preface

This is a considerably revised version of the first two sections of the authors' *Documents on Nazism 1919–1945* (J. Cape London 1974), now out of print. This volume covers the period from the founding of the Nazi Party in 1919 to Hitler's assumption of the office of 'Führer and Reich Chancellor' on 1 August 1934. The documents, drawn from a wide range of sources—official and party documents, memoirs, diaries, letters, and newspapers—are linked with a commentary. This new edition has given us the opportunity to include a new introduction, to present some new documents, and where necessary to revise the commentary in the light of the research of the past decade. To save space we have dispensed with document headings. References to the sources of documents will be found at the back.

We are extremely grateful to Dr Peter Morris for invaluable help with the editing, to Dr Michael Duffy for helpful comments on the manuscript, to Mike Rouillard for designing the cover, and to Ingrid Noakes for help with the translation.

July 1983   J. NOAKES AND G. PRIDHAM

PREFACE TO THE FIFTH IMPRESSION

We have taken the opportunity of this reprint to update the bibliography.

September 1991   J. NOAKES AND G. PRIDHAM

PREFACE TO THE SIXTH AND SEVENTH IMPRESSIONS

Once again we have taken the opportunity of a reprint to update the bibliography.

September 1994 and February 1996   J. NOAKES AND G. PRIDHAM

Introduction

Nazism was as a political movement essentially a product of the First World War, of defeat and of the revolutionary upheaval which followed. Its ideological roots, however, go back to pre-war Germany. They lay, firstly, in the new wave of antisemitism which began with the 'great depression' of 1873–1896; and secondly, in the emergence of a new radical form of right-wing movement which began in the 1890s and found expression in imperialist pressure groups and anti-democratic organisations such as the Pan-German League. Both of these developments were, in turn, responses to the social dislocation produced by the rapid and uneven industrialisation and urbanisation which followed national unification.

Pre-war German antisemitism appealed to those social and economic groups whose lives were being most seriously disrupted by economic and social change. There were peasant farmers who found it difficult both to adjust to the rapid price fluctuations of a full market economy and to adapt their crops to the changing demand patterns created by urban growth; there were artisans under pressure from the cheap mass produced goods pouring from the new factories; and finally, there were small shopkeepers who were confronted with growing competition from new developments in retailing—the growth of chain and department stores and consumer cooperatives. All these groups, who had traditionally regarded themselves as the backbone of society, the healthy 'middle estate' (*Mittelstand*), now found their economic existence threatened by forces which they could not really understand. Moreover, these economic forces confronted them in the human guise of cattle dealers, corn brokers, department store owners, and money lenders, many of whom—for historical reasons—were Jewish. Furthermore, as the local economy became more and more integrated into the national and international economies, the whole issue acquired a new dimension. For, behind the local dealer or money lender who, at least would be a familiar figure, perhaps resented but difficult to regard as a demon, there appeared to lurk the anonymous forces of high finance—the banks and the stock exchange in which the Jewish presence was well-known to be strong. Against this background, theories of a Jewish conspiracy to destroy the German *Mittelstand* could acquire a certain plausibility. An important aspect of pre-war German antisemitism then represented a revolt by traditional economic and social groups against the economic forces of the modern world, which the Jew came to symbolise and provide a focus of hostility for.

Not only the traditional German *Mittelstand* felt under pressure during the pre-war decades. The German professional classes and intelligentsia were also faced with disturbing changes. The numerical expansion of the traditional professions as well as the creation of new professions or quasi-professions to meet new needs associated with the modernisation process—architects, surveyors, accountants etc.—was often interpreted by traditional professional families as a threat to their professional and social status. Simultaneously, there occurred an influx of Jews into the professions. They took advantage of the process of emancipation associated with the Liberal era of the 1860s to move into occupations hitherto barred to them. Many of these Jewish doctors, lawyers and so on were not only able but also highly motivated to succeed in their new careers and, therefore, were liable to pose strong competition for the established professional community.

Unfortunately, however, the Jews achieved their emancipation just at the moment when the liberal values to which they owed it were about to go into eclipse. Liberalism was discredited firstly, by the fact that national unification had been achieved through the diplomacy and the military power of the conservative Prussian establishment rather than through the pious aspirations of Liberal politicians; secondly, by the economic crisis of the 1870s, which undermined confidence in the basic tenets of Liberal economic theory, and finally, by the failure of Liberalism to respond adequately to the demands of a modern industrial society. The political culture of the new German nation state was to be shaped not by the relatively enlightened liberalism of the years of unification but by a hybrid combination of traditional authoritarian values with a strong militarist flavour and an increasingly influential form of integral nationalism. This integral nationalism had no place for the Jews in its conception of German national identity; indeed, to some extent it defined itself in opposition to them and what they were conceived to represent. But, before looking at this new form of nationalism, there is one other aspect of pre-war antisemitism which needs to be considered—a particularly ominous one.

Towards the end of the nineteenth century, a new pseudo-biological form of antisemitism began to appear which defined Jews not in terms of religion, culture, or ethnicity but as a distinct, biologically determined, and inferior race. Attempts to divide human beings into distinct races and to assign to each a particular rank in a scale of quality have a long history. The first influential modern racial theory was that of the Frenchman, Count Joseph Arthur de Gobineau (1816–1882). Gobineau transformed the term 'Aryan', used by philologists to describe the Indo-Germanic peoples whose languages had been discovered to have a common root, into a racial term. He attributed superior physical and cultural qualities to this 'Aryan race' which he associated with the Germanic as opposed to the Latin or Semitic peoples. Later in the century Gobineau's theory was taken up by influential intellectuals such as Houston Stewart Chamberlain who claimed the Germans were the purest form of Aryans.

Racist theories received encouragement from new advances in biology during the second half of the century which encouraged the attempt to understand human beings and their behaviour primarily in biological terms. Such biological theories did not necessarily imply an antisemitic attitude, just as antisemitism was not necessarily racially motivated. But, by the end of the century, the racist form of antisemitism was becoming an increasingly influential strain within the movement. There was a growing literature, mostly in pamphlet form, which described the Jews as a parasitic race, acting as an element of decomposition within their host nations, and engaged in a conspiracy to achieve world domination.

This theory had important implications for the position of the individual Jew. For since, according to this theory, the Jews were a biologically distinct race, their evil was inherent in each individual Jew. Just as it was impossible for a leopard to change his spots, so it was impossible for a Jew to cease being a Jew i.e. evil. By definition, there could be no such a thing as a good Jew. When, as in the past, antisemitism had been motivated by religious or economic factors, it had been possible for Jews to escape persecution by religious conversion or, at any rate after emancipation, by changing their occupations. But, if racist antisemitism had its way, there could be no possibility of escape. Indeed, racist antisemites were already beginning to draw the logical conclusions from their own premises. Thus, the Hamburg programme of the 'Union of Antisemitic parties', formed in 1899, stated that 'since the Jewish question in the course of the twentieth century will become a question of world significance, it must be finally solved by the separation and finally by the extermination of the Jewish people.'

Before 1914, antisemitism as an organised movement was by no means unique to Germany. Indeed, by comparison with Austria-Hungary and even France, it was relatively insignificant. Its organisations were divided and their membership comparatively small and this was reflected in their tiny political representation in the Reichstag. Nevertheless, in the form of a basic dislike of the Jews and of what they were felt to represent, it had succeeded in permeating broad sections of German society from the Kaiser down to the lower middle class. Ominously, it was particularly strongly entrenched within the academic community, thereby influencing the next generation.

Above all, antisemitism had become accepted as an essential component of a new definition of German nationalism which had become dominant by 1914. This new populist (*völkisch*) form of nationalism emerged during the 1890s and radicalised German right-wing politics. It reflected the increasing politicisation of the mass of the population as a result of rapid industrialisation and urbanisation. On the one hand, this politicisation found expression in the rise of the Social Democratic Party on the Left, representing industrial workers. On the other hand — partly in response — it also saw the political mobilisation of petty bourgeois groups and the consequent emergence of a basis for a mass politics of the Right.

This 'new Right'—like its French counterpart—developed outside the political parties in pressure group-type organisations known as 'leagues'— the Pan-German League, the Navy League etc. Its ideology reflected the ideas and political aspirations of the middle-class generation which had grown up in the immediate aftermath of German unification and came to maturity in the 1890s and 1900s. These men had discarded the remnants of the enlightened 1848 Liberalism of their fathers and grandfathers. According to Heinrich Class, who became chairman of the Pan-German League, three ideals had characterised the liberalism of his father's generation: 'patriotism, tolerance, humanity'. However, 'we youngsters had moved on: we were nationalist pure and simple. We wanted nothing to do with tolerance if it sheltered the enemies of the *Volk* and the state. Humanity in the sense of that liberal idea we spurned, for our *Volk* was bound to come off worse.'[1] For men like Class the fortunes of the new German state had acquired paramount importance; their own self-esteem came to be bound up with the prestige of the new Reich.

The populist flavour of this new nationalism derived from their sense of exclusion from the traditional Prusso-German establishment. As successful businessmen, professionals and bureaucrats who had benefited from the rapid economic development following unification, they resented the patronising attitudes of the traditional elites who tended to regard them as parvenus. Moreover, they felt that the elitist nature of the political establishment weakened Germany by alienating the masses, encouraging the growth of class spirit and dividing the nation. In their view, this fragmentation of the nation was also encouraged by the existing political

---

[1] Quoted in G. Eley, 'Reshaping the Right: Radical Nationalism and the German Navy League 1898–1908' in *Historical Journal* 21.2.1978 p.348. This section owes much to the work of this author.

system of parliamentary and party government. This, it was felt, simply reinforced the divisions between Germans and led to the sacrifice of national interests for the benefit of sectional advantage. They rejected the idea central to liberal democracy that the national interest could only emerge out of the free interplay of differing interests and groups. Instead, they proclaimed a mythical concept of the *Volk*—an equivalent to the *pays reél* of pre-1914 French integral nationalism—as the real source of legitimacy and claimed that current political institutions (the Reichstag, parties etc.) were distorting the true expression of national will. In their view, the key to uniting the nation was the indoctrination of an ideology of extreme nationalism; above all, the goal of imperial expansion would rally and unite the nation.

For the völkisch movement the Jews represented the 'golden international' of high finance and Western liberalism which, together with the 'black international' of the Roman Catholic Church and the 'red international' of Socialism, threatened to undermine German national unity and the German cultural identity. In other words, they saw behind their domestic opponents—the left Liberals, the Catholic Centre party, and the Social Democrats—a foreign threat; domestic opposition was a form of treason. This way of thinking had been prepared to some extent by Bismarck's habit of labelling his same political opponents 'enemies of the Reich'. It was also to bedevil the Weimar Republic when the Versailles settlement instead of uniting the nation fatally divided it.

By 1914, the völkisch Right had begun to impose their radical intolerant stamp on German right-wing politics. Faced with the apparently inexorable rise of the Social Democratic Party, which in the 1912 election had become the largest single party in the Reichstag, and faced with a government which not only appeared weak in foreign affairs but, above all, seemed increasingly willing to seek an accommodation with the moderate Left, the old traditional, conservative Right began to make common cause with the new radical Right.

It was, however, during the course of the First World War that this new Right seized the initiative. The main focus of their efforts was a campaign to commit the Government to a so-called *Siegfrieden* in which Germany would use her expected victory to demand large-scale territorial annexations in both East and West and in the form of overseas colonies. This was regarded as vital not simply in order to reestablish Germany as a world power, but also as a means of diverting pressure for democratic reform at home. As the pressure for a compromise peace and for constitutional reform increased after 1916, the Right responded with even more vigorous agitation. The main emphasis of this campaign was on trying to reach a mass audience. On 24 September 1917, in a direct response to the Reichstag Peace Resolution of 17 July, a new party was founded—the Fatherland Party. Financed by heavy industry, and organised by the

Pan-German League and similar bodies, its aim was to mobilise mass support for a *Siegfrieden* and to resist moves towards parliamentary democracy. The party soon acquired over a million members, mainly among the middle class.

The Pan-Germans were, however, particularly anxious to reach the working class. Already, in the summer of 1917, a 'Free Committee for a German Workers' Peace' had been established in Bremen by the leader of a 'yellow' i.e. pro-employer workers' association in the Krupp dockyards, which carried out imperialist propaganda suported by the Army author-ities. Among its claimed 290,000 members was a skilled worker in the railway workshops in Munich named Anton Drexler, who established a Munich branch of the organisation on 7 March 1918 and who soon was to become a co-founder of the Nazi Party. Its success, however, was limited; it only acquired forty members. Drexler's failure to mobilise the working class for Pan-German policies reflected a general pattern and this lack of success prompted the Pan-German leadership to seek more effective propaganda themes.

From the autumn of 1917 onwards, antisemitism came to play an increasing role in Pan-German propaganda until, by the spring of 1918, it had become a key factor. On 13 April 1918, at a meeting of the executive committee of the Pan-German League, Heinrich Class noted 'a satisfactory growth in the antisemitic mood which had already reached an enormous extent...Our task will be to bring this movement out on to the national political arena...for the Jews the struggle for existence has begun.' This trend increased as Germany moved towards defeat and as the threat of democratic reforms increased. At another meeting on 20 October, Class argued that 'if the political goal of the war can be achieved through a dictatorship then it will be unnecessary to bring up the Jewish question.' But, if it could not be, he went on, then it would be vital to do so. For, in a struggle with the parliamentary system 'one of the most effective means of influencing people is through fear of the Jews'. In which case it should 'not be treated simply in an academic-political fashion but also in a demagogic-practical one'. They should exploit the 'situation for fanfares against the Jews and use the Jews as a lightning conductor for all injustices'. In short the Jews were to be made the scapegoat for the national humiliation of defeat, a defeat for which in reality the German establishment bore full responsibility. Class concluded: 'I will not be afraid to use any means and, in this connexion, will follow Heinrich von Kleist's dictum [which referred to the French]: 'Strike them dead; at the last Judgment you will not be asked for your reasons'.[2]

---

[2] Quoted in W. Jochmann, 'Die Ausbreitung des Antisemitismus' in W. E. Mosse and A. Paucker, eds. *Deutsches Judentum in Krieg und Revolution 1916–1923* (Tübingen 1971) pp. 438–440.

CHAPTER 1

From the Founding of the Party to the Putsch 1919–1923

(i) The Founding of the Party

The German military collapse in the Autumn of 1918 was followed by a revolution at the beginning of November, forcing the Kaiser to abdicate. The semi-autocratic regime of the Second Reich was replaced in 1919 by a constitution accepted by a National Assembly meeting at Weimar, establishing a parliamentary democracy similar to those of Germany's enemies in the West. This represented a victory for the opposition forces of the Empire—Social Democrats, Catholics, and left-wing Liberals. They benefited from the fact that the majority of the population associated the Kaiser and his government with defeat and felt Germany needed a new start. Many hoped democratic reforms would conciliate the Allies and produce more favourable peace terms.

The *völkisch* movement, however, refused to accept the triumph of the Left and determined to reverse it. They saw the key to this in the mobilisation of the masses against the Left through a campaign of antisemitism. The Pan-German League had already established a special committee in September to coordinate antisemitic propaganda, including representatives from the various antisemitic organisations. From December 1918 onwards, a flood of antisemitic propaganda in the form of leaflets, pamphlets, speeches, and lectures—all paid for by sections of heavy industry—poured over Germany. Its main theme was that the Jews had conspired to defeat Germany and promote revolution as a stage on the path towards their goal of world domination.

Although the working class remained largely resistant to this propaganda, it did achieve some resonance among the middle class. Defeat had come as a great shock to the German people; until the last moment they had been lulled into believing all was well. The revolution had alarmed and dismayed the middle class. Since the German establishment had lost its credibility and was paralysed by the events of November 1918 there were no satisfactory explanations for what had happened from traditional opinion leaders. So, for a time at least, the antisemitic agitators were operating in a political vacuum. In this chaotic situation, ideas of a conspiracy by Jewish international capital in league with the West, and of a 'stab in the back' by Jewish-Bolshevik agitators could seem plausible to desperate and bewildered middle class people, particularly since latent antisemitic feelings were already widespread and deep-rooted.

During 1919, as the population became increasingly disillusioned with the moderate Left government, the political mood in Germany shifted further and further to the extremes. The Peace Settlement of Versailles had imposed severe conditions on Germany and had met with a wave of protest. In particular, the 'war-guilt clause' by which Germany was obliged to accept full blame for the war stuck in the throats of the German people. Some of the unpopularity of the treaty was transferred to the Government, which had been obliged to sign it and to the new democratic system itself, which had been expected to pacify the Allies but was now associated with national humiliation.

Particular foci of Pan-German antisemitic agitation were the Army, which was particularly anxious to counter left-wing or even democratic subversion in its ranks, and also the Free Corps. The Free Corps were paramilitary formations composed of ex-army officers and volunteers, mostly young men from the middle- and lower-middle classes. They were recruited by the government to suppress left-wing revolutionary activity, to defend the eastern borders against Polish incursions, and to retain German influence in the Baltic states. The Free Corps proved extremely fertile soil for *völkisch* propaganda. It was not surprising, therefore, that the first major challenge to the new democratic order—in March 1920—came from an attempted coup carried out by a Free Corps, resisting its disbandment under the terms of the Versailles settlement. It operated in collaboration with high-ranking army officers and Conservative politicians and, significantly, the coup or 'putsch' was led by a prominent Pan-German, the Prussian civil servant, Friedrich Kapp. The putsch proved unsuccessful, partly as a result of a general strike called by the deposed Socialist government and the Trade Unions, partly because of the refusal of cooperation by key civil servants and Army leaders, and partly because of the incompetence of its leaders. But, though it failed to establish its authority at national level, the Right was far more successful in the state of Bavaria.

The Founding of the Nazi Party

The Nazi Party was merely one of a number of similar *völkisch* groups which sprang up all over Germany during 1919. It had, however, the particular advantage of being based in Bavaria, where events had been especially turbulent. The swing to the Left had been more marked than elsewhere; the swing to the Right was correspondingly strong. From the beginning of November 1918, there were four different left-wing regimes within a period of six months. But, on 1 May 1919, all revolutionary activity was crushed by troops sent by the Socialist central government, including the Free Corps. This force put down the revolution with considerable ferocity and restored the previous moderate Socialist government in Bavaria. In the meantime, however, the revolutionary events of these months had alienated the traditionally conservative population, many of whom were Catholic peasants. They also resented the removal of some of Bavaria's constitutional privileges by the Weimar Constitution. In March 1920, a right-wing group exploited the disorder caused by the Kapp putsch to carry out their own coup in Bavaria and replaced the Socialist government by a right-wing regime under a Conservative, Gustav von Kahr. Under the Weimar Constitution the police were responsible to the federal states rather than to the central or Reich government. So, for the next few years, Bavaria became a haven for right-wing extremists from all over Germany. In many other states and particularly in Prussia (which covered three-fifths of Germany), they were harried by the police at the orders of Socialist-dominated state governments. But in Bavaria the state authorities regarded their activities with benevolence. The early months of left-wing extremism had produced an excessive preoccupation with the threat of Bolshevism and an atmosphere in which the Nazi Party could flourish.

The defeat and revolution of November 1918 created favourable conditions for the birth of Nazism; the *völkisch* movement and the Army were to act as midwives. As elsewhere, the Army in Bavaria held indoctrination courses for its personnel, addressed by Pan-Germans and other supporters of the *völkisch* Right. Among the soldiers who attended such a course in Munich was a thirty year old private, Adolf Hitler. The son of an Austrian customs official, Hitler had been influenced by the Pan-German nationalism current among much of the German-speaking population of pre-war Austria-Hungary and of which his history teacher in Linz had been an

TRTP-B

ardent supporter. He despised the multi-national Habsburg empire as an ethnic mishmash and his consciousness of his German cultural identity was no doubt reinforced by his years spent among the rootless in the men's hostels of pre-war Vienna after failing his entry examination to the Art Academy. It was presumably comforting to feel that, although he was living among the socially deprived, he was at least a member of the master race of the empire. He had also acquired the Pan-German dislike for Catholic politics and, above all, their hostility to the Social Democrats. His dislike of the 'reds' was no doubt reinforced by his desperate struggle to maintain his petty bourgeois status above the ranks of the workers. During his Vienna years, Hitler also appears to have adopted the racist form of antisemitism which was to form the core of his future ideology. Various forms of antisemitism were virulent in pre-war Vienna including its racist version which was popularised in numerous pamphlets which Hitler eagerly devoured. It evidently provided him with an answer to the problems of identity and purpose which had troubled him.

After moving to Munich in 1913 to try and improve his prospects as an artist and also to escape National Service for the despised Habsburg Empire, he eked out a precarious existence selling his paintings. His artistic ambitions had been frustrated; his petty bourgeois social pride was being constantly humiliated through the circumstances of his daily life; like many a young man in his position, his only refuge from his colourless existence lay in day-dreaming about grandiose future achievements, in his case in the field of architecture. In this situation the outbreak of war came as a godsend. He immediately volunteered for the Bavarian Army in which he was to prove a loyal, brave, and efficient soldier. At last he had found a purpose and order in his life. Ironically, however, his C.O. did not recommend the future Führer for promotion on the grounds that 'he lacked leadership qualities'! Wounded by a gas attack in the Spring of 1918, he emerged from hospital to find his world in ruins: Germany had been defeated and the old order overthrown. He was still in the Army, but was not likely to be kept on for long and what then? The prospect of a return to his aimless, hand-to-mouth pre-war existence must have seemed bleak. In fact, however, the chaos produced by defeat and revolution was to offer opportunities to a man of Hitler's background and qualities which would have been inconceivable in the stable order of the pre-war world. In the historical conjuncture of Hitler's return to Munich after the war the man, the place, and the moment were made for one another.

Soon after his arrival in Munich Hitler was assigned by the Army to one of the political indoctrination courses being run with the assistance of the Pan-German League. Here he flourished. His endless arguments with fellow inmates of the men's hostels in pre-war Vienna had laid the foundations of his abilities as a mass orator; and now he found in lectures to other members of the course that he had a real talent for public speaking. His oratorical abilities drew him to the attention of Captain Mayr, head of the Press and Propaganda section in the Bavarian section of the Army. Mayr decided to use Hitler as an agent to keep an eye on the various political activities going on in Munich.

As part of this activity, Hitler was assigned to report on the German Workers' Party (DAP), led by the railway mechanic, Anton Drexler, and a journalist, Karl Harrer. The party had been founded on 9 January 1919 on Drexler's initiative and under the auspices of the so-called Thule Society, a cover name for the headquarters of the *völkisch* movement in Munich, of whom Harrer was effectively the representative on the Party's executive committee. Drexler later described what happened at the meeting which Hitler attended:

1

On 12 September 1919, the German Workers' Party held a monthly meeting in the Veterans' Hall of the Sterneckerbräu, in the so-called 'Leiber Room'. Gottfried Feder spoke on the 'Breaking of Interest Slavery'. The first National Socialist pamphlet, *My Political Awakening: From the Diary of a German Socialist Worker*, had just appeared. I had collected a few proof copies from the publisher, Dr Boepple, and was standing with five copies in my hand at the bar of the pub, listening with growing enthusiasm to the second speaker in the evening's discussion, who was a guest. He was dealing with the first speaker in the discussion, a Professor Baumann, who had urged the secession of Bavaria from Germany, and he was tackling the Professor in a way which it was a joy to watch. He gave a short but trenchant speech in favour of a greater Germany which thrilled me and all who could hear him. When the speaker had finished I rushed towards him, thanked him for what he had said and asked him to take the pamphlet I had away with him to read. It contained, I said, the rules and basic ideas of the new movement; if he was in agreement with them, he could come again in a week's time and work in a smaller circle, because we could do with people like him.

This was Hitler. He was persuaded to join the Party, whose membership was still very small and, by the end of the year, had become its propaganda chief. The DAP provided him with an outlet for his political energies and it was small enough to enable him to make his influence felt immediately. It attracted him because of its emphasis on antisemitism and on the need to win over the masses. His experience as a soldier had taught him the importance of morale and of the part played by propaganda in influencing morale. He believed the Allies had been more successful at mobilising the energy and enthusiasm of their own people and that the Germans had lost because of Socialist propaganda which had undermined their morale in the interests of international Jewry. He believed that Germany must learn from the Allies and that the first task must be to win the masses for nationalism and antisemitism. Only when this had been achieved would she be able to assert herself abroad.

His military superiors were happy to encourage his political activity and it was at their request that, on 16 September 1919, he wrote his first major political statement in reply to a letter asking for information on the Jewish problem from one of his fellow-participants in the Army indoctrination course, Adolf Gemlich. It expressed a number of ideas which were to remain basic to his thought for the rest of his life. Important, for example, was his emphasis on the fact that the Jews were a racial community rather than a religious group. Secondly, there was the emphasis on the need for the 'rebirth of the moral and spiritual energies of the nation...through the ruthless action of personalities with a capacity for national leadership', though there is no evidence that he yet saw himself in such a role.

2

If the danger represented by the Jews today finds expression in the undeniable dislike of them felt by a large section of our people, the cause of this dislike is on the whole not to be found in the clear recognition of the corrupting activity of the Jews generally among our people, whether conscious or unconscious; it originates mainly through personal relationship, and from the impression left behind him by the individual Jew which is almost invariably unfavourable. Antisemitism thereby acquires only too easily the character of being a manifestation of emotion. But this is wrong. Antisemitism as a political movement must not be, cannot be, determined by emotional criteria, but only through the recognition of facts. The facts are as follows: First, the Jews are definitely a race and not a religious community. The Jew himself never calls himself a Jewish German, a Jewish Pole, a Jewish American, but only a German, a Polish, an American Jew. From the foreign nations in whose midst he lives the Jew has adopted very little more than their language. A German who is compelled to use French in France, Italian in Italy, Chinese in China, does not thereby become a Frenchman, an Italian, or a Chinese; similarly a Jew who happens to live among us and is thereby compelled to use the German language cannot be called a German. Even the Mosaic faith, however important for the maintenance of this race, cannot be considered as absolutely decisive in the question of whether or not someone is a Jew. There is hardly a single race whose members belong exclusively to one particular religion.

Through a thousand years of inbreeding, often practised within a very narrow circle, the Jew has in general preserved his race and character much more rigorously than many of the peoples among whom he lives. And as a result, there is living amongst us a non-German, foreign race, unwilling and unable to sacrifice its racial characteristics, to deny its own feeling, thinking and striving, and which none the less possesses all the political rights that we ourselves have. The feelings of the Jew are concerned with purely material things; his thoughts and desires even more so. The dance round the golden calf becomes a ruthless struggle for all those goods which, according to our innermost feelings, should not be the highest and most desirable things on this earth.

The value of the individual is no longer determined by his character, by the importance of his achievements for all, but solely by the amount of his possessions, by his money.

The value of the nation is no longer to be measured in terms of the sum of its moral and spiritual forces, but solely on the basis of the wealth of its material goods.

From this feeling emerges that concern and striving for money and for the power which can protect it which makes the Jew unscrupulous in his choice of means, ruthless in his use of them to achieve this aim.

In an autocratically governed state he whines for the favour of the 'Majesty' of the prince and abuses it to batten on his subjects like a leech. In a democracy he courts the favour of the masses, crawls before the 'majesty of the people' and yet knows only the majesty of money.

He destroys the character of the prince with byzantine flattery, and national pride, which is the strength of a nation, with mockery and shameless training in vice. His weapon is that public opinion which is never given utterance by the press, but is always led by it and falsified by it. His power is the power of money which in the form of interest effortlessly and interminably multiplies itself in his hands and forces upon nations that most dangerous of yokes, the sad consequences of which are so difficult to perceive because of the initial gleam of gold. Everything which makes men strive for higher things, whether religion, socialism or democracy, is for him only a means to an end, to the satisfaction of a lust for money and domination. His activities produce a racial tuberculosis among nations.

And this has the following result: Antisemitism stemming from purely emotive reasons will always find its expression in the form of programs [sic]. But antisemitism based on reason must lead to the systematic legal combating and removal of the rights of the Jew, which he alone of the foreigners living among us possesses (legislation to make them aliens). Its final aim, however, must be the uncompromising removal of the Jews altogether. Both are possible only under a government of national strength, never under a government of national impotence.

The Republic in Germany owes its birth not to the united national will of our people but to the cunning exploitation of a series of circumstances which combined to produce a deep general discontent. But these circumstances were independent of the form of the State, and are still active today; more active, indeed, today than before. And a large section of our people is aware that no mere change in the form of the State as such can alter or improve our position, but only the rebirth of the moral and spiritual energies of the nation.

This rebirth will be set in motion not by the political leadership of irresponsible majorities under the influence of party dogmas or of an irresponsible press, nor by catchwords and slogans of international coinage, but only through the ruthless action of personalities with a capacity for national leadership and an inner sense of responsibility.

But this fact robs the Republic of the internal support of the spiritual forces of the nation which are so necessary. And so the present leaders of the State are compelled to seek support from those who alone benefited from the changed situation in Germany and do so now, and who for this reason have been the driving forces of the revolution, namely, the Jews. Taking no account of the Jewish peril, which has certainly been recognised by present-day leaders—proof of this is the various statements of present leading figures—they are compelled to accept the support readily offered by the Jews for their own benefit, and therefore to pay the required price. And this price consists not only in giving the Jews every possible encouragement, but above all in hampering the struggle of the duped nation against their brother Jews—in the neutralising of the antisemitic movement.

Apart from antisemitism, extreme nationalism and a form of anti-capitalism predominated in the Party's propaganda at this stage. All these elements were present in the Party programme which was presented on 24 February 1920 to a public meeting in the Hofbräuhaus, a big Munich beer cellar. The programme, often erroneously ascribed to Gottfried Feder who played an influential role in the early years of the Party, was in fact almost certainly composed by Drexler and Hitler and only Point 11 derives from Feder.

3

The Programme of the German Workers' Party is designed to be of limited duration. The leaders have no intention, once the aims announced in it have been achieved, of establishing fresh ones, merely in order to increase, artificially, the discontent of the masses and so ensure the continued existence of the Party.

1. We demand the union of all Germans in a Greater Germany on the basis of the right of national self-determination.

2. We demand equality of rights for the German people in its dealings with other nations, and the revocation of the peace treaties of Versailles and Saint-Germain.

3. We demand land and territory (colonies) to feed our people and to settle our surplus population.

4. Only members of the nation may be citizens of the State. Only those of German blood, whatever their creed, may be members of the nation. Accordingly, no Jew may be a member of the nation.

5. Non-citizens may live in Germany only as guests and must be subject to laws for aliens.

6. The right to vote on the State's government and legislation shall be enjoyed by the citizens of the State alone. We demand therefore that all official appointments, of whatever kind, whether in the Reich, in the states or in the smaller localities, shall be held by none but citizens.

We oppose the corrupting parliamentary custom of filling posts merely in accordance with party considerations, and without reference to character or abilities.

7. We demand that the State shall make it its primary duty to provide a livelihood for its citizens. If it should prove impossible to feed the entire population, foreign nationals (non-citizens) must be deported from the Reich.

8. All non-German immigration must be prevented. We demand that all non-Germans who entered Germany after 2 August 1914 shall be required to leave the Reich forthwith.

9. All citizens shall have equal rights and duties.

10. It must be the first duty of every citizen to perform physical or mental work. The activities of the individual must not clash with the general interest, but must proceed within the framework of the community and be for the general good.

We demand therefore:

11. The abolition of incomes unearned by work.

The breaking of the slavery of interest

12. In view of the enormous sacrifices of life and property demanded of a nation by any war, personal enrichment from war must be regarded as a crime against the nation. We demand therefore the ruthless confiscation of all war profits.

13. We demand the nationalisation of all businesses which have been formed into corporations (trusts).

14. We demand profit-sharing in large industrial enterprises.

15. We demand the extensive development of insurance for old age.

16. We demand the creation and maintenance of a healthy middle class, the immediate communalising of big department stores, and their lease at a cheap rate to small traders, and that the utmost consideration shall be shown to all small traders in the placing of State and municipal orders.

17. We demand a land reform suitable to our national requirements, the passing of a law for the expropriation of land for communal purposes without compensation; the abolition of ground rent, and the prohibition of all speculation in land.

18. We demand the ruthless prosecution of those whose activities are injurious to the common interest. Common criminals, usurers, profiteers, etc., must be punished with death, whatever their creed or race.

19. We demand that Roman Law, which serves a materialistic world order, be replaced by a German common law.

20. The State must consider a thorough reconstruction of our national system of education (with the aim of opening up to every able and hard-working German the possibility of higher education and of thus obtaining advancement). The curricula of all educational establishments must be brought into line with the requirements of practical life. The aim of the school must be to give the pupil, beginning with the first sign of intelligence, a grasp of the notion of the State (through the study of civic affairs). We demand the education of gifted children of poor parents, whatever their class or occupation, at the expense of the State.

21. The State must ensure that the nation's health standards are raised by protecting mothers and infants, by prohibiting child labour, by promoting physical strength through legislation providing for compulsory gymnastics and sports, and by the extensive support of clubs engaged in the physical training of youth.

22. We demand the abolition of the mercenary [i.e. professional] army and the formation of a people's army.

23. We demand legal warfare on deliberate political mendacity and its dissemination in the press. To facilitate the creation of a German national press we demand:

    (a) that all editors of, and contributors to newspapers appearing in the German language must be members of the nation;

(b) that no non-German newspapers may appear without the express permission of the State. They must not be printed in the German language;

(c) that non-Germans shall be prohibited by law from participating financially in or influencing German newspapers, and that the penalty for contravening such a law shall be the suppression of any such newspaper, and the immediate deportation of the non-Germans involved.

The publishing of papers which are not conducive to the national welfare must be forbidden. We demand the legal prosecution of all those tendencies in art and literature which corrupt our national life, and the suppression of cultural events which violate this demand.

24. We demand freedom for all religious denominations in the State, provided they do not threaten its existence nor offend the moral feelings of the German race.

The Party, as such, stands for positive Christianity, but does not commit itself to any particular denomination. It combats the Jewish-materialist spirit within and without us, and is convinced that our nation can achieve permanent health only from within on the basis of the principle: *The common interest before self-interest.*

25. To put the whole of this programme into effect, we demand the creation of a strong central state power for the Reich; the unconditional authority of the political central Parliament over the entire Reich and its organisations; and the formation of Corporations based on estate and occupation for the purpose of carrying out the general legislation passed by the Reich in the various German states.

The leaders of the Party promise to work ruthlessly—if need be to sacrifice their very lives—to translate this programme into action.

When Hitler joined the DAP the Party was small and insignificant. No doubt he later exaggerated its weakness in order to emphasise his own impact upon it, but the following description, written in a newspaper article in 1929, is probably fairly accurate, at least for the very early period up to about October 1919:

4

Our little committee, which with its seven members in reality represented the whole party, was nothing but the managing committee of a small whist [*Skat*] club. The procedure was very simple. Every Wednesday a committee meeting took place. To start with, we met in a pathetic little room in a small pub, 'Rosenbad', in the Herrenstrasse... . In 1919, Munich was still in a bad way. Not much light, a good deal of dirt, refuse, shabby people, down-at-heel soldiers, in short the sort of picture which could be expected after four-and-a-half years of war, especially if, as in the case of Germany, the war had been followed by a shocking revolution. So it was a very poor 'committee room' in which we met... . The committee's proceedings consisted in reading out letters received, discussing replies to them, and registering the letters that were sent off following this discussion, i.e., reading them out also. Since that time I have developed a deadly hatred of writing letters and of letter writers.

It was always the same people, probably the chairmen of associations similar in

size. We were sent comradely greetings, we were told that in their particular place
the seed had been sown or had even sprouted. We were asked if we could say the
same of ourselves and the necessity of joint action was stressed.
We had also 'association funds'. These consisted of material goods and cash. The
cash fluctuated around 5 marks, and when times were good it rose to 12, 13, 15, and
once, I remember, even to 17 marks. The material goods consisted of a cigar box in
which the money was kept, notepaper, envelopes, a few stamps and the 'statutes' of
the association.

Hitler's main contribution to the Party in this early period was his ability
as a political speaker and his drive and energy. The following excerpt from
a speech by Hitler on 26 October 1920, based on notes taken by a member
of the Bavarian political police, indicates some of the main themes which
he emphasised during this period. The speech, entitled 'National Welfare
and Nationalist Idea' was given in the Kindlkeller, a Munich beer cellar:

5

We need some national pride again. But who can the nation be proud of these
days? Of Ebert[3] perhaps? (*laughter*) Of the Government? We need a national will
just as much. We must not always say: We can't do that. We must be able to do it.
In order to smash this disgraceful peace treaty, we must regard every means as
justified (*loud applause*). First, there must be a nationalist mood and then will come
the economic prosperity of the nation. We must have blind faith in our future, in
our recovery.
    Now Hitler turned to deal with the Right and the Left. The Nationalists on the
Right lack a social sense, the Socialists on the Left a nationalist one. He appeals to
the parties on the Right: If you want to be nationalist then come down among your
people and put away all your class pride. To the Left he appeals: You who proclaim
your solidarity with the whole world, first show your solidarity with your own
compatriots, be Germans first and foremost. Do they look like heroes who want to
smash the world and yet crawl before foreigners for fear they might not like
something they see here? (*applause*) You who are real revolutionaries, come over
to us and fight with us for our whole nation (*loud applause*). Your place is not over
there with the procurers of international capital, but with us, with your own
people!! (*stormy applause*).
    Then Hitler turned to the future of Germany, to the youth of Germany, and, in
particular, with warm words for their intellectual leaders, the German students.
Your place is with us, with the people. You who are still young and still have the
fire of enthusiasm in your veins, come over to us, join our fighting party, which
pursues its aims ruthlessly, with every means, even with force! (*loud applause*) We
are not a class party, but the party of honest producers (*Schaffenden*). Our strength
does not lie in the International but in our own strength, that is to say in our people!
(*long and stormy applause*)

---

[3] Friedrich Ebert, Social Democrat President of the Weimar Republic, 1919–25.

Hitler succeeded in establishing a notable *rapport* with the Munich masses whose economic plight was worsening owing to progressive inflation. He showed remarkable intuition in sensing and articulating their hopes and fears. He succeeded in projecting himself as a representative figure—an ex-soldier now drifting without a regular job, filled with hatred and resentment against those he considered responsible for the plight of Germany, which he in turn identified with the personal plight of his audience. He not only showed that he understood his hearers' mood and their predicament and gave them an emotionally convincing explanation for their problems; he also conveyed his own willpower and determination to change things, to restore Germany to her former greatness and to destroy those who were responsible for the present situation. Kurt Ludecke, one of Hitler's early associates, later recorded his impressions on first hearing him speak in 1922:

6

My critical faculty was swept away. Leaning from the rostrum as if he were trying to impel his inner self into the consciousness of all these thousands, he was holding the masses, and me with them, under an hypnotic spell by the sheer force of his conviction.... I do not know how to describe the emotions that swept over me as I heard this man. His words were like a scourge. When he spoke of the disgrace of Germany, I felt ready to spring on any enemy. His appeal to German manhood was like a call to arms; the gospel he preached, a sacred truth. He seemed another Luther. I forgot everything but the man; then glancing around, I saw that his magnetism was holding these thousands as one. Of course I was ripe for this experience. I was a man of thirty-two, weary with disgust and disillusionment, a wanderer seeking a cause, a patriot without a channel for his patriotism, a yearner after the heroic without a hero. The intense will of the man, the passion of his sincerity, seemed to flow from him into me. I experienced an exaltation that could be likened only to religious conversion.

In February 1920 the Party had changed its name to 'National Socialist German Workers' Party' (NSDAP), thereby emphasising its attempt to combine both a nationalist and a socialist appeal. An early membership list of some 200 names showed a fair cross-section of the city's population: tradesmen, craftsmen, shopkeepers, bank and post-office employees, and a few doctors and engineers as well as a number of soldiers and workers. Largely as a result of Hitler's successful oratory, membership gradually increased to 2,000 at the end of 1920, 3,300 by August 1921 and branches were beginning to be founded outside Munich. The first was established in Rosenheim, forty miles from Munich, as early as April 1920. In July 1921 a branch was founded in Hanover and one or two others followed elsewhere. In November 1922, however, the Party was banned in Prussia and in some other states; Bavaria, and Munich in particular, remained the main centre. The success of the Party drew the attention of military circles. At the end of 1920, with the assistance of funds from the Reichswehr, the Party purchased a newspaper. Having appeared since 1887 as the *Münchener Beobachter*, a racialist weekly, the *Völkischer Beobachter* (*VB*), as it had been renamed on 9 August 1919, was now published twice a week as the organ of the NSDAP. It did not become a daily until 8 February 1923. The state of the Party's finances was at the moment precarious. Funds were derived from membership dues, very small, collections at meetings and occasional contributions from wealthy sympathisers. Nearly all the staff were unpaid.

(ii) Hitler takes over the Party leadership, August 1921

By mid-1921 Hitler had clearly established himself as the key figure in the Party. It owed its rise in membership to his abilities as a speaker, and he also possessed extremely useful connexions with the Army, which he had left on 31 March 1920, through Captain Ernst Röhm, who acted as a political liaison officer for the Army HQ and was a member of the NSDAP. Yet Hitler was still officially only the propaganda chief. In January 1920 Harrer had been obliged to resign as chairman of the Party. He had disagreed with Hitler and Drexler about the intensive propaganda activities of the Party, wishing it to remain a select group on the lines of a Masonic lodge. Harrer had been replaced as chairman by Drexler, who recognised Hitler's ability and, as he told Feder on 13 February 1921, wanted him to assume more responsibility in the organisation, 'though without my being pushed into the background in consequence'. Hitler himself, however, rightly regarded his propaganda activities as the most important function in the Party, particularly since he still saw his objective as the winning of 'the masses' for more important nationalist figures. He was not tempted by the routine work of chairman and declined Drexler's offer of the post. Shortly after, however, the question of the Party organisation and Hitler's position within it was brought to a head when the committee began to pursue a course of action to which Hitler strongly objected. This brought home to him for the first time the importance of the formal distribution of power within the organisation and forced him not only to take over the chairmanship but to establish a new structure of authority in which the chairman was no longer merely *primus inter pares* within a committee, but a leader, superior to the committee. The crisis persuaded him that only in this way could he ensure that the Party pursued the policies which he believed were the right ones. And then, having established his position as leader, he rationalised this development with a theory of political leadership which condemned the traditional form of committee organisation and insisted on the need for a dominant leader. The fusion of the NSDAP with other National Socialist parties, discussed at conferences in August 1920 at Salzburg and in March 1921 at Zeitz brought the conflict to a head. Other parties involved were the German Socialist Party (DSP), whose organisation was more widespread throughout Germany than that of the NSDAP, and National Socialist groups from Austria and Bohemia such as the German National Socialist Party. Drexler and other NSDAP leaders favoured a union, believing a unified *völkisch* movement would be more effective than various groups operating on their own. Hitler, however, was contemptuous of the other racist groups which he regarded as too bourgeois in their political style and too academic in their antisemitism. A merger would dilute the energy and drive of the Nazi Party and threaten the position which he had built up for himself as the indispensable motor of the Nazi Party, a role where at last he had found personal fulfilment.

During a long absence of Hitler in Berlin in the early summer of 1921, Drexler was persuaded by a Dr Dickel, the leader of a *völkisch* group in Augsburg, to merge the NSDAP with Dickel's own group, the *Abendländischer Bund* (Western League). Informed of this, Hitler returned at once from Berlin and tried to persuade the committee to change their minds. When they refused, he resigned on 11 July and threatened to set up his own party, three days later issuing an ultimatum stating his conditions for rejoining. These included a stipulation that the headquarters of the Party should remain in Munich and not be moved to Augsburg or Berlin, thereby depriving him of much of his influence since his main personal following was in Munich. The terms of his ultimatum were as follows:

7

---

1. That an extraordinary membership meeting be immediately summoned within eight days from today with the following agenda: The present committee of the Party to resign their offices. At the new election I demand the post of chairman with dictatorial powers for the immediate establishment of an action committee which must ruthlessly purge the Party of foreign elements which have now penetrated it. The action committee to consist of three people.

2. That the unalterable rule be laid down that the headquarters of the movement is and always shall be Munich. Finally, that the Party leadership shall be vested in the Munich local branch until the movement has reached a size sufficient to enable it as a whole to finance its own Party leadership.

3. That any further alteration of the name or programme of the Party shall be absolutely avoided for the next six years. Members working in this direction or to this end shall be excluded from the movement.

4. All further attempts at such a fusion between the National Socialist German Workers' Party and the movement which unjustifiably calls itself the German National Socialist Party must in the future cease. The Party can never agree to a fusion with those who wish to make contact with us; they must join the Party. Reciprocal gestures on our part are out of the question... .

I do not make these demands because I am hungry for power, but rather because recent events have convinced me now more than ever that without iron leadership the Party will in a very short time cease to be what it ought to be: a National Socialist German Workers' Party and not an *Abendländischer Bund*.

A sharp struggle followed, during which Drexler attempted to defeat Hitler by expelling some of his colleagues from the Party. Hitler's victory was swift for Drexler changed his mind and threw in his lot with Hitler. He had long agreed with Hitler on the need for vigorous mass propaganda and he realised that the Party could not dispense with Hitler's superior talent as a public speaker. Hitler had also the backing of the younger and more activist element in the Party, attracted by his drive. The dispute had already been settled when a special meeting of the Party was called on 29 July. Hitler dominated the meeting and was elected chairman of the Party. According to the minutes:

8

The chairman of the meeting was the previous chairman of the association, Herr Anton Drexler...
1. Report on recent events.
2. Amendments or additions to the statutes.
3. A new election of the committee.
He then read out the draft of the new statutes. Comrade Hitler as chairman of the meeting then proceeded to take the vote on the new statutes. The statutes were with one exception (Comrade Posch) unanimously adopted (*enthusiastic applause*). Comrade Drexler then began to speak and proposed the election of Comrade Hitler as Chairman of the Party. The election is unanimously confirmed with loud applause.

Drexler was made honorary president. The statutes adopted at this meeting formalised the dictatorial powers of the Party chairman. The committee of Party officers created by the first statutes of 1920 was retained merely for the purposes of registration of the NSDAP as a legal organisation, while Hitler's responsibility to the membership meeting was a formality. Article 5 read as follows:

9

The headquarters of the National Socialist German Workers' Association is in Munich. The leadership of the Party as such will be combined with the leadership of the Munich branch so long as the Association does not have sufficient funds flowing in from the individual branches to finance a leadership for the Party itself.

Since the Munich branch is the mother group of the whole movement, generous use will be made of its income as before in order to promote the movement as a whole.

The association is subdivided into local branches which are subordinate to the main headquarters.

These will be combined to form *Gau* organisations and the *Gaue* to form state organisations as required.

In order to facilitate a decisive leadership of the movement, the I. Chairman is made responsible for the leadership of the movement as a whole. The leadership of the individual branches is the responsibility of the chairmen of the local branches.

The I. Chairman of the movement as a whole is its legal representative. In his absence the II. Chairman will deputise for him.

The Party headquarters section

The Party headquarters section consists of: (1) the committee to be legally elected by the membership meeting and composed of the first and second chairmen, the first and second treasurers, and the first and second secretaries; (2) the subordinate committees. Since the real responsibility for the leadership of the association lies in the hands of the first chairman, his position must be regarded as standing above the committee. He is responsible solely to the membership meeting.

Hitler placed his leading supporters in positions of authority. Hermann Esser was put in charge of propaganda, and Max Amann, Hitler's former army sergeant, became business manager.

(iii) The development of the Party, 1921–23

In a memorandum of 7 January 1922 Hitler emphasised the fundamental differences of character between the traditional parties and the NSDAP. The NSDAP had not the limited appeal of the bourgeois parties of prewar Germany—it was a new kind of party, a party of action, a movement of the people:

10

The ninth of November[4] meant above all the complete collapse, not of the party life in itself but of bourgeois party life, of that mixture of goodwill, harmless naïvety, theoretical knowledge and utter lack of instinct. The racialist movement also, just like the bourgeois national parties, utterly failed in its main task of winning the broad masses for the national cause. Responsibility for the collapse lies with the bourgeoisie. The racialists [*Völkisch*] were not capable of drawing the practical conclusions from correct theoretical judgements, especially in the Jewish question. In this way the German racialist movement developed a pattern similar to that of the 1880s and 1890s. As in those days, its leadership gradually fell into the hands of highly honourable but fantastically naïve men of learning, professors, district councillors, schoolmasters and barristers—in short a bourgeois, idealistic and refined class. It lacked the warm breath of the nation's youthful vigour. The impetuous force of headstrong fire-eaters was rejected as demagogy. The new movement was therefore a nationalist movement but no longer a movement of the people... . There reappeared in the new movement the distressing characteristics of our bourgeois parties, lacking any uniform discipline or form...

This utter failure in all the matters mentioned led to the founding of the NSDAP. The new movement aimed at providing what the others did not: a racialist movement with a firm social base, a hold over the broad masses, welded together in an iron-hard organisation, instilled with blind obedience and inspired by a brutal will, a party of struggle and action... . If this new kind of movement is to become great and important, its aims must be propagated with fanatical ardour and the total energy of its few supporters must be placed at the service of its propaganda as there is nothing there yet to organise.

With power in Munich, Hitler determined to consolidate his authority by abolishing the autonomy enjoyed by the local branches under Drexler. By May 1922 there was a total of forty-five branches, though most of them in Bavaria. At a meeting of branch leaders in January 1922 Hitler insisted on their subordination to the Munich headquarters. In fact he found it impossible to exercise effective control over the Party outside Bavaria because the situation in the racialist movement elsewhere was so confused. Nevertheless, his authority over the Party in Munich was now absolute.

In the summer of 1921, the armed squads employed to protect Party meetings from disruption by opponents were formally organised in a special unit under the cover name of 'Gymnastic and Sports Section', renamed in October the 'Storm Detachments' (SA). It appealed to the considerable number of ex-soldiers and ex-Free Corps men who had no use for conventional political activity, but were looking for the type of violent action not possible since the dissolution of the Free Corps by the Government. The SA, paramilitary in both organisation and appearance,

---

[4] 9 November 1918—the date of the declaration of the Republic.

had military ranks, wore uniforms and marched in formation. The founding of the unit was formally announced in the *Völkischer Beobachter* on 3
August 1921.

11

The NSDAP has created its own gymnastic and sports section within the framework
of its organisation. It is intended to bind our young party members together to form
an organisation of iron, so that it may put its strength at the disposal of the whole
movement to act as a battering ram. It is intended to uphold the idea of the
importance of the military for a free people. It is intended to provide protection for
the propaganda activity of the leaders. But above all it is intended to develop in the
hearts of our young supporters a tremendous desire for action, to drive home to
them and burn into them the fact that history does not make men, but men history,
and that he who allows himself to be put in the chains of slavery without any
resistance deserves the yoke of slavery. But it [the SA] will also encourage mutual
loyalty and cheerful obedience to the leader.

A good indication of the nature of the organisation is provided by the
pledge which every stormtrooper was obliged to make on joining:

12

As a member of the storm troop of the NSDAP I pledge myself by its storm flag
[*Sturmfahne*]: to be always ready to stake life and limb in the struggle for the aims
of the movement; to give absolute military obedience to my military superiors and
leaders; to bear myself honourably in and out of service; to be always companion-
able towards other comrades!

The SA protected Nazi meetings from disruption, assisted in propaganda
activities, and disrupted the meetings of other parties. On 14 September
1921, for example, a meeting of the federalist Bavarian League was
disrupted, as described by a correspondent of the *Münchner Neueste
Nachrichten*:

13

The meeting, which was well attended, came to a premature end owing to an attack
systematically planned by the National Socialists. National Socialist youths had
early on taken the seats near the speakers' platform, and numerous National
Socialists were distributed as well throughout the hall. When Hitler, the leader of
the National Socialists, appeared in the hall, he was greeted by his followers with
demonstrative applause. His arrival gave the cue for the violence that followed.

The former editor of the *Völkischer Beobachter*, Esser, climbed on a chair and declared that Bavaria owed the situation it was in to the Jews. Ballerstedt had always avoided the Jewish question. The National Socialists therefore saw themselves 'forced' to stop Ballerstedt from speaking and let Hitler speak instead. Hitler's followers, bent on making it a National Socialist meeting, thereupon occupied the platform. But a large section of the meeting protested and demanded that Ballerstedt should speak. He had pushed his way through to the platform, but could not begin because the National Socialists were all the time shouting, 'Hitler!' The uproar grew even worse when someone tried to prevent the fight which was feared by switching off the electricity. When the lights came on again, Ballerstedt declared that anybody who tried to disturb the meeting would be charged with disturbing the peace. After this the young people on the platform, many of them hardly in their teens, surrounded him, beat him up and pushed him down the platform steps. Ballerstedt received a head injury which bled badly. As the audience were naturally growing more and more excited, three members of the state police appeared in the hall. A [plain-clothes] detective declared the meeting dissolved. A fairly strong group of state police then cleared the hall; this operation went smoothly without further incident after an announcement that the charge for admission would be refunded.

Regular SA intimidation of political opponents involved especially members of left-wing parties—as with the vicious brawl with Social Democrats in the Hofbräuhaus in November 1921. Opponents who demanded the right to speak in the so-called 'discussion' at Nazi meetings were often given rough treatment.

Jews were banned from Nazi functions. Political violence, whatever its outcome, gave Hitler and his party publicity, and the Bavarian authorities were remarkably tolerant of such disorder. After the assassination of the Jewish German Foreign Minister, Walther Rathenau, by right-wing fanatics in June 1922, the NSDAP was prohibited in almost every state in Germany. Yet no action was taken by the Government in Bavaria, where the Party's activities continued unabated. In the autumn of 1922, Julius Streicher a notorious antisemite from Nuremberg, declared his allegiance to Hitler. Streicher, who controlled the DSP in northern Bavaria, was an important acquisition and became one of the Party's most popular speakers.

The NSDAP arranged for its first Party rally in Munich in January 1923. The Bavarian Government took fright at the possible consequences and declared martial law in the city. The rally was banned, but on Röhm's intercession and a last-minute assurance by Hitler that he would not attempt a 'putsch', the meetings went ahead as planned. Karl Alexander von Müller, a Munich professor of history, was present at the rally.

14

On the 28th, 6,000 SA men instead of 5,000 lined up on the Marsfeld. The previous evening Hitler had dashed in his car from one meeting to another. In the 'Löwenbräu' I heard him speak in public for the first time. How often I had attended public meetings in this hall! But neither during the war nor during the revolution had I been met on entering by so hot a breath of hypnotic mass excitement. It was not only the special tension of these weeks, of this day. 'Their own battle songs, their own flags, their own symbols, their own salute', I noted down, 'military-like stewards, a forest of bright red flags with black swastika on white ground, a strange mixture of the military and the revolutionary, of nationalist and socialist—in the audience also: mainly of the depressed middle class of every level—will it be welded together again here?' For hours, endless booming military music; for hours, short speeches by subordinate leaders. When was he coming? Had something unexpected happened? Nobody can describe the fever that spread in this atmosphere. Suddenly there was a movement at the back entrance. Words of command. The speaker on the platform stopped in mid-sentence. Everybody jumped up, saluting. And right through the shouting crowds and the streaming flags the one they were waiting for came with his followers, walking quickly to the platform, his right arm raised stiffly. He passed by me quite close and I saw. This was a different person from the one I had met now and then in private houses; his gaunt, pale features contorted as if by inward rage, cold flames darting from his protruding eyes, which seemed to be searching out foes to be conquered. Did the crowd give him this mysterious power? Did it emanate from him to them? 'Fanatical, hysterical romanticism with a brutal core of willpower', I noted down. 'The declining middle class may be carrying this man, but he is not of them; he assuredly comes from totally different depths of darkness. Is he simply using them as a jumping-off point....?

(iv) The Hitler–Putsch 8–9 November 1923

The French and Belgian occupation of the Ruhr in January 1923 alarmed the Army authorities, who became increasingly concerned lest France or other states on Germany's borders try to annex parts of German territory. In an attempt to mobilise all available German forces to meet this threat the Army secretly took under its wing many extreme right-wing paramilitary leagues to form a so-called 'Black Reichswehr'. Among these was the SA, which became increasingly militarised during 1923, a tendency to which it had been prone from the beginning. Hitler himself did not approve, believing the Ruhr occupation and soaring inflation were polarising public opinion in Germany and that civil war was imminent. Consequently, he now felt obliged to work with other nationalist groups without wishing to be forced into a position of cooperating with the Government against the French. He wished the nationalist forces to be used to defeat any coup from the Left and to replace the Republican regime with a right-wing dictatorship.

By August 1923, it had become clear that the policy of passive resistance to the French had failed and the rather conservative government of Wilhelm Cuno resigned, being replaced by a government under a right-wing Liberal, Gustav Stresemann, which included the Social Democrats. On 26 September, it announced the ending of passive resistance in the Ruhr. Hitler believed these developments represented the first stage in the establishment of a Communist regime, as Communists had already allied with Socialist state governments in Thuringia and Saxony to form proletarian paramilitary units. In the meantime, Hitler had become political head of the *Kampfbund*, which coordinated the activities of the NSDAP and other paramilitary groups in Bavaria. Under its pressure the Bavarian Government declared a state of emergency and appointed Kahr State Commissioner with dictatorial powers. There now developed an uneasy relationship between the Bavarian authorities and the *Kampfbund*. Both groups shared a determination to bring down the national government in Berlin, through a march on Berlin along the lines of Mussolini's 'March on Rome' of October 1922. They would use the excuse of the need to crush the left-wing governments in Thuringia and Saxony which lay between Bavaria and Berlin. They hoped to coordinate action with right-wing groups in north Germany and in particular the Army.

The attitude of the Army authorities in Bavaria, vitally important to the success of such an enterprise, was soon tested. The national government in Berlin had replied to the declaration of a state of emergency in Bavaria by declaring a state of emergency in the Reich as a whole, handing over emergency powers to the Army Commander General von Seeckt. Acting under these emergency powers, the Reich authorities now attempted to get the Bavarian authorities to ban the *Völkischer Beobachter* for its bitter and mendacious attacks on Stresemann. Kahr refused to comply and persuaded General von Lossow, Commander of the Bavarian military district, to support him. After refusing point blank an order from Berlin to ban the paper, Lossow was dismissed. However, after swearing an oath of loyalty to the Bavarian government, he was promptly reinstated by them. Berlin and Munich appeared to be on a collision course.

Although Kahr and the *Kampfbund* basically agreed on objectives—the overthrow of the Weimar constitution, they differed on the necessary tactics. In October 1923, the Reich government's preemptive stroke, ordering the Army to crush the left wing governments in Saxony and Thuringia, caused the authorities in Bavaria to hesitate since they no longer had an excuse to march on Berlin. The right-wing groups in north Germany were also hesitant. In particular, the Army commander, von

Seeckt, although sympathetic to the idea of a right-wing coup, was ultra-cautious—the example of Kapp was not exactly encouraging. Kahr, therefore, decided to warn the leaders of the Kampfbund against independent and precipitate action, at a meeting with them held on 6 November:

15

To introduce the discussion, Kahr said the first priority is the creation of a nationalist government. We agree on that. Now we have to divide the work between us. The Stresemann Government is not nationalist and therefore must be fought from the start. Kahr then dealt with the fact that various leagues—the *Kampfbund* was not mentioned by name—had acted somewhat independently during the last few days and it was rumoured that the leagues would start the attack independently. He warned them against this, for he counted on the support of the leagues if the abnormal path was chosen. For, in the present situation, it was doubtful whether the normal path could be followed. The abnormal path would have to be prepared. Preparations had already been made. But if this abnormal path was to be followed everybody must stand together. A uniform well-prepared and well-thought-out plan must be followed...

While Kahr could afford to wait, Hitler could not, having worked the enthusiasm and expectations of his followers up to fever pitch. Furthermore, the crisis would not last for ever; there were signs that the national government was getting a grip on the situation. Once conditions had returned to normal, Hitler would have lost his opportunity possibly for ever. He decided, therefore, to take the initiative himself by creating a situation in which Kahr and Lossow would be forced to join him. He used the opportunity of a public meeting in the Bürgerbräukeller, a big Munich beer cellar, on the evening of 8 November. At the meeting, held to protest against the growth of Bolshevism in Germany, Kahr was to speak and General von Lossow, Colonel von Seisser (the head of the Bavarian Landespolizei or paramilitary police) and other leading citizens of Munich were to be present. Some six hundred armed SA men were posted outside the meeting hall as Hitler burst in and interrupted Kahr's speech to announce that 'the national revolution' had begun. The historian von Müller, who later on was a witness at Hitler's trial, gave the following account:

16

Herr von Kahr had spoken for half an hour. Then there was movement at the entrance as if people were wanting to push their way in. Despite several warnings, the disturbance did not die down. Herr von Kahr had to break off speaking.

Eventually, steel helmets came into sight. From this moment on, the view from my seat was rather obscured. People stood on chairs so that I didn't see Hitler until he had come fairly near along the main gangway; just before he turned to the platform, I saw him emerge between two armed soldiers in steel helmets who carried pistols next to their heads, pointing at the ceiling. They turned towards the platform, Hitler climbed on to a chair on my left. The hall was still restless, and then Hitler made a sign to the man on his right, who fired a shot at the ceiling. Thereupon Hitler called out (I cannot recollect the exact order of his words): 'The national revolution has broken out. The hall is surrounded.' May be he mentioned the exact number, I am not sure. He asked the gentlemen Kahr, Lossow, Seisser to come out and guaranteed their personal freedom. The gentlemen did not move. The General State Commissioner [Kahr] had stepped back and stood opposite Hitler, looking at him calmly. Then Hitler went towards the platform. What happened I could not see exactly. I heard him talk to the gentlemen and I heard the words: Everything would be over in ten minutes if the gentlemen would go out with him. To my surprise the three gentlemen went out with him immediately... .

Hitler took Kahr, Lossow and Seisser into a side room to persuade them to throw in their lot with him. His excited behaviour contributed to the melodramatic atmosphere of the evening, but Kahr refused to be brow-beaten when Hitler threatened violence. The whole affair was very much improvised. General Ludendorff, who was to play a major part in Hitler's plans for a national government, had not yet arrived. According to the official account prepared by the Bavarian police:

17

After the three gentlemen had entered the room, Adolf Hitler called out: 'No one leaves the room alive without my permission'. At the door a member of the bodyguard walked up and down continually, holding a pistol.

Then Hitler turned to Excellency von Kahr with the statement: 'The Reich Government has been formed, the Bavarian Government has been overthrown. Bavaria is the springboard for the Reich Government. There must be a Reich governor in Bavaria. Pöhner[5] is to become Minister-President with dictatorial powers. You will be Reich governors. Reich Government—Hitler; national army—Ludendorff; Lossow—army minister; Seisser—police minister.

'I know this step is a difficult one for you, gentlemen, but the step must be taken, it must be made easier for the gentlemen to make the leap. Everybody must take up the post which he is allotted. If he does not, then he has no right to exist. You must fight with me, achieve victory with me, or die with me. If things go wrong, I have four bullets in my pistol, three for my colleagues if they desert me, the last bullet for myself.' While saying this, he put the pistol which he had been holding all the time to his head. While he was speaking to Excellency von Kahr, he noticed Major

---

[5] Ernst Pöhner, the Munich police chief was sympathetic to the Nazis.

Hunglinger[6] in the room and motioned with his hand for him to leave. Kahr declared to Herr Hitler: 'You can arrest me, you can have me shot, you can shoot me yourself. Whether I live or die is unimportant.' Whereupon Hitler turned to Colonel von Seisser who accused him of not keeping his promise [not to attempt a putsch]. Hitler replied: 'Yes, that's true, but I did it in the interests of the fatherland. Forgive me.'

Herr von Lossow tried to say something to the other two gentlemen. But this was prevented by a shout: 'You gentlemen are not allowed to talk to one another.'

Lossow then stepped back to the window, disgusted with the proceedings. While looking out between the curtains, he noticed in front of every window a group of armed men, some of whom looked into the room with their guns at the ready. Hitler, who clearly saw the unpleasant impression made, waved them away with his hand. Excellency von Lossow asked: 'What is Ludendorff's attitude to the affair?' Hitler replied: 'Ludendorff is ready and will soon be fetched.' Hitler then left the room. He got no answer during this time, either from Herr von Kahr or from the other gentlemen... .

The crowd in the hall was becoming impatient. Hitler could not go back on his plans as he had staked his prestige on success and his supporters expected much of him. He returned to the hall and, in an effort to put pressure on Kahr and his colleagues, announced that they had agreed to his plans. The effect of Hitler's speech was electric. According to von Müller, the crowd was not entirely on Hitler's side and was aware of his clever tactics:

18

...The general mood—I can of course only judge from my surroundings, but I think that this represented the general feeling in the hall—was still against the whole business. One heard: 'Theatrical!' 'South America!' 'Mexico!' That was the prevailing mood. The change came only during Hitler's second speech when he entered about ten minutes later, went to the platform and made a short speech. It was a rhetorical masterpiece. In fact, in a few sentences it totally transformed the mood of the audience. I have rarely experienced anything like it. When he stepped on to the platform the disturbance was so great that he could not be heard, and he fired a shot. I can still see the gesture. He got the Browning out of his back pocket and I think it was on this occasion that the remark about the machine gun was made. When things did not become quiet, he shouted angrily at the audience: 'If you are not quiet, I shall have a machine gun put up on the gallery.' In fact he had come in to say that his prediction of everything being over in ten minutes had not come true. But he said it in such a way that he finally went out with the permission of the audience to say to Kahr that the whole assembly would be behind him if he were to join. It was a complete reversal. One could hear it being said that the whole thing had been arranged, that it was a phoney performance. I did not share this

6 Major Franz Hunglinger, Seisser's adjutant.

opinion because Kahr's attitude seemed to contradict it. Seeing him at close quarters, one got the impression of confusion, of great dismay... .

Ludendorff arrived, pretended to be surprised by the affair and joined him in persuading Kahr, who, after much hesitation finally agreed. The official police account continues:

19

...Ludendorff then entered the room in a hat and coat and, without asking any questions, with obvious excitement and with a trembling voice, declared: 'Gentlemen, I am just as surprised as you are. But the step has been taken, it is a question of the fatherland and the great national and racial cause, and I can only advise you, go with us and do the same.'

With the appearance of Ludendorff the character of the proceedings in the adjoining room changed completely. The pistols had disappeared. It took the form of friendly persuasion. (Because of this, Ludendorff, who was not a witness of the initial attack in the hall, may have got the impression that no force had been used, whereas Kahr, Lossow, and Seisser had no doubt that Ludendorff was accessory to the enterprise which had been essentially arranged for him.)

Shortly after Ludendorff, Pöhner entered the room. Hitler, Ludendorff and Weber[7] now began a process of urgent persuasion. Excellency von Kahr, in particular, was besieged on all sides. Moved by the feelings previously described, Lossow at last gave Ludendorff the consent he wanted with the dry comment, 'All right'. After some hesitation, Colonel von Seisser also nodded his agreement. Then Hitler, Ludendorff, and Dr Weber, with Pöhner also, worked on Excellency von Kahr with coaxing and pleading. Lossow and Seisser were asked to take part in the coaxing, but neither replied. Ludendorff took Major Hunglinger on one side and asked him to persuade Herr von Kahr. But still no discussion with Ludendorff or discussion between the three gentlemen was allowed; they only wanted to hear 'Yes' from them. Hitler could no longer go back, whatever the position of Kahr, Lossow, and Seisser might prove to be. Hitler kept bringing this out with statements like: 'The deed has been done, there is no going back. It has already passed into history.'

After long urging, Kahr declared: 'I am ready to take over the destiny of Bavaria as the representative of the monarchy.' Hitler insisted that this statement should be made in the hall. Herr von Kahr replied that after the way in which he had been led out of the hall he refused to go back into the hall. He wanted to avoid any public fraternising. But Hitler insisted with the words: 'You will be carried shoulder high, you will see what jubilation will greet you: the people will kneel before you.' Kahr replied: 'I can do without that.' They then went into the hall.

The leaders of the putsch returned to the hall and put on a show of

---

[7] Dr Friedrich Weber, leader of the paramilitary league, Bund Oberland, was also taking part in the putsch.

solidarity, but von Müller noticed the difference in behaviour between them:

20

...An hour after Hitler's first appearance the three gentlemen came back into the hall with Hitler and Ludendorff. They were enthusiastically received. On the platform Kahr began to speak first without being requested to and gave the speech which was printed word for word in the papers. Ludendorff too in my opinion spoke without being requested to, whereas Lossow and Seisser only spoke after repeated requests—I can't remember the words, but only the gestures—on Hitler's part. If I am to depict the impression made by the gentlemen on the platform, I would say that Kahr was completely unmoved. His face was like a mask all evening. He was not pale or agitated, he was very serious, but spoke very composedly. I got the impression that there was a melancholy look about his eyes. But that is perhaps being subjective. Hitler, on the other hand, during this scene was radiant with joy. One had the feeling that he was delighted to have succeeded in persuading Kahr to collaborate. There was in his demeanour, I would say, a kind of childlike joy, a very frank expression which I shall never forget. Excellency Ludendorff by comparison was extremely grave; when he came in he was pale with suppressed emotion. His appearance as well as his words were those of a man who knew it was a matter of life and death, probably death rather than life. I shall never forget his expression. It was such that when I heard in town on the following day the rumour that he had been killed, I said to myself: That's what he looked like last night. Lossow's expression was very different; there was something detached, relaxed about his whole attitude. I don't want to make a party point but, if I am to describe it, it struck me that he made a slightly ironical fox face. A certain impenetrable smile never left his features. Seisser was pale and upset. He was the only one who gave the impression of personal agitation, of external agitation. His words were merely a variant of Lossow's. The report in the papers of the words of these two gentlemen was not correct: it was somewhat touched up. .

Hitler's apparent triumph was short-lived. The situation changed completely overnight. Ernst Röhm had occupied Army headquarters in Munich and there was sympathy for the putsch among junior officers, but the attitude of the Reichswehr as a whole never remained in doubt and when Lossow returned to his headquarters reinforcements were ordered to the Bavarian capital. Kahr followed suit by revoking the agreement he had been forced to make at gunpoint. In spite of these setbacks, arrangements went ahead for a march into the city centre of a few thousand supporters of Hitler in the forlorn hope of winning sufficient support among the population to force Kahr, Lossow and Seisser to join them. Hitler and Ludendorff led the procession. An official report prepared for the subsequent committee of inquiry related what happened:

21

...The column of National Socialists about 2,000 strong, nearly all armed, moved on through the Zweibrückenstrasse across the Marienplatz towards the Theatinerstrasse. Here it split up, the majority going down the Perusastrasse to the Residenz, the rest going on along the Theatinerstrasse.

The police stationed in the Residenz tried to cordon it off as well as the Theatinerstrasse by the Preysingstrasse. Numerous civilians hurried on ahead of the actual column in Residenzstrasse and pushed the police barricade. The ceaseless shouts of 'Stop! Don't go on!' by the state police were not obeyed. Since there was the danger of a breakthrough here, a police section, originally in the Theatinerstrasse, hurried round the Feldherrenhalle to give support. They were received with fixed bayonets, guns with the safety catches off, and raised pistols. Several police officers were spat upon, and pistols with the safety catches off were stuck in their chests. The police used rubber truncheons and rifle butts and tried to push back the crowd with rifles held horizontally. Their barricade had already been broken several times. Suddenly, a National Socialist fired a pistol at a police officer from close quarters. The shot went past his head and killed Sergeant Hollweg standing behind him. Even before it was possible to give an order, the comrades of the sergeant who had been shot opened fire as the Hitler lot did, and a short gun battle ensued during which the police were also shot at from the Preysingpalais and from the house which contains the Café Rottenhöfer. After no more than thirty seconds the Hitler lot fled, some back to the Maximilienstrasse, some to the Odeonsplatz. General Ludendorff apparently went on towards the Odeonsplatz. There he was seen in the company of a Hitler officer by a police officer barring the Briennerstrasse, who went up to General Ludendorff and said to him: 'Excellency, I must take you into custody.' General Ludendorff replied: 'You have your orders. I'll come with you.' Both gentlemen were then accompanied into the Residenz.

The putsch had failed. Its leaders were arrested and the Nazi Party, its membership grown to 55,000, was banned. Hitler, a prisoner of the public enthusiasm which he had encouraged, had not succeeded in gaining control over events. The attempt failed because of the lack of support from the Army and the police.

On 26 February 1924, Hitler, Ludendorff, Pöhner and the leaders of the Kampfbund were put on trial for high treason in Munich, with the conservative nationalist leaders, Kahr, Lossow and Seisser, as the chief witnesses for the prosecution. The trial received enormous publicity and Hitler's bravado enabled him to turn the ignominious failure of the putsch into a considerable propaganda victory. For, while asserting that Kahr and the others had pursued a similar goal, he did not deny his own part—but claimed it was a patriotic act. He blamed the failure of the enterprise on the pusillanimity of the nationalist leaders. As a result of this stand, Hitler now became a hero to many antisemites in other parts of Germany who before had never heard of him. They saw him as the one man who had had the courage and energy to act. This ensured that when the Party was refounded after his release, numerous new branches could be established outside Bavaria.

22

...Lossow said here that he had spoken with me in the spring and had not noticed then that I was trying to get something for myself and had thought that I only wanted to be a propagandist and a man who would rouse people.

How petty are the thoughts of small men! You can take my word for it, that I do not consider a ministerial post worth striving for...

From the very first I have aimed at something more than becoming a Minister. I have resolved to be the destroyer of Marxism. This I shall achieve and once I've achieved that, I should find the title of 'Minister' ridiculous. When I first stood in front of Wagner's grave, my heart overflowed with pride that here lay a man who had forbidden any such inscription as 'Here lies State Councillor, Musical Director, His Excellency Richard von Wagner'. I was proud that this man and so many others in German history have been content to leave their names to posterity and not their titles. It was not through modesty that I was willing to be a 'drummer' at that time for that is the highest task [*das Höchste*]: the rest is nothing.

Mr Public Prosecutor! You emphasise in the indictment that we had to wait with clenched teeth until the seed ripened. Well, we did wait and when the man came, we cried: 'The seed is ripe, the hour has come.' Only then, after long hesitation, did I put myself forward. I demanded for myself the leadership in the political struggle; and secondly, I demanded that the leadership of the organisation for which we all longed and for which you inwardly long just as much should go to the hero who, in the eyes of the whole of German youth, is called to it. The witness Seisser declared cynically that we had to have Ludendorff so that the Reichswehr would not shoot. Is that a crime? Was it treason that I said to Lossow, 'The way you are beginning it must come to a conflict; as I see it, there need be no conflict'?...

...What did we want on the evening of 8 November? All these gentlemen wanted a Directory in the Reich. If one has striven for something in the Reich, one cannot condemn it in Bavaria. The Directory already existed in Bavaria, it consisted of Messrs Kahr, Lossow and Seisser. We no longer knew anything of a legal government, we only feared that there might be scruples over the final decision.

I am no monarchist, but ultimately a Republican. Pöhner is a monarchist, Ludendorff is devoted to the House of Hohenzollern [Prussia-Germany]. Despite our different attitudes we all stood together. The fate of Germany does not lie in the choice between a Republic or a Monarchy, but in the content of the Republic and the Monarchy. What I am contending against is not the form of a state as such, but its ignominious content. We wanted to create in Germany the precondition which alone will make it possible for the iron grip of our enemies to be removed from us. We wanted to create order in the state, throw out the drones, take up the fight against international stock exchange slavery, against our whole economy being cornered by trusts, against the politicising of the trade unions, and above all, for the highest honourable duty which we, as Germans, know should be once more introduced—the duty of bearing arms, military service. And now I ask you: Is what we wanted high treason?...

Now people say: But His Excellency von Kahr, von Lossow and von Seisser did not want the events of the evening of 8 November. The bill of indictment says that we pushed these gentlemen into an embarrassing situation. But it was through these gentlemen that we ourselves had got into an embarrassing situation; *they* had pushed *us* into it. Herr von Kahr should have said honourably: Herr Hitler, we understand something different by a *coup d'état*, we mean something different by a march on Berlin. He had a duty to say to us: In what we are doing here we mean something different from what you think. He did not say that, and the consequences should be borne solely by these three gentlemen...

...The army which we have formed grows from day to day; it grows more rapidly from hour to hour. Even now I have the proud hope that one day the hour will come when these untrained [*wild*] bands will grow to battalions, the battalions to regiments and the regiments to divisions, when the old cockade will be raised from the mire, when the old banners will once again wave before us: and the reconciliation will come in that eternal last Court of Judgement, the Court of God, before which we are ready to take our stand. Then from our bones, from our graves, will sound the voice of that tribunal which alone has the right to sit in judgement upon us. For, gentlemen, it is not you who pronounce judgement upon us, it is the external Court of History which will make its pronouncement upon the charge which is brought against us. The verdict that you will pass I know. But that Court will not ask of us, 'Did you commit high treason or did you not?' That Court will judge us...as Germans who wanted the best for their people and their fatherland, who wished to fight and to die. You may pronounce us guilty a thousand times, but the Goddess who presides over the Eternal Court of History will with a smile tear in pieces the charge of the Public Prosecutor and the verdict of this court. For she acquits us.

The judges, right-wing and sympathisers with the motives of the conspirators, acquitted Ludendorff and gave Hitler the minimum sentence of five years' imprisonment, with the clear understanding that he would be released early on probation.

CHAPTER 2

The Creation of a Nationwide Party Organisation 1924–28

During Hitler's imprisonment the banned Nazi Party disintegrated into rival factions. Hitler had nominated Alfred Rosenberg, editor of the *Völkischer Beobachter*, to act as his deputy during his imprisonment. Rosenberg, however, was unable to assert his authority and was soon challenged by rivals, notably Esser and Streicher. Outside Bavaria the dominant racialist party was the German Racialist Freedom Party, or DVFP, founded in 1922 by three Reichstag deputies, former members of the main extreme right-wing party, the German National People's Party (DNVP). Although during elections, the DVFP worked with former Nazis in an electoral alliance, the so-called *Völkisch*-Social Block, its ambitions were bitterly resisted by many other former Nazis, particularly young people, who considered the party too bourgeois in its social composition and political style. For a time they worked with Esser and Streicher until personal differences caused a bitter row. These opponents of the DVFP looked to Hitler as their leader and appealed to him for support. But Hitler, finding that he could not control events from prison and unwilling to compromise himself with any commitments, decided to withdraw from active politics until his release. The confusion in the *völkisch* movement strengthened his own position.

In Landsberg Prison, Hitler was working out his plans for the Party after his release. The coalition of antisemitic groups formed for the Reichstag election of May 1924 won 9 per cent of the vote and thirty-two deputies, although of these only ten were former Nazis. In the spring election to the Bavarian state diet the racialists became the second largest party in the diet. This impressed Hitler. The putsch had proved unsuccessful because the Army did not cooperate and the end of the political and economic crisis made an attempt to seize power by force look less and less feasible. A new policy was necessary as Hitler told Ludecke when he received a visit from him in Landsberg:

23

...I noticed that he barred in particular any reminder of the putsch and any question concerning his policy towards the Party schism...I gladly eschewed the subject as too delicate. But the lesson it taught was another matter, which Hitler himself took up.

'From now on,' he said, 'we must follow a new line of action. It is best to attempt no large reorganisation until I am freed, which may be a matter of months rather than years.'

I must have looked at him somewhat incredulously. 'Oh yes', he continued, 'I am not going to stay here much longer. When I resume active work it will be necessary to pursue a new policy. Instead of working to achieve power by armed conspiracy, we shall have to hold our noses and enter the Reichstag against the Catholic and Marxist deputies. If outvoting them takes longer than outshooting them, at least the results will be guaranteed by their own Constitution! Any lawful process is slow. But already, as you know, we have thirty-two Reichstag deputies under this new programme, and are the second largest party in the Bavarian Landtag diet. Sooner or later we shall have a majority and after that we shall have Germany. I am convinced that this is our best line of action now that conditions in the country have changed so radically...

Although now ready to participate in elections and to enter Parliament, Hitler did not in any way give up his hostility to it. The putsch attempt made it much easier for him to pursue a constitutional course since he could never be accused of weakness. This was important. For it was the extremism of the Nazis which distinguished them from similar groups and contributed so much to their success.

(i) The Refounding of the Party, 27 February 1925

Hitler was released in December 1924 and, after promising to work within the Constitution, was permitted to refound the Nazi Party at a meeting in the same Bürgerbräu beer cellar in Munich on 27 February 1925. Hitler made it clear in the *Völkischer Beobachter* of 26 February that he was interested only in what the individual could offer him in terms of abilities and in whether he was prepared to obey the leader without preconditions. He justified this demand for absolute control with a promise to render an account in a year's time and take the responsibility whatever the outcome. Finally, unlike other antisemitic groups, particularly in north Germany, he was not interested in fighting Roman Catholicism. This would only limit the potential support of the Party particularly in Bavaria itself and it would antagonise the Bavarian Government, now dominated by the Catholic Bavarian People's Party, which he was trying to conciliate in order to secure freedom for the Party to operate effectively:

24

National Socialists! Party Comrades!

...In this hour we do not only want to remember again those who in November 1923 became blood witnesses of our political beliefs and aims; we also want to thank all those who in this past year did not despair of the movement and what it stands for, but laboured in its service regardless of whatever camp they felt drawn to.

Above all, we want to remember the one man who had nothing to gain but rather stood to lose the fame of being the undying leader of the heroic German armies in the greatest war on earth, and who despite all this decided to make the great sacrifice of giving his name and his energy to a movement which had no leader.

In General Ludendorff the National Socialist movement will for ever honour its most faithful and unselfish friend. The movement will be bound to him not by the memory of friendship given in happy times but by loyalty maintained in persecution and misery.

My task as leader of the movement is not to look for the causes of a previous quarrel or to assess who was right, but to mould the movement into a unified weapon regardless of the interests of individuals. Thus I shall not inquire into the past of those comrades who rejoin, but only work to ensure that the past will not repeat itself in the future. From our supporters I demand that if they are willing to join the new movement they should feel themselves once more to be brothers in a great fighting community and stand together loyally shoulder to shoulder as before.

But I expect the leaders, in so far as they come from the old camp, to give me the same obedience as we all give to the common idea.

Those who cannot forget the past are not worthy of serving a better future.

I myself promise to render an account to the comrades in a year's time as to whether the Party has become a movement or whether the movement has suffocated by being a party.

In either case I shall take the responsibility.

Long live the National Socialist German Workers' Party!

Long live our German fatherland!

25

'On the revival of our movement'
...I do not consider it to be the task of a political leader to try and improve, let alone make uniform the human material which he has at hand. The temperaments, characters, and talents of individual people are so various that it is impossible to unify a large number of completely similar people. It is also not the task of a political leader to try and remove these deficiencies by 'training' people to be united. All such attempts are condemned to failure. Human nature is a given quantity which does not lend itself to alteration in particulars, but can only transform itself through a process of development lasting for centuries. But even then the prerequisite for such a change is generally alterations in the basic racial elements...

If a political leader departs from this awareness and if instead he attempts only to seek people who come up to his ideal, he will not only wreck his plans, but also in a very short time leave behind him chaos instead of an organisation. The guilt which he then attributes to individual supporters or subordinates is in reality only his own lack of awareness and ability.

For this very reason, if I try today to revive the old NSDAP, I cannot recognise commitments which derive from past events. I am not prepared to accept conditions, whose fulfilment would only represent that lack of psychological awareness and ability which I described above.

I shall, therefore, see it as my particular task to direct the various temperaments, talents and qualities of character in the movement into those channels in which by supplementing one another they benefit everybody.

In the future, the movement's struggle must once more take the form which we intended at its foundation. With all its forces concentrated together it must be turned against that power to which above all we owe the collapse of our fatherland and the destruction of our people. This does not mean an alteration in or a 'postponement' of the old and main aim of our struggle, but simply its reassertion.

At this point, I must object particularly to the attempt to drag religious quarrels into the movement, or even to go so far as to equate the movement with such things. I have always opposed the collective description 'racialist' [*völkisch*], because the extremely vague definition of this term has opened the way to damaging activities. For this reason, earlier on, the movement placed more emphasis on its clearly defined programme as well as on the unified trend of its struggle than on a term which was incapable of being clearly defined and which was conducive to a more or less verbose interpretation.

I see in the attempt by various people to turn the racialist movement into a struggle about religion the beginning of the end of that movement.

Religious reformations cannot be carried out by political infants and these people are rarely anything but that.

I am quite clear about the possibility of beginning such a struggle, but I doubt if the gentlemen involved are clear about its probable end result.

In any case, it will be my main task to make sure that in the newly awakened NSDAP members of both confessions can live peacefully side by side and can stand together in the common struggle against that power which is the deadly enemy of every form of Christianity, no matter what confession.

No movement has fought harder against the Centre Party and its supporting groups than our own, not for religious reasons but solely from political considerations. And so from now onwards we must fight the Centre not because it claims to be 'Christian' or 'Catholic' but solely because a party which has allied itself with atheistic Marxism for the suppression of its own people is neither Christian nor Catholic.

We do not declare war on the Centre for religious reasons, but solely for national-political ones.

History will pass judgement on who will be successful, we or the advocates of a cultural struggle.

Finally, I demand of the movement's supporters that from now onwards they direct all their energies outwards and do not weaken themselves in a fratricidal struggle.

The best local branch leadership is not the one which 'unites' the other nationalist organisations or 'wins them over' to the movement, but the one which wins antinationalists back to the German people.

The success of our movement must be measured not by the number of Reichstag or Landtag seats we win, but by the extent to which Marxism is destroyed and by the degree of enlightenment about its originator, the Jews.

Let those who wish to join in this struggle do so; let those who do not, stay away.

(ii) The assertion of the primacy of the 'Führer'

After the refounding of the Party, Hitler, soon banned from public speaking in Bavaria and many other states, concentrated on writing the second volume of *Mein Kampf*. During the summer of 1925, the Munich branch of the Party became involved in bitter factional squabbles in which personalities played a major part. Hitler had left the day-to-day running of the Party in the hands of the Party officials—Bouhler (the secretary), Schwarz (the treasurer), Amann (the head of the publishing house) and Esser (the propaganda chief). In addition, Julius Streicher, the branch leader of Nuremberg, and Artur Dinter, Gauleiter or regional leader of Thuringia, were influential. This group had fought a bitter feud with other Bavarian antisemites and former Nazis during 1924 and this feud now broke out again. But Esser, Streicher and Dinter were also extremely unpopular among many Party members throughout Germany and particularly in the north and west. Some of the Gauleiters here, where the Party was now growing more rapidly than in Bavaria, resented the authority of what they regarded as an unsavoury Munich clique. This conflict dated back to the previous year when Esser's abrasive personality had alienated many Nazis, particularly when he committed the cardinal sin of washing the Party's dirty linen in the pages of the influential 'Jewish' newspaper, the *Frankfurter Zeitung*.

But apart from questions of personality, important issues of principle now emerged. Some leading members of the Party outside Bavaria disagreed on aspects of Party policy. In the first place, the Party leaders in Göttingen and Hanover disagreed with participation in elections. This represented a challenge to the new parliamentary tactics now being followed by the Party. Secondly, Gregor Strasser, the Gauleiter of Lower Bavaria, who had met many of the north and west German Party leaders while acting as Hitler's deputy in the refounding of the Party there, felt that the Party programme was too vague and should be defined more concretely in a 'Socialist' direction. He was supported by some of the local Party leaders in the industrial areas of north and west Germany who wanted to compete with the Left for the support of the workers.

The 'Socialism' of Gregor Strasser was in fact typical of that of most racialists—a determination to try to win the workers for nationalism by giving them a greater sense of belonging to the nation. It sprang from his experience in the trenches during the war, as he told a meeting in 1927:

26

...How did all those tens of thousands in all parts of Germany become National Socialist? Perhaps I may be allowed to recall how I became one...because I am a test case here! Before the war we did not bother with politics. I grew up the son of a low-ranking civil servant. I had no ambition other than to get on through hard work. In the war we became Nationalists, that is to say, out of that vague feeling that the fatherland had to be defended, that it was something great and sacred, the protector of the existence of the individual, out of this vague notion which for many of us was not clear, we became nationalists on the battlefield. When I saw all the nations of the earth rushing against the German trenches with bloodthirsty destruction, when the international stock exchange armed one country after another and set them going against the single German nation in the trenches— Americans, Portuguese, Blacks, Yellows, against the little group of Germans fighting for their existence, it became clear to me: if Germany wants to survive, every German must *know what it means to be a German and must defend this idea to the limits of self-sacrifice.* Companies and batteries reduced from 250 to 60 men did not have to be told about the *community of need*; they knew: if we do not stand together the Blacks will be on us. We knew that the first priority of manhood is to defend oneself, and the second, all who speak the same language must stick together, must organise themselves to be strong by being united!

And why did we become Socialists?

This notion was still as far from many who today stand in our ranks as the notion of nationalism in terms of its real significance. We learnt all sorts of things at school. But nobody told us that half the German people were hostile to the nation *because they had been denied the most basic needs of life by the other half.* Not a word were we told about that tragic hour for the German people *when the growing German workers' movement was nothing but the cry of millions of German fellow countrymen for acceptance into the nation on equal terms (loud applause).* So these millions of people were left to the Jew Marx who created Marxism out of the German workers' movement, who intended to do nothing but *destroy the German nation* with the strength of these millions *and to make it a colony of world capital.*

We must always regard *one* principle as fundamental: to be ready to recognise mistakes, to see that when a nation goes under, it is mainly the *fault of the rulers* of that nation. They had the power to prevent everything which in the long run forced people to become hostile to the nation and state.

This person, whom the Jew Marx had perverted into a 'Social Democrat', a Marxist, was suddenly found standing next one in the platoon, in the battery, by the guns. During the long hours of sentry duty there would be discussion: What are you? A mechanic. Politically? A red, a Marxist. And we who came from the bourgeoisie, we who had been told nothing, were surprised.

Why am I a Marxist? Because you have never bothered with us! Then one started thinking, then came the great realisation how brave the man is, and how well he does his duty! It was my experience that the best soldiers were frequently those who had least to defend at home *(applause).* He cooperated, he did his duty unfailingly, and from conversations with him we understood *the mistakes of our great-grandfathers. Because we had become nationalists in the trenches we could not help becoming Socialists in the trenches,* we could not help coming home with the brutal intention of gathering the whole nation round us and teaching them that the greatness of a nation depends on the willingness of the individual to stand up for this nation and say to it: Your fate is indissolubly linked with the fate of your people, with the fate and greatness of your nation. We could not help coming home from this war with this resolve: *Those who have fought together with us and who are hostile towards the nation because it has not bothered with them must be emancipated so that Germany will in future be strong and the master of her enemies! (loud applause).*

In order to further his attempt to change the programme and as a counterweight to the Party bureaucracy in Munich, Strasser now took the initiative in establishing a so-called 'working group' (*Arbeitsgemeinschaft*) of the Gauleiters in north and west Germany. In fact, however, as is clear from the following report, written by Fobke, a Göttingen leader, of the first meeting, held at Hagen in Westphalia on 10 September, there were deep disagreements between these Gauleiters over the various points at issue, particularly over the question of elections which was the main issue for the Göttingen leaders. The only aim on which most of them were agreed was cooperation in matters of organisation among regions with similar problems and the development of new ideas appropriate to their needs which the bureaucrats in the Munich headquarters 'Esser & Co' were apparently incapable of doing. These would, it was hoped, meet with Hitler's approval and it is significant that Point 4 of the statutes of the working group shows that they had been careful to gain Hitler's general approval for the organisation:

27

...The movement is at the moment undergoing a crisis associated mainly with the name of Hermann Esser. This extremely dubious character, of obscure political as well as moral background, is at the moment absolute boss in the Party leadership. The result is a continual diminution of all the good elements in the movement, which today, for example, in the city of Munich only comprises 700 members. Thousands stand aside without joining any group, others—the smaller part—have joined together in the National Socialist People's League [*Nationalsozialistische Volksbund*] under the leadership of Dörfler and Anton Drechsler [*sic*], which parted from the NSDAP some time ago under the slogan 'With Hitler but without Esser!' when Hitler did *not* do without Esser. In the last few days, an open conflict has developed between Alfred Rosenberg, editor of the *Völkischer Beobachter* and publisher of the *Weltkampf*, and Adolf Hitler, the origin of which must be sought in the prominent position in the Party of Esser, Amann and Streicher. Of my personal acquaintances with me in the prison in Landsberg, the best are standing aside in convinced opposition.

Hitler himself, whom I met on 26 and 27 August, adopts a completely passive attitude towards the business; this, under the circumstances, is equivalent to supporting Esser. At the moment his activity is entirely confined to the completion of the second volume of his book, *Mein Kampf*. Any suggestion of getting rid at last of Esser & Co., including above all Streicher and Dinter, he counters with the insubstantial objection that for him their usefulness is the decisive factor. He overlooks the fact that the total rejection of them throughout the Reich is being outweighed by their theoretical usefulness within a limited area. Outside Bavaria too the movement is in my opinion in a stagnant condition, which, apart from the general political indifference, has its origin in the sorry state of things at the Munich headquarters.

Opposition to the Esser dictatorship is naturally making itself evident. To create a counterbalance to this dictatorship was the purpose of a meeting which Gregor Strasser, Hitler's honest and extremely hard-working, even if not exactly inspired colleague, summoned for 10 September at Hagen in Westphalia. Strasser himself was prevented from attending, with the result that the discussion was perhaps not as far-reaching as it would have been had he been there... .

As convener, Herr Strasser originally intended to use the negotiations at the meeting to play off the block formed by those invited against the pernicious Munich line. Of this plan, apart from Haase [Gauleiter] of Göttingen, only Dr Goebbels[8] and a man unknown to us by name who chaired the meeting,[9] were aware. Since Strasser did not attend, the real purpose of the meeting was not touched on; instead, to begin with, the only decision reached was the setting up of a close

---

[8] A party activist in Elberfeld.

[9] Dr Hellmuth Elbrechter, a Nazi from Elberfeld.

association between the *Gaue* mentioned above, with the name 'Working Group of the north and west German Gauleiters of the NSDAP'. Cooperation was planned through an exchange of speakers, and organisational help of every kind was arranged by setting up a headquarters and by the publication of the 'National Socialist Letters' [*NS Briefe*]. These are intended for the leadership and are meant to effect a uniform clarification of basic questions, to be achieved by a free exchange of views. At the head of this working group is Strasser.

When it looked as if in Strasser's absence the question of Esser would not be mentioned, I brought it up with the agreement of Herr Haase. This produced a general reaction of horror. Some people strongly opposed such a 'palace revolution', and the representative from Rhineland-North, who was chairing the meeting, suggested postponing discussion of the matter. Haase and I agreed to this postponement intentionally because by pressing the point we had sown a seed which could be cultivated at the monthly meetings which were planned to follow. Consultation with the chairman who was deputising for Strasser and with Dr Goebbels produced unanimity on this point.

Haase had travelled to Hagen with the firm intention of bringing about at all events a clarification of the question of participation in any elections, whether local council, county council, regional diet or Reichstag, in view of the Prussian elections which were coming up. A preliminary sounding produced the situation that at the moment Telschow (Hanover-East) and Lohse (Schleswig-Holstein) were supporting us in opposing, whereas Vahlen (Pomerania) and Haake (Cologne) were against us and in favour of electoral participation. Already some time back we had had Rust's (Hanover-Brunswick) pledge to support non-participation.

Haase therefore made a short statement to the effect that we and those gentlemen who agreed with our position *would under no circumstances participate in any elections, no matter what directives had been given by Munich headquarters. The other* Gaue *would have to adapt themselves to our attitude.* This declaration produced a shocked and embarrassed pause. But the discussion produced a majority agreement on a resolution to Hitler which this time was unanimously approved. This stated that *all* the Gauleiters meeting in Hagen absolutely rejected participation in elections and demanded a clear statement from the Party leadership, which so far had sent three different sets of instructions to three different places... .

To conclude, the newly founded working group offers the possibility of securing further recognition for our position in the National Socialist movement. Haase is determined to exploit this possibility to the limit and, next to the question of Parliament, to try also to settle the case of Esser, that is the purging of the movement in accordance with our views...

28

Statutes of the working group

1. The Working Group of the North and West German *Gaue* of the NSDAP comprises the *Gaue*: Rhineland-North, Rhineland-South, Westphalia, Hanover, Hanover-South, Hesse-Nassau, Lüneberg-Stade, Schleswig-Holstein, Grea-

ter-Hamburg, Greater-Berlin and Pomerania.
2. The aim and purpose of the Working Group is: the greatest possible uniformity among the affiliated *Gaue* in organisation and propaganda; the creation of uniform propaganda methods, the swapping of speakers; the good-neighbourly encouragement of friendly personal relations among the Gauleiters; the exchange of ideas on questions of politics and organisation by letter and by regular meetings; when necessary, joint statements on current political issues.
3. The journal of the Working Group is the bi-monthly *NS Briefe*, to be published by Comrade Gregor Strasser and edited by Comrade Dr Goebbels.
4. Both Working Group and *NS Briefe* exist with the express approval of Adolf Hitler.
5. The director of the Working Group is Comrade Gregor Strasser, Landshut.
6. The secretary of the Working Group is Comrade Dr Goebbels, Elberfeld.
7. The office of the Working Group is until further notice at Elberfeld, Holzerstrasse 4. Tel. 6526.
8. The Gauleiters affiliated to the Working Group meet for joint discussions, when necessary, in a city in one or another of the above-mentioned *Gaue*... .

The meeting of the Working Group in Hanover on 22 November 1925 invited Gregor Strasser to draft a new Party programme. Two months later, however, on 24 January 1926, a second meeting in Hanover set up a sub-committee to consider a new programme after rejecting Strasser's draft as too vague and verbose. He had clearly proved unable to reconcile the differing views on such questions as the structure of the future National Socialist state and foreign policy. A number of members, including Goebbels, favoured an alliance with Russia against the 'Jewish-capitalist' West, regarding Russia under Stalin as a 'nationalist' power. The Göttingen group, on the other hand, regarded Russia as a field for German expansion.

Another important issue discussed was the need to decide whether or not to support a referendum organised by the Left to demand the expropriation of the royal princes. The Party's attitude on this question would be regarded as a test of Nazi claims to be considered a genuinely workers' and Socialist party. The meeting passed the following resolution which, despite its equivocation, went some way towards committing the Party to the principle of expropriation. This did not prove sufficient to persuade many workers to support the Nazi Party but it does indicate that the Working Group, led by Strasser, Goebbels and the other Elberfeld leaders, were serious in their intention of winning working class support.

29

The study group holds the view, without in any way wishing to anticipate the decision of Party headquarters, that the so-called question of compensation for the princes is not a question of fundamental importance for the Party as such.

It is guided by the view that the question of so-called compensation for the princes is not only a legal but also a social matter. In a state in which law and justice prevailed, one would obviously regard it only from the legal standpoint. This state of Weimar, however, which has perpetrated upon pensioners, war-loan recipients and state creditors the enormous injustice of confiscating their property and calling it revaluation, has violated the very basis of law and property, and this not in the interests of the community, but, on the contrary, in the service of speculative, immoral stock exchange capital which is in the hands of only a few.

The distressing circumstances in which the German people find themselves, owing to the criminal policy of the government parties of all shades, do not permit, simply with reference to formal law, the granting of hundreds of millions of Reichsmarks to former princes, the majority of whom did not understand or further the racial tasks of Germany.

But this attitude makes it doubly necessary to point out the crude mendacity of the parties of the Left, who want to exploit this question for sordid party purposes...

For such wealth, which is immoral in view of the present distress of the German people, is not only in the hands of former princes, but above all is in the possession of Jewish financiers great and small. Therefore, if the Marxist petition for the expropriation of the Royal Houses without compensation is accepted, we demand also the expropriation without compensation of all Eastern Jews who have entered Germany as immigrants since 1 August 1914, as well as the confiscation of all increases in property after 1 August 1914, paying particular attention to bank and stock exchange profits.

We ask all Party members in public discussions to adopt on this question a position in accordance with this point of view.

Hitler's representative, Gottfried Feder, regarded himself as the leading ideologist of the Party and resented the criticism levelled at the programme by the Working Group. His report on the support given by the meeting to the referendum, on their determination to rewrite the programme, and above all on their critical attitude towards the Munich headquarters, which may or may not have included the leader himself, forced Hitler to act. His attempts to win the approval of businessmen, a tactic which would be undermined by Party support for the expropriation of the princes, would be threatened. Furthermore, while Hitler regarded the details of the Party programme as of relatively minor significance, he was not prepared to have the programme itself discussed since this would give it undue importance. If the programme could be altered as a result of discussion and pressure from the membership, the Party would be liable to endless doctrinal disputes such as those that bedevilled the parties of the Left. This would detract from the main aim of winning power. Above all, if the programme was made to appear so important and was subject to alteration by the membership, then it would inevitably restrict the freedom of the leader to act as he thought fit in any given circumstances. Instead of the party line being defined by the leader, he would be bound by a party programme whose interpretation would be in the hands of the party membership. The issue at stake was whether the party was to be a 'Führer party' in which the leader was the source of all authority, or whether authority was to be ultimately derived from the programme as interpreted by the membership. Finally, Hitler feared the growth of the Working Group into a regional organisation which might challenge the authority of Munich headquarters. To meet this challenge, therefore, he summoned a conference of Party leaders on 14 February at Bamberg in Bavaria at which, without actually attacking the Working Group, he made it clear that their policies were unacceptable. Goebbels described the occasion in his diary:

30

Leaving Saturday morning. In Bamberg we shall have to act the part of the bashful maiden and lure Hitler on to our territory. I am glad to notice that our [i.e. the Socialist] spirit is on the march in all towns. Not a soul has faith in Munich. Elberfeld must become the Mecca of German Socialism... .
...Sunday morning. Strasser comes to fetch me in the morning. He is hopeful. Plan for action ready. With Rust and Vahlen. Then tour of Bamberg. Charming town. Old, Jesuit. Hitler's car tears past us. A handshake. Well, well, Schlange-Berlin,[10] Streicher, Esser, Feder. Then to work. Hitler speaks for two hours. This pretty nearly finishes me. What kind of Hitler? A reactionary? Amazingly clumsy and uncertain. Russian question: altogether beside the point. Italy and Britain are natural allies. Horrible! It is our job to smash Bolshevism. Bolshevism is a Jewish creation! We must become Russia's heirs! A hundred and eighty millions!!! Compensation for princes! Law is law. Also for the princes. Question of not weakening private property [sic]. Horrible! Programme will do! Happy with it. Feder nods. Ley[11] nods. Streicher nods. Esser nods. It hurts me deeply to see you in that company!!! Short discussion. Strasser speaks. Hesitant, trembling, clumsy, good, honest Strasser; Lord, what a poor match we are for those pigs down there! Half an hour's disussion after a four-hour speech! Nonsense, you will win! I cannot say a word! I am stunned! By car to the station. Strasser is quite beside himself! Waving and *Heil*. My heart aches! Farewell from Strasser. We meet again in Berlin the day after tomorrow. I want to cry! Journey home. Sad journey home. With Haake and Dr. Ley. I say hardly a word. A horrible night! Probably one of my greatest disappointments. I can no longer wholly believe in Hitler. This is terrible. I have lost my inner support. I am only half myself. Grey dawn appears. Elberfeld. A few hours' sleep. Kaufmann.[12] I want to embrace him. We all say all there is to be

---

[10] Dr Schlange, Gauleiter of Berlin 1925–26.
[11] Dr Robert Ley, Gauleiter of Rhineland-South 1925–31; 1931–33, posts in Munich headquarters; after 1933, head of the German Labour Front and of Party organisation.
[12] Karl Kaufmann, Gauleiter of the Ruhr 1926–28, Gauleiter of Hamburg 1929–45.

said. Schmitz and Toni join us. The result: we are Socialists. We don't want to have been it in vain! Telegram from Lohse, Strasser, Vahlen. Do nothing hasty. Tomorrow discussion in Göttingen. Then Wednesday to Strasser. Proposal: Kaufmann, Strasser and I go to Hitler to impress on him: he must not allow those rogues down there to tie him hand and foot. Well then, train again tomorrow. Into battle. I despair! Sleep! Sleep! Sleep!

Although for a few weeks Goebbels and some other members of the Working Group still hoped that they would win over Hitler, this proved impossible. The Party Congress in May 1926 declared the programme once again immutable and in July working groups within the Party were forbidden. In the meantime Goebbels had made his peace with Hitler and in November was appointed Gauleiter in Berlin.

(iii) The creation of the Party cadre

The importance of the period 1925–29 in the history of the Nazi Party lies in the creation of a cadre of dedicated activists scattered in towns and villages throughout Germany. The basic framework had been laid before 1925 for the Party began with a number of supporters already involved in the *völkisch* movement either in the Nazi Party before its ban or in the German *Völkisch* Freedom Party (DVFP). These, rather than join the new DVFP, joined the refounded Nazi Party largely because of its reputation for activism and of the prestige won by Hitler during his trial. Significantly, those who joined the Nazi Party tended to be younger than those joining its rival. The basic pattern of Nazi organisation was regional. Germany was divided into *Gaue* or regions, and regional Party leaders or Gauleiters were appointed, usually men already successful in establishing their leadership in the area who were in effect confirmed by Party headquarters in Munich. Until 1928, the boundaries of the *Gaue* had been arranged on a largely *ad hoc* basis depending partly on the existing political and administrative divisions, partly on the extent of the area over which respective Gauleiters had established their authority. In 1928, however, the *Gaue* were reorganised to correspond with the thirty-five Reichstag electoral districts. Below the *Gaue* came the local branches and 'strongpoints' varying from a few hundred members down to one or two, who, not forming a branch, carried out propaganda in their area as best they could. In time, a district (*Kreis*) organisation developed between the *Gau* headquarters and the local branches but this only became fully effective after 1929. The main burden of Party work during this period fell on the *Gau* headquarters, in touch with both Munich and the local branches. In the early period the main correspondence with Munich concerned membership forms and subscriptions. As for propaganda, the *Gaue* could expect only an occasional speaker from headquarters. Most propaganda work was carried out by the Gauleiters and a few leading local activists, speaking at meetings arranged by the local branches, often in neighbouring towns and villages as yet without a branch. Such meetings might produce enough new members to found a branch—usually a minimum of fifteen. Once a branch had been founded it would canvass support in neighbouring villages by holding periodic meetings and distributing pamphlets.

A typical example was the village of Affinghausen in the district of Diepholz in Lower Saxony. The history of the local branch written in 1937 records the founding as follows:

31

In the year 1928–29 the National Socialist speaker, Jan Blankemeyer [a peasant] from Oldenburg came and talked to us about Adolf Hitler and his movement. Comrade Blankemeyer then came every two months and in winter even more frequently. He was living then in Uenzen, Kreis Grafschaft Hoya [a neighbouring district]. Comrades from the Uenzen branch ran the meetings here. Then Dincklage, the deputy Gauleiter, came. In October 1929, after a Blankemeyer meeting, eleven people joined the Party. Then in November 1929 the SA from Borstel near Nienburg [in a neighbouring district] held a propaganda march, which was followed by a meeting with Comrade Leister from Nienburg, and a branch was founded with farmer Hermann Menke as branch leader. Then we carried out propaganda in the surrounding villages.

Before 1928–29 it was a slow process, characterised by much conflict within the various local Party organisations. But a cadre organisation was being created, which provided the organisational framework essential if the Party was to be capable of successfully exploiting the economic and social discontent of 1929–33. The character of these men, who were to form the political leadership of the Third Reich, helped shape the future development of National Socialism. Their youth, radicalism, and sense of commitment, helped to determine the charismatic nature of the Party organisation, expressed in the emphasis on the absolute authority of Hitler as leader. This had ensured the failure of the Working Group, whose members themselves and notably its most dynamic leader, Joseph Goebbels, shared this commitment to Hitler's leadership. They wanted a leader and they recognised that Hitler was by far the most effective leader in the *völkisch* movement. He offered them the type of political action which they enjoyed. Politics for them was not a matter of discussion, bargaining and compromise within established bodies and procedures, but the thrill of physical action in the streets and beer halls or of inspiring an audience with a speech; the sense of comradeship induced by the struggle against an enemy; the glow of self-righteousness springing from a comparison of one's own self-sacrifice for the sake of the nation with the 'philistinism' of the citizen going about his ordinary daily life. This style of politics appealed to many young people and to many uprooted during the post-war crisis from normal ties of family and job whose alienation now became a source of pride rationalised by an ideology which condemned the established order and glorified them as an elite. These men ousted the older generation of *völkisch* leaders whose political style had been shaped by the pre-war years, as the young Dr. Albert Krebs, who became for a short time Gauleiter in Hamburg, later recalled:

32

Characteristic of this period was the steady disappearance of all leaders and subordinate leaders (with the exception of a few parliamentary deputies) whose views and methods of struggle were still rooted in prewar days. Their places were taken by the young men of what was known as the front generation of 25–35 years old.

The importance of this changing of the guard can hardly be overemphasised. The openness of the feeling and judgement of these young men, their unweakened power of faith, their sheer physical energy and pugnacity lent the Party an impetus which the bourgeois parties above all could not match. Only rarely can the attack of youth be parried with the wire entanglement of grey-haired experience or the barbed-wire barricades of bitter scepticism. For the youth of the twenties these were nothing but a new provocation to their defiance and revolutionary enthusiasm. The quickest to feel it were those racialist groups and parties whose leadership represented conservative, or rather reactionary, views taken over from the past. Within only two short years they no longer had any political role whatsoever, even though such of them as the 'German Racialist League of Defence and Defiance'[13] had at one time several hundred thousand followers. Even in Hamburg, where the development of the NSDAP progressed rather slowly, the Racialist Freedom Party was already after one year in total disintegration. 'Without young people', one of their representatives confessed to me, 'nothing can be organised, not even the distribution of leaflets'.

A young member from Bad Harzburg who joined the SA during this period described his 'conversion' as follows:

33

For me this was the start of a completely new life. There was only one thing in the world for me and that was service in the movement. All my thoughts were centred

---

[13] A large antisemitic organisation established by the Pan-German League in 1919.

on the movement. I could talk only politics. I was no longer aware of anything else. At the time I was a promising athlete; I was very keen on sport, and it was going to be my career. But I had to give this up too. My only interest was agitation and propaganda.

This created problems of discipline. Indeed the structure of the local Party organisations during these early years bore in some ways a closer resemblance to a street gang than to a conventional political party. The post of leader was fiercely competitive, the incumbent being constantly required to prove himself in the eyes of his followers by his drive and radicalism. When things were going well this competition contributed to the dynamic of the Party. When things went badly, it could cause serious internal conflict as the following account by Ludolf Haase, Gauleiter of Göttingen, indicates:

34

When in the year 1914 our magnificent army went to war, leadership was conferred by rank... . But as the years went by, and the period of the great *Materialschlachten* arrived with their incredible spiritual and physical demands, the only real leader, so far as his troops were concerned, was the man who proved himself in a crisis. The thing that now counted in an officer was not his uniform but the example he set people and his readiness to die for them. Here in blood, pain and mud, was born National Socialism, to which similar laws later applied, though under apparently quite different conditions. But basically in the movement it is only the true man, not the official, who is leader.

This explains why there was very often tension in the Party. The movement wanted to see men at the top who understood how to master conflict and opposition and who would yield to no one. If the leadership appeared to fall short, they were soon discontented and, because their obedience had been voluntarily given, there was risk of serious disturbance. The falling short might not even be real, only suspected; but still, if some individual had personal designs and spread accusations in the attempt to secure a following, serious damage could be done.

The quieter things were, the greater was this continual threat of internal unrest in the still immature party; the revolutionary spirits wanted to find an outlet, and as soon as the external enemy was less active or less under attack they turned their energy inwards. This hidden process, constantly at work within the movement, was the death of many a local branch in the early period and more than one Gauleiter fell victim to it. The leader of an area grew in the struggle and learned his lessons both from his opponents and from his own troop.

This reflection of his own Social Darwinist view of life won Hitler's approval. Indeed, he himself encouraged the emergence of leaders through a type of natural selection. Gustav Seifert, a Party member who had founded the Hanover branch in 1921 and who asked to be reappointed leader in 1925, was told by Max Amann from Munich headquarters in a letter dated 27 October 1925:

35

You know from your earlier activity as a branch leader of the National Socialist German Workers' Party that Herr Hitler takes the view on principle that it is not the job of the Party leadership to 'appoint' Party leaders. Herr Hitler is today more than ever convinced that the most effective fighter in the National Socialist movement is the man who wins respect for himself as leader through his own achievements. You yourself say in your letter that almost all the members follow you. Then why don't you take over the leadership of the branch?

Hitler did not like intervening personally in such conflicts, preferring to leave one or other combatant to come out on top. He believed leaders would prove themselves by the success with which they maintained and extended their position and he particularly admired ruthlessness in the pursuit of power. On the other hand, he qualified this approach by a tendency to show loyalty to those associated with him from an early stage even if later they had shown themselves not entirely competent.

Sometimes, for the sake of the stability of the organisation, it became necessary for Party headquarters to intervene to uphold the authority of a local leader who was being threatened with faction, and very occasionally Hitler would have to intervene personally and appoint someone from outside to restore order. This occurred, for example, in 1926 with the Berlin branch. Hitler appointed Joseph Goebbels as the new Gauleiter of Berlin. He recognised Goebbels's ability and was anxious to conciliate him after the affair of the Working Group. Goebbels, who had soon become reconciled to the failure of the Working Group and whose admiration for Hitler was unbounded, accepted with alacrity. The following reports written by Reinhold Muchow, a leading member of the Berlin organisation, describe the impact of Goebbels's appointment. The first is for October 1926:

36

The internal party situation has not been good this month. The state of affairs which has developed in our *Gau* reached such a climax this time that a complete disruption of the Berlin organisation seemed likely. The tragedy of the *Gau* has been that it has never had a proper leader, particularly necessary in this city of millions. With all respect to the first Gauleiter, Comrade Dr Schlange, who has worn himself out, he never succeeded in establishing a clear line in the *Gau*. He lacked the gift of oratory and his work was paralysed by much unjust hostility...There began slowly to develop in the *Gau* an opposition which strongly criticised the bad state of affairs.... . This opposition was partly justified, but it was unruly rather than positive or objective, and when Comrade Dr Schlange transferred the management of the *Gau* to the deputy Gauleiter, Comrade Schmiedicke, it spread further and further. This comrade was even less capable of the determination required to master the confused situation. The result was that the opposition gathered fresh strength...The fighting efficiency of the Party sank to nil. Only a very few branches in the *Gau*—Neukölln and Spandau—looked at things dispassionately and persevered patiently, partly on their own responsibility. The unity of both these branches was preserved by the complete isolation of their membership from the details of the personal intrigues which went on in the meetings of the branch leaders. These two branches have an especial significance in that both, particularly Neukölln, are situated in the largest centres of Marxism.

When it proved impossible to establish order in the general chaos and when the local opposition groups went so far as to ignore all the decisions of the deputy Gauleiter, negotiations were started with the Reich party leadership in Munich with the request for a new Gauleiter. We received at length the news that Comrade Dr Goebbels would probably become the future Gauleiter of Berlin. A genuine sigh of relief went up from the disorganised *Gau*, proving how much all the comrades had felt the lack of a real leader. An official statement has not yet been made, but all Berlin comrades confidently hope that Comrade Dr Goebbels will definitely come.... .

Goebbels diverted the energy and violence of the Party activists against the Party's political opponents in Berlin, of whom the Communists were the most active. It was an uphill struggle, but the important fact was that the members were now engaged against the enemy under a leader whose energy and radicalism they could admire. This is clear from the following report dated 'February 1927':

37

On the 11th of this month the Party held a public mass meeting in the Pharus [Beer] Halls' in Wedding, the real working class quarter, with the subject: 'The Collapse of the Bourgeois Class State'. Comrade Dr Goebbels was the speaker. It was quite clear to us what that meant. It had to be visibly shown that National Socialism is determined to reach the workers. We succeeded once before in getting a foothold in Wedding. There were huge crowds at the meeting. More than 1,000 people filled the hall whose political composition was four-fifths SA to one-fifth KPD. But the latter had gathered their main forces in the street. When the meeting was opened by Comrade Daluege, the SA leader, there were, as was expected, provocative shouts of 'On a point of order!'. After the KPD members had been told that *we*, not they, decided points of order, and that they would have the right to ask questions after the talk by Comrade Dr Goebbels, the first scuffling broke out. Peace seemed to be restored until there was renewed heckling. When the chairman announced that the hecklers would be sent out if the interruptions continued, the KPD worked themselves into a frenzy. Meanwhile, the SA had gradually surrounded the centre of the disturbance, and the Communists, sensing the danger, suddenly became aggressive. What followed all happened within three or four minutes. Within seconds both sides had picked up chairs, beer mugs, even tables, and a savage fight began. The Communists were gradually pushed under the gallery which we had taken care to occupy and soon chairs and glasses came hurtling down from there also. The fight was quickly decided: the KPD left with 85 wounded, more or less: that is to say, they could not get down the stairs as fast as they had calmly and 'innocently' climbed them. On our side we counted 3 badly wounded and about 10–12 slightly. When the police appeared the fight was already over. Marxist terrorism had been bloodily suppressed... .

As a result of his success in reviving the Berlin *Gau*, Goebbels was later appointed head of the Party's propaganda organisation on 27 April 1930.

The following document written, significantly by Gregor Strasser, on 9 January 1927 for his paper *Der Nationale Sozialist für Sachsen* indicates the progress already made by the cult of the Führer. Despite the frequent tensions within local Party organisations, Hitler had now succeeded in establishing for himself an unchallenged position, and the respect of the rank and file for his leadership now provided the main cohesive force within the Party:

38

...The tremendous superiority which the NSDAP has as a fighting instrument compared with all the other formations which instinctively pursue the same aim of German liberty and the rebirth of the German people, is due to the fact that we have the outstanding leader, who holds not only supreme power but also the love of his followers—a much stronger binding force.

'Duke and vassal!' In this ancient German relationship of leader and follower, fully comprehensible only to the German mentality and spirit, lies the essence of the structure of the NSDAP, the driving force of this aggressive power, the conviction of victory!

Heil Hitler! This is our first salute in the new year as it was the last one in the old year: Heil Hitler! In this salute lies the pride in the success of the past year which in all the *Gaue* of our beloved fatherland saw the powerful, irresistible progress of the National Socialist idea! In thousands of public meetings, members' evenings, in many hundreds of mass meetings the idea of National Socialism, the name of Adolf Hitler, was hurled among the masses of the German people and a hush fell on the ranks of this enslaved, exploited, starved people. An awareness of this glowing will for the struggle, the struggle to preserve the German people, the struggle for that people's freedom, freedom both within and without—for the one is worthless and impossible without the other—an awareness of those metallic accents of a brutal harshness which call things by their real names and challenges those things to a

struggle, a relentless struggle giving no quarter... .
Friends, a new year lies before us. Let us join hands in a silent vow to struggle in
the new year with redoubled, with threefold vigour, each one at his post, for the
victory of National Socialism, that is for the inward and outward freeing of the
German people, to struggle without wavering, without flinching, in selfless
devotion and true comradeship. And then, friends, raise your right arm and cry out
with me proudly, eager for the struggle, and loyal unto death, 'Heil Hitler'.

The Annual General Meeting on 2–3 September 1928 illustrated the
Party's pride in its rejection of democratic procedures in favour of the
acclamation of a leader:

39

...Above all, Hitler notes the gradual penetration of the whole movement with the
basic concepts of our ideas. He stresses primarily the gradual consolidation of the
leadership principle [*Führer prinzip*]. The movement can be proud of the fact that it
is the only one based on a logical foundation. This was necessary in order to make
up for our numerical minority by a maximum degree of inner discipline, stability,
fighting power, in short, energy... .
...The disintegration spreads slowly but surely; there is hardly any serious
resistance. But antisemitism grows as an idea. What was hardly there ten years ago
is there today: the Jewish question has been brought to people's notice, it will not
disappear any more and we shall make sure that it becomes an international world
question; we shall not let it rest until the question has been solved. We think we
shall live to see that day (*enthusiastic applause*)... .
The chairman of the meeting, Gregor Strasser, expresses the mood of the
meeting very well by remarking that any other party would now say that they had
heard the reports of the chairman, whereas we National Socialists have heard the
speech of the leader. And there is the same difference between the chairman of the
old parties and the leader of the movement as there is between the report of a
chairman of a party and the speech we have just heard.
The party business is now quickly dealt with according to the regulations. First,
'the election of the statutory executive committee'. To the amusement of the
audience, Strasser proposes NSDAP member Hitler as Chairman. He notes that he
has been unanimously elected by a show of hands (*laughter*). In the place of
Comrade Schneider, who has been transferred by his employer away from the city,
Comrade City Councillor Fiehler is elected Secretary in the same way. Also Reich
treasurer Comrade Schwarz, who had 'resigned', is elected as first Treasurer,
whereupon Strasser declares the acceptance of the election by the person nominated.

The main burden of Party activity fell on the SA to which at this period
nearly all fit and active members of the Party belonged. Hitler took his
time about its refounding, which officially took place in the autumn of 1926

under a former Free Corps leader, von Pfeffer. He wanted to ensure it did not become either a military-style formation, as had happened during 1923, or a group of revolutionary conspirators, since in either event the Government might use this as an excuse to ban the Party. In his first orders to the new SA, therefore, on 1 November 1926, he made it clear it was to be purely a propaganda weapon and strong-arm squad:

40

Letter from Adolf Hitler to Captain von Pfeffer (SA Order I)
To conclude our discussions about the programme of your reorganisation, I would like to sum up briefly my main instructions.

The training of the SA must be carried out, not on a military basis, but in accordance with the needs of the Party.

In so far as the members undergo physical training, the main emphasis must be, not on military drill, but far more on sports activities. Boxing and Jiu-Jitsu have always seemed to me far more important than any ineffective, because only incomplete, shooting practice. Physical training must implant in the individual the conviction of his superiority and give him that self-assurance which lies only in confidence in one's own strength; furthermore, it should give him those athletic skills which serve as a weapon for the defence of the movement.

The organisation of the SA as well as its clothing and equipment must accordingly be carried out, not on the model of the old army, but in a way appropriate to its task.

In order right from the start to prevent the SA acquiring any secretive character, quite apart from the fact that its clothing is recognisable to everybody, the size of its membership must define the path which assists the movement, one which is known to the public. It must not meet in secret but should march in the open air and thereby be channelled into activities which conclusively destroy all legends of a 'secret organisation'. To provide a mental diversion from any temptation to satisfy its activism by petty conspiracies, it must from the very beginning be initiated into the great idea of the movement and be trained in the task of representing this idea to such a degree that the horizon is widened right from the start and the individual SA man does not see his mission in the elimination of some crook or other whether big or small, but in helping to build a new National Socialist racialist state. Thereby the struggle against the present state will be raised above the atmosphere of petty acts of revenge and conspiracy to the greatness of an ideological war of extermination against Marxism, its constructions and its string pullers.

What we need is not a hundred or two hundred daring conspirators, but a hundred thousand and hundreds of thousands more fanatical fighters for our *Weltanschauung*. We must not work in secret conventicles but in huge mass marches, and neither by dagger nor poison nor pistol can the path be cleared for the movement, but only by conquering the street. We have to teach Marxism that National Socialism is the future master of the streets, just as it will one day be master of the State.

[signed] ADOLF HITLER
I hereby bring this letter to the notice of the SA leaders as a directive.

CHAPTER 3

The Emergence of Nazism
as a Mass Movement
1928–1933

By 1928, the Weimar Republic had superficially acquired a degree of political stability and economic prosperity. Yet, although these years 1928–29 are often seen as the high point of economic prosperity before the Wall Street crash and ensuing slump, this view requires qualification. Firstly, this economic prosperity was based on very insecure foundations. During the years 1924–28 German industry, agriculture, and local government had borrowed extensively on the American market at high rates of interest and largely on a short-term basis. If economic difficulties occurred in the United States, many of these loans were liable to recall at short notice.

Secondly, by the end of 1927, agriculture and the *Mittelstand*—artisans and small retailers—were already in economic difficulties. The years 1924–29 saw something of a shift in the economic balance of power towards big business on the one hand and organised labour on the other and against agriculture and the *Mittelstand*. It was a period of rationalisation in German industry, involving an acceleration of the historical trend towards the concentration of firms into big trusts and cartels against which small businesses found themselves competing at a disadvantage. At the same time, organised labour in the shape of the Trade Unions and the Social Democrats had some success in pressing demands for higher wages and improved welfare measures. Thus, a major new unemployment insurance scheme was introduced at the end of 1927, financed by contributions from employers and employees. *Mittelstand* groups found that, in addition to the burden of high interest rates on their loans, they had to pay high taxes and social security contributions for their employees.

Finally, at the end of 1927, a world-wide agricultural depression began, whose effects were exacerbated by trade treaties with countries such as Poland, by which Germany agreed to import agricultural produce in return for German industrial goods. These treaties were a response to pressure both from the dominant export-oriented sections of industry—chemicals, electrical goods, and machinery—and also from organised labour which wanted cheap food. Inevitably, this agricultural crisis soon involved groups dependent on agriculture such as artisans and small traders in rural areas.

The economic difficulties of peasants and *Mittelstand* groups, which had already suffered the effects of hyperinflation in 1923, imposed increasing strains on the political system. The Protestant middle class electorate, already divided between several major parties began to fragment still further as new parties emerged offering to provide more determined representation of their specific interests—a process facilitated by the extreme form of proportional representation enshrined in the Weimar Constitution. The problem was that, although these special interest parties—for peasants, landlords, tenants, etc.—could sometimes play a pivotal role in Parliament, ultimately this fragmentation was bound to weaken the political weight of these groups. The growing awareness of this led to further disillusionment with the whole political system, a disillusionment which the Nazis were quick to exploit.

(i) The Breakthrough 1928–30

The relative prosperity and political stability of 1924–28 had created a climate unconducive to the growth of Nazism. The tactics followed by the Party in concentrating on trying to win over the industrial workers made things worse. By the end of 1927 this policy had manifestly failed to achieve results. Workers remained loyal to the Social Democrats and the Communists. Moreover, the majority of the middle class suspected the Party's working class, 'Socialist' image. It had built up a nucleus of diehard supporters but they were still fewer than 75,000 in the whole of Germany. Its seven deputies made the Party a negligible quantity in Parliament. The Nazi Party was a fringe group on the far right of German politics and without influence.

A new tactic was clearly necessary if the energies of the Party were not to turn inwards in self-destructive internal conflict. In fact, a change of emphasis by the beginning of 1928 led the Party, while continuing to try to attract workers, to concentrate increasingly on the middle class, now recognised as more responsive. In December 1927 the deputy Gauleiter of

Hanover-North, Karl Dincklage, wrote to Franz Stöhr, a Nazi Reichstag deputy, and referred to the line which Hitler had taken at a conference of Party leaders in Weimar on 27 November:

41

...In full agreement with the remarks of our leader in Weimar we too believe that we shall not yet succeed in winning much ground from the Marxists in the coming election. We shall receive most sympathy from the small businessman as the strongest opponent of department stores and consumer cooperatives. Further, from the white-collar worker, who being in the DHV,[14] is already an antisemite...

In the winter of 1927–28 discontent began among the rural population of north-west Germany and soon spread. It was sparked off by an increase in the salaries of civil servants on 16 December 1927. This infuriated the rural population which regarded itself as grossly overtaxed. The Nazis were quick to exploit the possibilities and in December 1927 Hitler made a major speech to a protest meeting of farmers from Schleswig-Holstein.

The following police report of a mass demonstration on 26 January 1928, in the city of Oldenburg, in the middle of a big livestock farming area in north-west Germany, describes these grievances. It also shows how the Nazis exploited them by trying to discredit the professional organisations which had organised the meeting, and to convince their members that the whole parliamentary system was at fault and that only a political movement dedicated to the overthrow of that system could bring relief:

42

...In meetings of the rural population which were held in many places in the state of Oldenburg during the past weeks, the majority of those participating demanded again and again that an open-air protest meeting should be held in the state capital of Oldenburg, in order to give weight to the demands of the rural population, outlined below, which emerged in the meetings and were in the meantime formulated by a committee. It would also open the eyes of the state government to the masses of discontented who stand behind these demands. The Rural League [*Landbund*], the Farmers' Association [*Bauernverein*], the League of Smallhold-ings, the Artisans' League, the Settlers' Association, and the Shopkeepers' Guild had therefore called their members to a combined mass demonstration which took place in the Horsefair on 26 January. According to fairly accurate estimates, approximately 20,000 country people had assembled in the Horsefair by 12 noon...

After the speeches of the representatives of various trade associations, the

---

14 Deutschnationaler Handlungsgehilfenverband: the German Nationalist Commercial Em-ployees' Association, a white collar workers' union with völkisch sympathies.

general secretary of the Oldenburg Farmers' Association, a farmer named Brende-
bach, announced the following fourteen demands of the rural population and said
that during the next few days a delegation was to go to Berlin to convey these
demands to the Reich Government and to demand radical measures for improving
the situation of the rural population:

1. An embargo on all superfluous foreign imports.
2. Protection of agriculture through tariffs equivalent to those already applied to
   industry.
3. Simplification of the tax system; replacement of current direct taxes by income
   tax and property tax after suitable alterations; furthermore, the right for states
   and parishes to impose surcharges on these taxes.
4. Tax remission for farmers, craftsmen, and shopkeepers who are in distress.
5. Speedy radical reduction of government activity and expenditure.
6. Economical management in all branches of public administration, and reduction in the number of officials.
7. Temporary suspension of the pay regulations for civil servants of 16 December
   1927.
8. We do not see in the incorporation of Oldenburg into Prussia a measure
   making for cheaper administration.
9. Reduction of social insurance contributions to a level which business can stand.
10. Permission for voluntary overtime work after the 8-hour working period. Loyal
    application of the Reich regulations on contracts. Radical measures against
    non-guild work.
11. Planned reduction of controlled housing policy and promotion of building
    programmes.
12. The prerequisite for any settlement activity must be its profitability.
13. Availability of long-term cheap credit for improvement of the debt situation
    with the aim of wiping out debts.
14. The privileged treatment of civil servants in Parliament who receive a salary in
    addition to allowances and a substitute must cease.

The reading out of the demands drew loud and prolonged applause from the
majority of the participants... .

A certain Münchmeyer,[15] formerly pastor of Borkum, as well as the National
Socialists, had used the assembly of large numbers of the rural population for
propaganda purposes for their parties. After ineffective appeals to the leadership of
the protest meeting to be allowed to speak at the Horsefair, Münchmeyer called a
public meeting at the Lindenhof for 10 a.m., which was attended by approximately
800 people... .

The NSDAP had scheduled two public meetings at the Lindenhof and the
Ziegelhof at 3 p.m. At the meeting at the Lindenhof which was attended by over
1,000 people, Reichstag Deputy Kube[16] of Berlin was the speaker; Reichstag
Deputy Gottfried Feder of Munich spoke at the meeting at the Ziegelhof which was
attended by about 500 people... .

---

[15] A leading antisemite who was to join the Nazis in April.

[16] Wilhelm Kube, Gauleiter of Kurmark 1928–1936, General Commissioner of White Russia
1941–43.

All the speakers at the Kube meeting expressed the view that the rural population could not be satisfied with the form and outcome of the demonstration. At the end the following resolution was read out and adopted unanimously:
    'The thousands of Oldenburg farmers and middle-class people assembled today in the Lindenhof, together with the tens of thousands of their fellow-countrymen, who have come here in the most bitter distress to give visible expression of their despair, having listened to the speech of the National Socialist Reichstag Deputy Wilhelm Kube of Berlin, declare their absolute determination not to be deceived, misled, exploited and expropriated.
    'We have recognised that the distress of agriculture is inseparably bound up with the *political misery* of the whole German people; that parliamentarism which is corrupt through and through and a weak government are unable to overcome the German political and economic emergency.
    'Let us do away with this Marxist-capitalist extortion system that has made Germany, our homeland, powerless, without honour, defenceless, and that has turned us free German farmers and middle-class people into poor, misused slaves of the world stock exchange.
    'But let us also do away with the professional federations who only throw dust in our eyes and neutralise any vigorous action because politically they stand in the camps of those parties who have caused all this misery by accepting the Dawes Plan. The middle class and the farmers of Oldenburg see in the German National Socialist Hitler movement the only salvation from the parliamentary morass, from the pathetic and cowardly fulfilment policy.
    'Only when Germany is reborn in power, freedom and honour, led by unselfish German men who are not burdened by the contemptible policy of the last few years, only then will the German farmer stand as a free man on free soil serving the great German community as the backbone of our people.'
    It was noted that after the meeting several farmers approached Reichstag Deputy Kube to secure him for talks in the countryside.

The Nazis' opponents stigmatised them as a radical, socialistic, working class party, the image it had tried to convey hitherto. Efforts to frighten the peasants with Point 17 of the Nazi programme led Hitler to 'clarify' it on 13 April 1928. This alteration indicates the significance attached by Hitler to the reorientation of the Party:

43

In view of the false interpretations on the part of our opponents of Point 17 of the Programme of the NSDAP, it is necessary to make the following statement:
    Since the NSDAP accepts the principle of private property, it is self-evident that the phrase 'confiscation without compensation' refers simply to the creation of possible legal means for confiscation, when necessary, of land acquired illegally or not managed in the public interest. It is, therefore, aimed primarily against Jewish companies which speculate in land.

This new orientation had insufficient time to have much effect before the Reichstag election in May 1928. The results appeared to reflect the improved situation. The extreme Right suffered a serious defeat compared with December 1924. The Nazis lost 100,000 votes and polled 2.6 per cent of the vote. The ultra-conservative German Nationalists with 78 seats had lost 25 seats. The Left increased their vote to over 40 per cent of the total. The Social Democrats gained 21 seats and had 152; the Communists with 54 gained 9 seats. Although greeted at home and abroad as a victory for Weimar democracy, the results in fact indicated the situation was by no means as satisfactory as appeared at first sight. Not only the Right lost support; the parties of the Centre—the Democrats or left-wing Liberals, the German People's Party or right-wing Liberals, and the Catholic Centre Party—all lost seats. Their voters had either stayed away—the percentage of those voting declined sharply—or supported the new economic interest parties established between 1924–28. The Business Party which catered for artisans and small shopkeepers increased its seats from 17 to 23.

This was an ominous result. For the past four years Germany had been ruled by a coalition of the Right and Centre—German Nationalists, German People's Party, Democrats, and Catholic Centre Party. The vote for the Left and against the Centre and Right, was not a vote of confidence in the existing government. If anything, it was a vote against or at least an abstention. Unfortunately, the conclusions which the Right and Centre parties drew led them to interpret the result to mean that participation in the Government would alienate their own supporters.

This reaction reflected the nature of the German party system. Parties tended to represent specific interests: the German Nationalists—agriculture, particularly the big arable landowners of the east, the Junkers; the German People's Party—industry, and particularly heavy industry; the Centre Party—the Catholics; the Social Democrats—the trade unions. At the same time, the parties competed with one another within a broad segment of the population—the German Nationalists, the People's Party and the Democrats competed for the support of the Protestant upper and middle classes; the Social Democrats and Communists competed for the support of the workers. Parties committed to specific interests and competing against rivals for support within the same segment of the population, made the formation of coalitions difficult at the best of times. The result of the election of 1928 made the position even worse. The parties were convinced that by participating in government they would damage their electoral prospects by compromising the interests of their voters and members to maintain a coalition with parties which represented other and often conflicting interests. This would play into the hands of rivals who were not members of the Government, as the growth of the economic interest parties, regarded as dangerous new competitors, showed. The party bureaucracies, primarily concerned about retaining the

backing of interests and voters, applied increasing pressure on the parliamentary groups to stay in opposition to enable the party to assert
without compromise the interests of their supporters. The parliamentary
party groups in turn put pressure on their colleagues in the Government
coalition to leave the Government rather than compromise.

These considerations determined the future trend of politics. The
German Nationalists had previously compromised their hostility to the
Republic, participating in government to protect the interests of their
mainly agrarian supporters in the formulation of tariff legislation. From
now onwards, they began to move to the Right, back to the uncompromisingly anti-Republican position they had adopted in the first years of the
Republic. The People's Party did not follow this trend to the Right
immediately. Indeed, it now entered a coalition with the Social Democrats,
largely because of Gustav Stresemann, who was aware that the democratic
system depended on a strong Centre and on a willingness to compromise
with the moderate Left. Pressure, however, continued to build up within
the party against this coalition, particularly in view of the competition from
the intransigent Nationalists on the Right. When Stresemann died on 3
October 1929, it was to be only a matter of time before the coalition broke
down under the strain of the rightward drift of the People's Party under the
influence of its strong industrial wing.

Finally, even the Catholic Centre Party began to move Right, particularly under its new and more conservative leader, Ludwig Kaas, from the end
of 1928. This drift of the parties of the Centre towards the Right was
paralleled by a leftward trend of the Social Democrats, the result of
increasing competition from the Communists, evident from their election
gains in 1928. In short, after the election of 1928 a polarisation of politics
began which threatened to paralyse the parliamentary system by making
coalition governments impossible. Whether or not it would continue would
depend on future economic developments; a deterioration in the economic
situation would force the parties to uphold, even more rigidly, the
particular interests of their members and voters.

Although the new middle-class campaign had not had time to take effect
before the election, the low average Nazi vote of 2 per cent disguises
district variations. In some north-west rural districts where the protest
movement had been strong, they gained over 10 per cent. The Party
summed up the lessons of the election in the *Völkischer Beobachter* on 31
May 1928:

44

...The election results from the rural areas in particular have proved that with a
smaller expenditure of energy, money and time, better results can be achieved
there than in the big cities. In small towns and villages mass meetings with good

speakers are events and are often talked about for weeks, while in the big cities the effects of meetings with even three of four thousand people soon disappear. Local successes in which the National Socialists are running first or second are, surprisingly, almost invariably the result of the activity of the branch leader or of a few energetic members...

Nazi Party membership steadily increased from 100,000 to 150,000 between October 1928 and 1 September 1929. The next turning-point came in the autumn of 1929. With the Wall Street crash, the economic situation in Germany rapidly deteriorated. American financiers, under pressure, called in the numerous short-term loans made to Germany since 1924. Bankruptcies followed. Moreover, since the crisis was international, export markets disappeared and businesses were forced to shed labour or close down. This reduced home demand, making the situation even worse. Unemployment figures began to soar. At this point, an issue emerged which was ideally adapted for a right-wing attack on the Republic.

Under the chairmanship of the American banker, Owen Young, the Allied Reparations Commission had devised a plan finally to settle German war reparations. Germany would pay less than originally intended but would still make substantial annual payments until 1988, a total of 34,500 million goldmarks. This was seen by the extreme Right as an excellent opportunity to exploit the growing discontent and regain the support lost in the 1928 election. They claimed Germany's children were being sold in slavery to the Allies. The German Nationalists had a new leader, the press and film magnate Alfred Hugenberg, a co-founder of the Pan German League. Hugenberg had used the Party's electoral failure and subsequent financial difficulties to impose himself and his extreme anti-Republican views on the Party. In the Autumn of 1929, he organised a referendum for a law rejecting the Young Plan and making any politican who agreed to the plan face trial:

45

§1. The Reich Government will solemnly inform the foreign powers without delay that the compulsory recognition of war guilt in the Versailles Treaty contradicts historical truth, is based on false preconceptions, and is not binding under international law.

§2. The Reich Government will endeavour to secure abrogation of the recognition of war guilt in Article 231 as well as of Articles 429 and 430 of the Versailles Treaty. It will also endeavour to secure the immediate and unconditional evacuation of the occupied territories and the removal of all controls over German territory, irrespective of the acceptance or rejection of the Hague Conference.

§3. New burdens and obligations vis-à-vis foreign powers on the basis of the recognition of war guilt may not be undertaken.
This also includes the burdens and obligations which are to be undertaken by Germany on the basis of the proposals of the Paris experts and the agreements deriving therefrom. [i.e. the Young Plan.]
§4. Reich Chancellors, Reich Ministers and their plenipotentiaries who sign treaties contrary to the regulation contained in §3.1 will be subject to the penalties contained in §92, No.3 of the Penal Code. [i.e. Penal servitude for not less than two years.]

To win maximum support for this draft law, Hugenberg invited the help of all willing to cooperate including the Nazis.

Hitler saw this as an ideal opportunity for his party, giving him access to the funds of the Right and national publicity in the Hugenberg press. More important, the association of the Nazis with the conservative and upper-class Nationalists would remove the stigma of being radical and working class and make it more acceptable to the middle class. Finally, the Nazis as the most active of all the groups participating in the campaign gave the impression of being the most dynamic of the anti-Republican groups on the Right. They appeared more attractive than their conservative rivals to the growing number of those discontented with the Republican parties owing to the deteriorating economic situation. The fact that the subsequent plebiscite failed to win anything like sufficient support—5.8 million instead of the necessary 21 million votes—did not detract from these advantages. Indeed, the Young Plan campaign coincided with the state and local government elections of November–December 1929, in which the Nazis made significant gains. In the election in the state of Thuringia, for example, they won 11.3% of the vote and participation in the Government. Nazi local government propaganda used rumour and scandal to discredit opponents. Whether the scandal was true or not did not matter; they hoped to benefit from the belief that 'there's no smoke without fire'. They aimed to discredit the local establishment whether Conservative or Social Democrat.

There were, however, some within the Party who resented this reorientation of its propaganda towards the middle class and rural areas. They continued to press for a more definite 'socialist' commitment; they also objected to the subordination of the Party and its ideology to the leader. A leading spokesman for this group was Otto Strasser, the brother of Gregor Strasser. The newspapers of the Kampfverlag, the Strasser publishing house, continued to adopt a comparatively 'left wing' line, complicating Hitler's appeal to the middle class. The issue was finally fought out at an interview between Hitler and Otto Strasser in 1930. First, Hitler challenged the claim of Strasser's associates that the 'idea', i.e. the ideology, of the Party was distinct from and superior to the leader, then the argument turned to the question of the definition of Socialism about which Hitler and Strasser had very different views:

46

How do you justify Blank's[17] theories?' Hitler demanded. 'His conception of loyalty, the distinction he makes between the Leader and the Idea, are incitements to Party members to rebel.'

'No,' I said, 'it is not a question of diminishing the Leader's prestige. But for the free and Protestant German the service of the Idea first and foremost is an ingrained necessity. The Idea is divine in origin, while men are only its vehicles, the body in which the Word is made flesh. The Leader is made to serve the Idea, and it is to the Idea alone that we owe absolute allegiance. The Leader is human, and it is human to err.'

'You are talking monumental idiocy. You wish to give Party members the right to decide whether or not the Führer has remained faithful to the so-called Idea. It's the lowest kind of democracy, and we want nothing to do with it! For us the Idea is the Führer, and each Party member has only to obey the Führer...'

'What you say would lead to the dissolution of our organisation, which is based on discipline. I have no intention of allowing our organisation to be disrupted by a crazy scribbler. You have been an officer; you see that your brother accepts my discipline, even if he doesn't always see eye to eye with me. Take a lesson from him; he's a fine man.'

He seized my hands, as he had done two years before. His voice was choked with sobs, and tears ran down his cheeks... .

'All that is very simple for you, Herr Hitler', Strasser continued, 'but it only serves to emphasise the profound difference in our revolutionary and Socialist ideas. The reasons you give for destroying the Kampfverlag I take to be only pretexts. The real reason is that you want to strangle the social revolution for the sake of legality and your new collaboration with the bourgeois parties of the Right.'

At this Hitler grew violent.

'I am a Socialist, and a very different kind of Socialist from your rich friend Reventlow.[18] I was once an ordinary working-man. I would not allow my chauffeur to eat worse than I eat myself. But your kind of Socialism is nothing but Marxism. The mass of the working classes want nothing but bread and games. They will never understand the meaning of an ideal, and we cannot hope to win them over to one. What we have to do is to select from a new master-class men who will not allow themselves to be guided, like you, by the morality of pity. Those who rule must know they have the right to rule because they belong to a superior race. They must maintain that right and ruthlessly consolidate it... .

'What you preach is liberalism, nothing but liberalism. There is only one possible kind of revolution, and it is not economic or political or social, but racial, and it will

---

[17] Herbert Blank was a friend of Otto Strasser.
[18] Count von Reventlow, a leading *völkisch* activist.

always be the same: the struggle of inferior classes and inferior races against the superior races who are in the saddle. On the day the superior race forgets this law, it is lost. All revolutions—and I have studied them carefully—have been racial... .'

'Let us assume, Herr Hitler, that you came into power tomorrow. What would you do about Krupp's? Would you leave it alone or not?'

'Of course I should leave it alone', cried Hitler. 'Do you think me so crazy as to want to ruin Germany's great industry?'

'If you wish to preserve the capitalist regime, Herr Hitler, you have no right to talk of Socialism. For our supporters are Socialists, and your programme demands the socialisation of private enterprise.'

'That word "socialism" is the trouble', said Hitler. He shrugged his shoulders, appeared to reflect for a moment and then went on:

'I have never said that all enterprises should be socialised. On the contrary, I have maintained that we might socialise enterprises prejudicial to the interests of the nation. Unless they were so guilty, I should consider it a crime to destroy essential elements in our economic life. Take Italian Fascism. Our National Socialist state, like the Fascist state, will safeguard both employers' and workers' interests while reserving the right of arbitration in case of dispute.'

Hitler, exasperated by my answers, continued: 'there is only one economic system, and that is responsibility and authority on the part of directors and executives. I ask Herr Amann to be responsible to me for the work of his subordinates and to exercise authority over them. Herr Amann asks his office manager to be responsible for his typists and to exercise his authority over them; and so on to the lowest rung of the ladder. That is how it has been for thousands of years, and that is how it will always be.'

'Yes, Herr Hitler, the administrative structure will be the same whether the state is capitalist or socialist. But the spirit of labour depends on the regime under which it lives. If it was possible a few years ago for a handful of men not appreciably different from the average to throw a quarter of a million Ruhr workers on the streets, if this act was legal and in conformity with the morality of our economic system, then it is not the men but the system that is criminal.'

'But that—' Hitler replied, looking at his watch and showing signs of acute impatience 'that is no reason for granting the workers a share in the profits of the enterprises that employ them, and more particularly for giving them the right to be consulted. A strong state will see that production is carried on in the national interest, and, if these interests are contravened, can proceed to expropriate the enterprise concerned and take over its administration.'

On 27 March 1930, the polarisation within the Reichstag finally brought the breakdown of the coalition government of the right-wing Liberal People's Party and the Social Democrats which had ruled Germany since 1928. The Government split on financing the deficit in the unemployment benefit fund, becoming daily larger as the numbers of unemployed rose. The interest groups behind the two parties made their weight felt. The People's Party under the influence of the industrialists wished to reduce the benefits, thereby putting the whole burden on the unemployed. The Social Democrats, on the other hand, under the pressure of the trade unions insisted on an increase in the social insurance contributions, of which the employers would have to pay half. After months of negotiation compromise proved impossible and the Government was forced to resign.

This was to mark the end of parliamentary government in Germany for nearly twenty years. The issue at stake in the conflict was: who would bear the main burden of the economic crisis—capital or labour? The trade unions regarded a cut in unemployment benefits as the thin end of the wedge. Were it accepted it would begin the erosion of the whole structure of wage and welfare concessions laboriously built up since 1918. It would discredit them in the eyes of their members and be grist to the mill of the Communists. The industrialists, on the other hand, saw the unemployment insurance issue as a classic demonstration of labour's success in exploiting the democratic system of Weimar to increase its share of the nation's wealth. Industry wanted a government that would cut back public expenditure and encourage profits. To achieve this would require the removal of the Social Democrats from the Government as a minimum goal. Many went further and wished to curb the power of the Reichstag.

Although the issue of unemployment insurance was the overt cause of the collapse of the coalition, behind the scenes negotiations had been going on since at least December 1929 for the removal of the Social Democrats. The Army had become increasingly disillusioned with the way the parliamentary system operated. It had drawn the lesson from the First World War that modern war required the total mobilisation of the nation's resources. It was vital, therefore, for the Army to have political support not simply for rearmament but also to create a climate of public opinion favourable to national mobilisation. The Weimar political system, already associated in their eyes with defeat and revolution, had discredited itself above all because of its failure to provide such a climate. Democracy enabled the Left with its strong pacifist sentiments to exert too much influence.

The Army's political expert, General Kurt von Schleicher, found sympathy for its view within the entourage of Reich President von Hindenburg. The weakness of coalition governments had been producing growing disillusionment with the system for several years. For some time the President's State Secretary, Otto Meissner, had been contemplating schemes to reduce the influence of the legislature. Hindenburg needed little persuading of the need to seize the opportunity of the anticipated breakdown of the coalition to remove the Social Democrats and establish a strong government of the moderate Right, which would be able to remain largely independent of the Reichstag by using the emergency powers contained in Article 48 of the Constitution.

Schleicher's candidate for the Chancellorship was the leader of the parliamentary group of the Catholic Centre Party, Heinrich Brüning, who had a reputation as a financial expert. Brüning's background as a volunteer machine-gun officer in the war had given him a great respect for the Army and he regarded Hindenburg, the old war hero, with considerable awe. He too was disillusioned with the operation of the parliamentary system and believed in strengthening the executive at the expense of the legislature, ideally culminating in a restoration of the monarchy. Initially he hoped to achieve this by a Right/Centre coalition with a majority in the Reichstag, excluding the Social Democrats from influence. The key, however, lay with the German Nationalists, split into those who supported Hugenberg in his intransigent opposition to the Republic and a more moderate rebel group. Brüning hoped to strengthen the moderates, thereby acquiring a majority. If he did not succeed, he could always use the emergency powers in paragraph 2 of Article 48 of the Weimar Constitution to issue legislation by Presidential decree:

47

§2. If a *Land* fails to fulfil the responsibilities assigned to it under the Constitution or the Reich Laws, the Reich President can take the measures necessary to restore law and order with the help of the armed forces.
   In the event of a serious disturbance of or threat to law and order, the Reich President can take the measures necessary to restore law and order, intervening if necessary with armed force. For this purpose he may provisionally abrogate either partially or completely the basic rights contained in Articles 114, 115, 117, 118, 123, 124, and 153.
§3. The Reich President is obliged to inform the Reichstag immediately of all measures taken under paragraphs 1 or 2 of this Article. The measures are to be revoked on the request of the Reichstag.
   In the event of an emergency a Land Government may provisionally implement the measures in paragraph 2 in its own area. The measures are to be revoked on the request of the Reich President or the Reichstag.
   Further details will be defined by a Reich Law.

Since the law mentioned in paragraph 3 was never passed, interpretation of when a threat to law and order existed was left to the Reich President himself.
   The new Government's policy for solving the economic crisis reflected the emphasis of traditional economic theory on the need to balance the budget, particularly after the experience of hyperinflation in 1923. It was, however, also determined by Brüning's desire to demonstrate to the Allies that even with the best will in the world Germany was incapable of coping with the burden of reparations. He hoped to secure the ending of reparations and thereby free Germany's hands to pursue a more aggressive

foreign policy both for its own sake and to take the wind out of the sails of the radical Right.

When, on 16 July 1930, part of the Government's tough budget was rejected by the Reichstag, the Nationalists voting against, Brüning implemented it by Presidential decree. When the Reichstag responded by demanding its revocation, it was dissolved and elections fixed for 14 September. Brüning hoped for a reduction in the Socialist vote, since they would probably be blamed for the economic crisis which had occurred under an SPD Chancellor. He also hoped the German Nationalist Party rebels would be strengthened and it would then be possible to form a Right/Centre coalition with a majority in Parliament. This disastrous miscalculation had far-reaching consequences.

At the Reichstag election on 14 September 1930 the most striking result was the increase in votes for the Nazi Party from 810,000 to 6½ million. Some of the increase came from new voters who had not voted in the previous election because they were disaffected or too young to qualify. Much, however, came from those who had previously voted for the middle class Liberal and Conservative parties (People's Party, Democrats, and Nationalists), who lost 67 seats between them. The Catholic parties (Centre and Bavarian People's Party) increased their support slightly, while the Social Democrats lost support mainly to the Communists who gained 23 seats. But there could be no doubt about the main significance of the result—the Nazi Party with 107 seats had become the second largest party in the Reichstag. The breakthrough for which the Party had been working for so long had at last been achieved.

(ii) Propaganda 1930–1932

An important factor in the Nazis' electoral success between 1930–33 was the Party's propaganda. Although there was not always a direct correlation between the areas of Nazis success and those of maximum propaganda activity, and although the propaganda effect was often indirect—for example through the recruitment of opinion leaders—rather than direct, there can be no doubt that the Party's propaganda made a major contribution to its success.

By 1930 Nazi propaganda was controlled by a special propaganda department represented at all levels of the Party. At the top was the Reich propaganda department headed by Goebbels after 27 April 1930. Each *Gau* or Party regional headquarters had its propaganda department with its own chief and, below that, each branch had an official in charge of propaganda. Although this propaganda department was subject to the overall authority of the political leadership at the various levels, it also had its own separate chain of command. Directives from the Reich propaganda department to the propaganda departments of the *Gaue* were relayed to the propaganda officials in the local branches in their region. Reports of propaganda activity, information on political opponents, and suggestions were passed up the chain in the reverse direction. The Reich propaganda headquarters exercised a tight control over all aspects of propaganda, particularly at election times.

As the following memorandum of the Prussian Ministry of the Interior of May 1930 indicates, Nazi propaganda was already geared to a high pitch of efficiency and the campaign had merely to be intensified for the September Reichstag election among a population now acutely anxious about their economic situation and disillusioned with the failure of their professional and political representatives. The rest of the parties, on the other hand, were obliged to turn from their legislative activities and face a hostile electorate which had little sympathy for their political manoeuvrings:

48

Hardly a day passes on which there are not several meetings even in narrowly restricted local areas. Carefully organised propaganda headquarters in the individual *Gaue* ensure that the speaker and subject are adapted to the local and economic circumstances. The Reichstag and Landtag deputies of the Party and many other Party speakers travel about every day to undertake and build up this agitation. Through systematic training courses, through correspondence courses and recently through a school for NSDAP speakers established on 1 July 1929, such agitators are trained for this task over a period of months, even years. If they prove themselves, they receive official recognition from the Party and are put under contract to give at least thirty speeches over a period of eight months and receive as an incentive a fee of 20 Reichsmarks or more per evening in addition to their expenses. Rhetorical skill combined with subjects carefully chosen to suit the particular audience, which in the countryside and in the small towns is mainly interested in economic matters, ensure, according to our observations, halls which are almost invariably overcrowded with enthusiastic listeners. Meetings with an audience of between 1000 and 5000 people are a daily occurrence in the bigger towns. Frequently a second or several parallel meetings have to be held because the halls provided cannot hold the numbers who attend... . On such occasions the network of local branches is extended as far as possible or at all events contact men are recruited who are intended to prepare the ground through intensive propaganda by word of mouth for the spread of the movement which can be observed everywhere. Frequently such propaganda squads stay in a certain place for several days and try to win the local population for the movement through the most varied sorts of entertainment such as concerts, sports days, tattoos in suitable places and even church parades. In other places an outside propaganda speaker is stationed for a certain time; with a car at his disposal, he travels systematically through the surrounding district. National Socialist theatre groups travelling from place to place serve the same purpose.

On 10 September 1930 the Party issued the following manifesto:

49

The victory of the national socialist movement will mean the overcoming of the old class and caste spirit. It will allow a nation once more to rise up out of status mania and class madness.

It will train this nation to have an iron determination.

It will overcome democracy and reassert the authority of personality.

It will restore justice to the German people through the brutal assertion of the principle that one has no right to hang the little ones so long as the biggest criminals go unpunished and untouched.

The other parties may have come to terms with the thievery of the inflation, may recognise the fraudulent revolution. National socialism will bring the thieves and traitors to justice. National socialism fights for the German worker by getting him out of the hands of his swindlers and destroying the protectors of international bank and stock exchange capital.

With its victory the national socialist movement will purge the German administration of the parasites who, though with no right to belong and without qualifications, have got in simply on the basis of their party card and are a burden on the nation. Anyone who talks of new taxes should first free the administration of the revolutionary parasites who have streamed in during the past twelve years. One protects the honest civil servant only by opening the way for his efficiency and honest labour and by removing the parliamentary profiteers from the civil service.

With its victory the national socialist movement will also seek to guarantee the economic protection of German people. As long as stock exchanges and department stores are inadequately taxed any further tax increases on the little man are a crime.

With its victory the national socialist movement will protect the peasant through the ruthless education of our people to consume our own products.

Our upper ten thousand will have to learn to eat black bread too, otherwise our rye will rot and wheat will have to be imported.

We will emphasise our national honour and national pride by avoiding all that is foreign as far as possible and giving preference to the results of our own hard work.

We will ensure that the reform of our attitude to defence and a change in our foreign policy will be at the top of the list of reforms.

After its victory the national socialist movement will no longer continue the policy of continually currying France's favours. Every hand which is offered to us in Europe which is in a similar plight and shares our way of thinking will be thankfully grasped.

We want to ensure that in future the importance of our nation once again corresponds to its natural worth rather than the pathetic representation of the past fifteen years.

The national socialist movement is not fighting a campaign on a short term basis. The path on which it has embarked may be a long one but victory will lie at the end... .

During the following three years, the party propaganda machine became increasingly sophisticated. The most modern techniques were used: highly coordinated press campaigns, whirlwind campaigns by air, film shows and so on. During election campaigns, a stream of directives specified precise details of what themes were to be emphasised and slogans to be used at different stages. Furthermore, a selection of standard leaflets and posters were produced which the *Gaue* were expected to order. The use of important speakers was centrally controlled and they were deployed where headquarters felt they would be most effective. The high degree of efficiency and attention to detail characteristic of the Nazi propaganda machine during these years is shown in the following excerpts from Reich Propaganda Department directives for the Presidential elections of March–April 1932 signed by Goebbels:

50

(a) Reich Propaganda Department to all *Gaue* and all *Gau* Propaganda Departments.
...A striking slogan:
Those who want everything to stay as it is vote for Hindenburg. Those who want everything changed vote for Hitler.
...
(b) Reich Propaganda Department to all *Gaue* and all *Gau* Propaganda Departments.
...Hitler Poster. The Hitler poster depicts a fascinating Hitler head on a completely black background. Subtitle: white on black—'Hitler'. In accordance with the Führer's wish this poster is to be put up only during the final days [of the campaign]. Since experience shows that during the final days there is a variety of coloured posters, this poster with its completely black background will contrast with all the others and wil produce a tremendous effect on the masses... .
(c) Reich Propaganda Department
Instructions for the National Socialist Press for the election of the Reich President
  1. From Easter Tuesday 29 March until Sunday 10 April inclusive, all National Socialist papers, both daily and weekly, must appear in an enlarged edition with a tripled circulation. Two-thirds of this tripled circulation must be made available, without charge, to the *Gau* leadership responsible for its area of distribution for propaganda purposes... .
  2. From Easter Tuesday 29 March until Sunday 3 April inclusive, a special topic must be dealt with every day on the first page of all our papers in a big spread. Tuesday 29 March: Hitler as a man. Wednesday 30 March: Hitler as a fighter

(gigantic achievements through his willpower, etc.). Friday 1 April: Hitler as a statesman—plenty of photos... .
3. On Sunday 3 April, at noon (end of an Easter truce), the great propaganda journey of the Führer through Germany will start, through which about a million people are to be reached directly through our Führer's speeches... . The press organisation is planned so that four press centres will be set up in Germany, which in turn will pass on immediately any telephone calls to the other papers of their area, whose names have been given them... .

The Party surpassed itself in the stage-management of mass rallies, particularly when Hitler himself was speaking. In the following account written at the time Frau Luise Solmitz, a Hamburg school teacher married to a former army officer, gives her impression of such a meeting in 1932:

51

...The April sun shone hot like in summer and turned everything into a picture of gay expectation. There was immaculate order and discipline, although the police left the whole square to the stewards and stood on the sidelines. Nobody spoke of 'Hitler', always just 'the Führer', 'the Führer says', 'the Führer wants', and what he said and wanted seemed right and good. The hours passed, the sun shone, expectations rose. In the background, at the edge of the track there were columns of carriers like ammunition carriers. What they carried were crates of beer. Aeroplanes above us. Testing of the loudspeakers, buzzing of the cine-cameras. It was nearly 3 p.m. 'The Führer is coming!' A ripple went through the crowds. Around the speaker's platform one could see hands raised in the Hitler salute. A speaker opened the meeting, abused the 'system', nobody listened to him. A second speaker welcomed Hitler and made way for the man who had drawn 120,000 people of all classes and ages. There stood Hitler in a simple black coat and looked over the crowd, waiting—a forest of swastika pennants swished up, the jubilation of this moment was given vent in a roaring salute. Main theme: Out of parties shall grow a nation, the German nation. He censured the 'system' ('I want to know what there is left to be ruined in this state!'). 'On the way here Socialists confronted me with a poster, "Turn back, Adolf Hitler". Thirteen years ago I was a simple unknown soldier. I went my way. I never turned back. Nor shall I turn back now.' Otherwise he made no personal attacks, nor any promises, vague or definite. His voice was hoarse after all his speaking during the previous days. When the speech was over, there was roaring enthusiasm and applause. Hitler saluted, gave his thanks, the Horst Wessel song sounded out across the course. Hitler was helped into his coat. Then he went.—How many look up to him with touching faith! as their helper, their saviour, their deliverer from unbearable distress—to him who rescues the Prussian prince, the scholar, the clergyman, the farmer, the worker, the unemployed, who rescues them from the parties back into the nation.

Although he spared no effort in his personal campaigning, particularly at the time of the Presidential elections in 1932, the main burden of propaganda lay on the *Gaue* and local Party organisations. Their energy and resourcefulness kept the Party firmly in the public eye. Numerous speakers from all classes, graded according to ability were deployed at local, regional or national level. Beside expenses they were paid a graded fee for their pains, and, since many were unemployed, they had an incentive to speak as often as possible.

An indication of the care devoted to local propaganda is provided by the instructions for the organisation of rural propaganda contained in the July 1931 issue of *Wille und Weg*, the monthly magazine of the Reich Propaganda Department:

52

The first meeting in a village must be prepared in such a way that it is well attended. A prerequisite is that the speaker should be fairly well informed about specifically rural questions. Then, it is most advisable to go to a neighbouring village some time after, but to advertise the meeting in the first village as well, then many people will certainly come over for it. After this, one holds a big German Evening in a central hall for a number of villages with the cooperation of the SA and the SA band... . The German Evening, provided it is skilfully and generously geared to producing a big public impact, has the primary task of making the audience enthusiastic for our cause; secondly, it is intended to raise the money necessary for the further build-up of propaganda. The preparation of the village meetings is best carried out in the following way: most effectively through written personal invitations to every farmer or inhabitant; in the bigger villages through a circular carried from farm to farm by Party comrades. For the meeting itself the question of finance has to be considered. Our movement is so poor that every penny counts. Collections must therefore be held during all discussion evenings and also in the big mass meetings if permitted by the police, either in the interval or at the end, even when an entrance fee has been taken at the beginning of the meeting. In this way, especially when plates and not caps are used, surprising amounts can sometimes be got out of a meeting.

One key to the Nazis' success in acquiring mass support was awareness of the extent to which German society had disintegrated into its sectional components, a process accelerated by postwar economic crises of inflation and then depression. By developing separate departments to organise the various economic interests and social groups, they successfully combined the pose of effectively representing individual interests and of a party of integration creating a unified national community of which they claimed the Party was already a microcosm. Thus, there were Party organisations for, among others, doctors, lawyers, teachers, war-disabled and war-pensioners, and civil servants. Perhaps the most successful were the

Agrarian Office and the *Mittelstand* Office (for artisans and retail traders), later known as the Combat League of Middle Class Tradespeople. Networks of specialists, often leading farmers or leading representatives of particular trades canvassed their colleagues and through the very fact of their own support for the movement provided invaluable propaganda.

The *Mittelstand* Office emphasised the Nazis' determination to preserve small businesses in face of the competition from the large department stores which had become intense during the depression. They were particularly astute at exploiting local issues:

53

Draft pamphlet [undated: c. April 1932]
Attention! Gravediggers at work!
Middle-class citizens! Retailers! Craftsmen! Tradesmen!
A new blow aimed at your ruin is being prepared and carried out in Hanover!
The present system enables the gigantic concern
WOOLWORTH (America)
supported by finance capital, to build a new vampire business in the centre of the city in the Georgstrasse to expose you to complete ruin. This is the wish and aim of the black-red[19] system as expressed in the following remarks of Marxist leaders.

The Marxist Engels declared in May 1890: 'If capital destroys the small artisans and retailers it does a good thing... .'

That is the black-red system of today!

Put an end to this system and its abettors! Defend yourself, middle-class citizen! Join the mighty organisation that alone is in a position to conquer your arch-enemies. Fight with us in the Section for Craftsmen and Retail Traders within the great freedom movement of Adolf Hitler!

Put an end to the system!
Mittelstand, vote for List 8!

These departments also encouraged the infiltration of the main profession-al organisations and purged their leadership by pressure from below. The agrarian office very successfully took over the main professional organisa-tion of agriculture, the *Landbund*. An example of the tactics used is provided by the Party's take-over of the North-West German Artisans' Association in 1932:

---

[19] Black for the Catholic Centre Party and red for the Social Democrats, who together formed the coalition government in the state of Prussia.

54

Urgent circular to the District Leaders and District Representatives of the Mittelstand
Office in Gau *Hanover-South-Brunswick*

The Gauleiter　　　　　　　　　　　　　　　　　*Hanover, 11 January 1932*
CONFIDENTIAL!
A discussion between the Gauleiter and the executive committee of the North-West German Artisans' Association resulted in a decision to arrange the entry of NSDAP members into the executive committee and Association leadership. Since the general meeting of the representatives of the Association is to be held in three weeks' time, the following must be clarified immediately:
1. The political attitude and personal qualities of the chairman and secretary of your particular district Artisans' Association.
2. Which Party members, or, if there aren't any available, which artisans of the National Socialist persuasion are eligible for membership of the executive committee and Association leadership.
3. Which members of the NSDAP are organised in the North-West German Artisans' Association and therefore what influence can be thrown into the scales.
The situation requires an immediate meeting of the district leaders and district experts with the *Gau* leadership on 14 January 1932 in Hanover.

Three weeks later Gauleiter Rust reported to Party headquarters in Munich that his attempt to penetrate the Artisans' Association from below had succeeded and that its leaders would be replaced by National Socialists or Nazi sympathisers:

55

Gau *Hanover–South-Brunswick*　　　　　　　　　　*1 February 1932*

The Gauleiter

Dear Herr Wagener,[20]
I take note with interest of your acceptance of the invitation to Brunswick. I hope to be able to introduce to you a mainly National Socialist executive committee of the North-West German Artisans' Association. For about ten weeks we have had a major fight to win control of the Association. On 8 amd 9 February an extraordinary meeting of delegates will take place in Hanover at which I have demanded the removal of the present president, Freidel of the Business Party, his replacement by a president who, though not a member of the NSDAP, is working completely along our lines, and two vice-presidential posts for members of the NSDAP. Meetings of

---

[20] Otto Wagener was head of the NSDAP's Economics Section in the Nazi Reich Headquarters.

artisans, usually overcrowded, have taken place in all the county towns [*Kreis-städte*] of the *Gau* which set things in motion. Furthermore, two meetings of all district experts of the *Mittelstand* Office have made this subject an issue in the *Gau*.

I take this opportunity of telling you that the executive committee of the Chamber of Industry and Commerce—a rare selection of first-rate economic reactionaries—have applied to me to arrange for the Führer to have a personal discussion with them. Here too the reason for this is pressure from below.

Heil!   BERNHARD RUST

The penetration and politicising of economic associations by the Nazi Party was a most effective way of winning new supporters and helped prepare the way for the 'coordination' of these groups after the Nazi takeover of power in Germany.

The Nazi appeal to youth proved particularly strong. Its dynamic and colourful style of politics, its proclaimed aim of breaking down class barriers, its leader-follower relationship, and its remarkably young membership and leadership offered young people the type of commitment in politics which they were seeking and which the other parties' traditional parliamentary methods did not offer. Only the Communists offered anything similar and they, because of their class commitment, remained largely confined to the working class, particularly the young unemployed. Young people, particularly from the middle class, saw the Nazi movement both as a means to destroy the hidebound conventions and social and occupational barriers associated with the older generation and as a national crusade to restore Germany to greatness. The basically emotional appeal to this group is shown by the following report from 1931 on the problems of containing the growth of Nazism in the Protestant youth movement:

56

The cause which at the moment is most closely associated with the name of National Socialism and with which, at a moderate estimate, certainly 70 per cent of our young people, often lacking knowledge of the facts, are in ardent sympathy, must be regarded, as far as our ranks are concerned, more as an ethical than a political matter. Our young people show little political interest. Fifth-formers are not really much concerned with the study of Hitler's thoughts; it is simply something irrational, something infectious that makes the blood pulse through one's veins and conveys an impression that something great is under way, the roaring of a stream which one does not wish to escape: 'If you can't feel it you will never grasp it... .'

To exploit this appeal to youth the Nazis developed the Hitler Youth movement for those under 18, a pupils league for boys in grammar schools, and a students' league. The activities of these organisations increasingly politicised schools and universities. In the state of Oldenburg, for example, there were complaints that the children of Republicans were being harassed by the fellow pupils:

57

To the Oldenburg Ministry for Churches and Schools: 21 November 1930

The Committee of the Oldenburg branch of the Reichsbanner Black-Red-Gold[21] submits the following matter to the State Ministry with a request for a prompt comment:

Leaflets have recently been distributed in the playgrounds of the schools of the city of Oldenburg and its vicinity, inviting people to join a National Socialist Pupils' Association. We enclose one of these leaflets.

A number of pupils have already followed the appeal to join this pupils' association. These consider themselves pledged, in the spirit of the leaflet, to bully those who disagree with them. In the playground these pupils join together and sing National Socialist combat songs. Children of Republicans are called names, their satchels are smeared with swastikas, and they are given leaflets with swastikas or 'Heil Hitler' or 'Germany awake' written on them. In the school in Metjendorf the son of a Republican was beaten up during the break by members of the pupils' association so badly that he had to stay at home for over a week. Grown-ups who are known to be members of a Republican party are called names by the pupils when they pass by the school. In one case this even happened out of the window of a classroom.

Since the children of Republicans are unfortunately in a minority in secondary schools they cannot defend themselves against these combined attacks. With an effort they preserve their self-control, but as soon as the child gets home, this too collapses. He then seeks refuge in tears and complaints. The parents find that lessons following breaks in which their child has been molested by his classmates are useless because he is too preoccupied with the events of the break. Sometimes teachers, not knowing the reason for the child's inattention, punish him as well. The same state of mind influences his homework, which therefore cannot be of a standard which a child in a good, cheerful mood would normally achieve. Again this has its effects at school.

It might be answered that parents and children have the right to make a complaint. This is true and yet at the same time not true. It must unfortunately be said that apart from a group of teachers who would treat such a complaint objectively, there are a number from whom this cannot be counted on and to whom one does not turn because they too are National Socialists or are active in other right-wing associations. The relationship of trust necessary between teachers and parents and their children has completely gone.

Since we have heard that some headmasters have already declared that they are

[21] The *Reichsbanner* Black-Red-Gold was a pro-Republican paramilitary organisation set up in 1924 by Social Democrats and Democrats to defend the Republic against the right-wing paramilitary organisations.

not in a position to deal with these incidents as required, since they have still received no instructions from the Ministry, we request that such instructions should be issued as soon as possible. We can presumably be sure that the State Ministry will adopt an attitude which does justice to all concerned and will decree that pupils' associations of political organisations are forbidden.
    Yours faithfully,
    The Committee of the Oldenburg Branch of the Reichsbanner Black-Red-Gold.

Although the Nazis concentrated much of their propaganda on specific groups, one of their main themes was a general appeal to nationalism and a claim that they, alone of all the parties, had succeeded in bridging the barriers between class and occupation. An example of such propaganda was the way they used the Kaiser's fourth son, Prince August-Wilhelm of Hohenzollern, as a speaker. He was always paired with an 'ordinary citizen', usually a farmer or a worker. At a meeting in Öttingen in central Bavaria in June 1931 such a meeting drew a crowd of between 900 and 1000 people, according to the police report:

58

The speakers were:
    Prince August-Wilhelm of Prussia
    Farmer Stegmann from Schillingsfürst
    Julius Streicher—NSDAP Gauleiter of Franconia

    The speech of Prince August-Wilhelm, which was kept short and matter-of-fact, was followed by the national anthem which was sung standing up in the hall, whereas the Streicher speech had been followed by the Hitler song. The meeting did not have the character of a political but rather of a patriotic meeting or rally. The audience had arrived in large numbers from far and wide on motor cycles and by car.

The effect of such propaganda is clear from an entry in the diary of the upper middle class Hamburg lady already referred to:

59

I. vi. 32

...I myself also know that not only the desperate but also those who purposely contract debts in our neighbourhood are enthusiastic Hitler people—as are all those who hope for something from a swing to the Left or the Right or anywhere.

Nevertheless, every person who thinks and feels as a German, the bourgeois, the farmer, the aristocrat, the prince, and the intelligentsia, stands by Hitler. It is the nationalist movement.

(iii) Statistics on the Social and Geographical Bases of Nazism

Between 1928 and 1930 the Nazi Party had concentrated largely on trying to win over sections of the middle class, notably the peasantry, the artisans, and the small retailers. After 1930, while still continuing much of their propaganda for these groups, they revived their pre-1928 efforts to win over the workers. In January 1931, for example, they established a Factory Cell Organisation (NSBO) in an attempt to challenge the Left in their factory strongholds. This organisation, however, had little success. Apart from white collar workers, the majority of workers remained loyal to the Social Democrats and Communists and, if under the pressure of unemployment they became more extreme, they tended to move to the Communists rather than the Nazis. Those blue collar workers who did support the Nazis tended to fall into one or more of the following categories: young, unorganised, employed in small workshops, in small towns or semi-rural areas, or in municipal or state enterprises e.g. gas works, railways. The middle classes proved much more vulnerable. They felt their economic position and their social status threatened by the Left, and the Social Democrats often appeared a more immediate threat than the Communists.

The statistics on party membership also show workers much under-represented in relation to their proportion of the population as a whole, while the middle-class occupations were correspondingly over-represented, though more peasants seem to have voted Nazi than become members. Between 1930 and 1933, the workers increased their proportion of the Party, while that of most other groups correspondingly declined. But this shift was marginal and workers continued to be heavily under-represented—32.5 per cent of the Party compared with 46 per cent of the population, although of course in terms of sheer numbers the workers formed a sizeable group within the Party. The statistics on age show the predominance of youth within the Party membership.

Electoral statistics confirm that while the Party drew support from all classes the middle class was significantly over-represented. They also show the significance both of religion and of the rural/urban division. The main strength of Nazism lay in the Protestant and predominantly rural areas of the north German plain stretching from East Prussia to Schleswig-Holstein. Eight out of the ten districts with the largest Nazi vote in July 1932 are in this area; the exceptions are Liegnitz (Silesia) and Chemnitz-Zwickau. Nazism was weakest in the big cities (e.g. Berlin and Leipzig) and in industrial areas generally, particularly in predominantly Catholic ones (e.g. Düsseldorf East and West). In the cities it tended to draw most support from upper middle class districts. It was also weakest in overwhelmingly Catholic rural areas (e.g. Koblenz-Trier). The religious factor is most evident in Bavaria, where the north (Franconia) contained many Protestants who tended to vote Nazi, while in the overwhelmingly Catholic south (Upper and Lower Bavaria) the Nazi vote was among the lowest in Germany, although the Party had originated and was still based there.

Exceptions to this general pattern were the high Nazi vote in much of Silesia (Liegnitz and Breslau), a predominantly Catholic area with industry, and in the Palatinate, mainly Catholic and rural. The border issue may have played a part here. Silesia had been hotly contested with Poland and, after a plebiscite ordered under the Versailles treaty, much of Upper Silesia was awarded to Poland. The Nazis probably benefited from the intense nationalism generated by this conflict. In the Palatinate, France's attempt to establish a separatist regime in the early 1920s had also generated nationalist feelings which may help to account for the vote. In mixed Protestant and Catholic areas such as Franconia Nazism tended to unify the Protestants, long resentful of the dominance of the Catholic Centre/Bavarian People's Party but whose vote, split among several parties, had been less able to influence events.

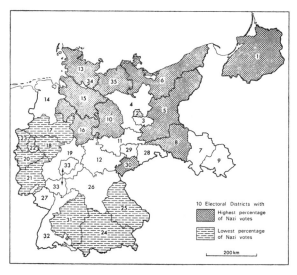

Electoral Map for 31 July 1932

60

Percentage of votes cast in favour of the NDSAP

Reichstag elections:	4.v.24	7.xii.24	20.v.28	14.ix.30	31.vii.32	6.xi.32	5.iii.33
Number of seats:	32	14	12	107	230	196	288
National vote:	6.5	3.0	2.6	18.3	37.3	33.1	43.9

District							
1 East Prussia	8.6	6.2	0.8	22.5	47.1	39.7	56.5
2 Berlin	3.6	1.6	1.4	12.8	24.6	22.5	31.3
3 Potsdam II	6.5	2.9	1.8	16.7	33.0	29.1	38.2
4 Potsdam I	5.8	2.8	1.6	18.8	38.2	34.1	44.4
5 Frankfurt a.d. Oder	5.0	3.2	1.0	22.7	48.1	42.6	55.2
6 Pomerania	7.3	4.2	1.5	24.3	48.0	43.1	56.3
7 Breslau	4.0	1.4	1.0	24.2	43.5	40.4	50.2
8 Liegnitz	1.5	1.5	1.2	20.9	48.0	42.1	54.0
9 Oppeln	2.6	1.5	1.0	9.5	29.2	26.8	43.2
10 Magdeburg	4.9	3.0	1.7	19.5	43.8	39.0	47.3
11 Merseburg	8.7	4.3	2.7	20.5	42.6	34.5	46.4
12 Thuringia	9.9	5.4	3.7	19.3	43.4	37.1	47.2
13 Schleswig-Holstein	7.4	2.7	4.0	27.0	51.0	45.7	53.2
14 Weser-Ems	7.4	4.8	5.2	20.5	38.4	31.9	41.4
15 East Hanover	8.6	4.4	2.6	20.6	49.5	42.9	54.3
16 South-Hanover-Brunswick	7.6	3.4	4.4	24.3	46.1	40.6	48.7
17 Westphalia-North	3.5	1.3	1.0	12.2	25.7	22.3	34.9
18 Westphalia-South	1.5	1.1	1.6	13.9	27.2	24.8	33.8
19 Hesse-Nassau	5.6	2.5	3.6	20.8	43.6	41.2	49.4
20 Cologne-Aachen	1.5	0.6	1.1	14.5	20.2	17.4	30.1
21 Koblenz-Trier	1.3	—	2.1	14.9	28.8	26.1	38.4
22 Düsseldorf-East	3.9	1.6	1.8	17.0	31.6	27.0	37.4
23 Düsseldorf-West	2.6	0.9	1.2	16.8	27.0	24.2	35.2
24 Upper Bavaria-Swabia	17.0	4.8	6.2	16.3	27.1	24.6	40.9
25 Lower Bavaria	10.2	3.0	3.5	12.0	20.4	18.5	39.2
26 Franconia	20.7	7.5	8.1	20.5	39.9	36.4	45.7
27 Palatinate	5.7	1.9	5.6	22.8	43.7	42.6	46.5
28 Dresden-Bautzen	4.5	1.5	1.8	16.1	39.3	34.0	43.6
29 Leipzig	7.9	1.8	1.9	14.0	36.1	31.0	40.0
30 Chemnitz-Zwickau	7.7	4.2	4.3	23.8	47.0	43.4	50.0
31 Württemburg	4.1	2.1	1.9	9.4	30.3	26.2	42.0
32 Baden	4.8	1.9	2.9	19.2	36.9	34.1	45.4
33 Hesse-Darmstadt	2.9	1.3	1.9	18.5	43.1	40.2	47.4
34 Hamburg	6.0	2.3	2.6	19.2	33.7	27.2	38.9
35 Mecklenburg	20.8	11.9	2.0	20.1	44.8	37.0	48.0

61

Age of Nazi Party membership as of 1 January 1935, divided according to date of joining

Date of birth	Age	Date of Party membership										Percentage of total population
		Before seizure of power						After seizure of power				
		Before 14.ix.30		From 14.ix.30 to 30.i.33		Total		After 30.i.33		Total		
		Number	Per cent	Number	Per cent	Number	Per cent	Number	Per cent	Number	Per cent	Per cent
1916–1914	18–20	468	0.5 / 0.4	14,972	17.0 / 2.1	15,440	17.5 / 1.8	72,648	82.5 / 4.4	88,088	100.0 / 3.5	5.8
1913–1904	21–30	47,167	5.5 / 36.4	296,438	34.8 / 41.3	343,605	40.3 / 40.4	508,869	59.7 / 31.0	852,474	100.0 / 34.1	25.3

Birth years	Age	No.	%	No.	%	No.	%	No.	%	Total	%	
1903–1894	31–40	40,700	5.9 / 31.4	193,937	28.0 / 26.9	234,637	33.9 / 27.8	459,780	66.1 / 27.9	694,417	100.0 / 27.9	22.0
1893–1884	41–50	22,835	4.7 / 17.6	122,884	25.2 / 17.1	145,719	29.9 / 17.2	342,338	70.1 / 20.8	488,057	100.0 / 19.6	17.1
1883–1874	51–60	12,546	4.5 / 9.7	66,454	23.9 / 9.2	79,000	28.4 / 9.3	199,491	71.6 / 12.1	278,491	100.0 / 11.2	14.5
1873 and earlier	61 and over	5,847	6.3 / 4.5	24,761	26.8 / 3.4	30,608	33.1 / 3.6	61,755	66.9 / 3.8	92,363	100.0 / 3.7	15.3
Total		129,563	5.2 / 100.0	719,446	28.9 / 100.0	849,009	34.1 / 100.0	1,644,881	65.9 / 100.0	2,493,890	100.0 / 100.0	100.0

NOTE. In the percentage columns, the upper of the two figures shows the percentage of Party membership on 1 January 1935; the lower figure shows the percentage of Party membership within the period of time covered by each pair of vertical columns.

62

Party members as of 1 January 1935, divided according to jobs and date of membership

Job	Date of Party membership								Total		Society June 1933
	Before seizure of power						After seizure of power				
	Before 14.ix.30		From 14.ix.30 until 30.i.33		Up to 30.i.33		After 30.i.33				
	No.	%	No.	%	No.	%	No.	%	No.	%	%
1 Persons in employment	121,151	5.1	669,678	28.4	790,829	33.5	1,567,055	66.5	2,357,884	100.0	
		93.5		93.1		93.1		95.3		94.5	
I Workers	33,944	4.5	233,479	30.8	267,423	35.3	488,544	64.7	755,967	100.0	46.3
		26.3		32.5		31.5		29.7		30.3	
2 White-collar employees	31,067	6.4	147,855	30.6	178,922	37.0	305,132	63.0	484,054	100.0	12.4
		24.0		20.6		21.0		18.6		19.4	
3 Self-employed	24,563	5.2	124,579	26.2	149,142	31.4	326,081	68.6	475,223	100.0	9.6
		18.9		17.3		17.6		19.8		19.0	
Artisans	11,059	5.3	55,814	26.8	66,873	32.1	141,309	67.9	208,182	100.0	
		8.5		7.7		7.9		8.6		8.3	
Tradesmen	9,918	5.3	48,920	26.0	58,838	31.1	128,776	68.7	187,614	100.0	
		7.6		6.8		6.9		7.8		7.5	
Professions	3,586	4.5	19,845	25.0	23,431	29.5	55,996	70.5	79,427	100.0	
		2.8		2.8		2.8		1.4		3.2	

	Count	%		Count	%		Count	%		Count	%		Total	%		Cat. %
4 Civil servants	10,015	3.3	7.7	46,967	15.3	6.5	56,982	18.6	6.7	250,223	81.4	15.2	307,205	100.0	12.4	4.8
Civil servants	7,992	3.6	6.2	36,088	16.2	5.0	44,080	19.8	5.2	179,033	80.2	10.9	223,113	100.0	9.0	
Teachers	2,023	2.4	1.5	10,879	12.9	1.5	12,902	15.3	1.5	71,190	84.7	4.3	84,092	100.0	3.4	
5 Peasants	17,181	6.7	13.2	89,800	35.2	12.5	106,981	41.9	12.6	148,310	58.1	9.0	255,291	100.0	10.2	20.7
6 Others	4,381	5.5	3.4	26,998	33.7	3.7	31,379	39.2	3.7	48,765	60.8	3.0	80,144	100.0	3.2	6.2
II Persons not in employment 7 Pensioners	2,453	6.5	1.9	11,684	30.7	1.6	14,137	37.2	1.7	23,736	62.8	1.4	37,873	100.0	1.5	
III Family dependents without a full-time job	5,959	6.1	4.6	38,084	38.8	5.3	44,043	44.9	5.2	54,090	55.1	3.3	98,113	100.0	4.0	
8 Housewives	4,706	7.3	3.6	29,304	45.3	4.1	34,010	52.6	4.0	30,617	47.4	1.9	64,627	100.0	2.6	
9 Students and school children	1,253	3.7	1.0	8,780	26.2	1.2	10,033	2.9	1.2	23,473	70.1	1.4	33,506	100.0	1.4	
Total	129,563	5.2	100.0	719,446	28.8	100.0	849,009	34.0	100.0	1,644,881	66.0	100.0	2,493,890	100.0	100.0	

NOTE. In the percentage columns, the upper of the two figures shows the percentage of Party membership on 1 January 1935; the lower figure shows the percentage of Party membership within the period of time covered by each pair of vertical columns.

CHAPTER 4

The Struggle for Power, 1930–33

Electoral success, a prerequisite for the acquisition of power, by itself was not enough in view of the Party's failure to achieve an absolute majority. Now that parliamentary government had broken down and power lay with the President under Article 48 of the Weimar Constitution, it was just as important to win the approval of the conservative elites whose influence increased in proportion to the decline of that of Parliament. The Army, senior members of the bureaucracy, big landowners and particularly the Junkers of east Germany (among whom the President could now count himself after industry's gift to him of his old family estate), industry itself—all these groups, had retained their economic and social power. They now found a sympathetic hearing from the President and from the camarilla which surrounded him, notably his State Secretary, Otto Meissner, and his son, Oskar. These groups saw an opportunity to replace Weimar democracy with a more authoritarian regime, to undo the results of the revolution. On what form such a regime should take there were different views. Some toyed with the idea of restoring the monarchy; others wished to restore the political system of the Second Reich but with a president in place of the emperor. But common to most of these views was the determination to reduce Parliament to a subordinate role and thereby to exclude the Left from effective political influence. In these plans the Nazi movement came to have an important function.

Initially, it had been hoped to secure a majority for a presidential regime with the moderate Right and Centre—this was Brüning's plan. But as the regime based on Article 48 established itself more and more firmly, and as political opinion became increasingly polarised, it became clear that it would be impossible to achieve a majority on such a basis. Instead the Brüning Government was sustained in a negative fashion by the unwillingness of the Social Democrats and all groups to the left of the German Nationalists to bring down the Government for fear of the election that would follow. But to permit the Social Democrats to wield influence had now become anathema to the German Right. The presidential regime, run by the bureaucracy, open to the influence of conservative pressure groups and largely independent of Parliament, had become congenial. It fitted in with the German tradition of the State ruling above the parties, though of course in practice the State invariably represented the conservatives. They wanted to give it a permanent basis, no longer dependent on the toleration of the moderate Left.

Yet it was realised that an authoritarian government seeking to secure a permanent basis would need mass support. When it became clear that the Brüning experiment had failed, and that its policies were beginning to threaten conservative interests, as with a plan to break up bankrupt Junker estates and settle them with peasants, the Right began to base their hopes on the Nazi movement as the means of acquiring mass support. Brüning himself had tried to use the Nazis and tame them by securing their participation in government; now the Right decided that Brüning had become an obstacle to this policy. There were many aspects of the Nazi movement of which the Right disapproved. It was too radical, too violent, its economic policies smacked too much of Socialism, and the characters of some of its leaders were dubious, to say the least. It was, however, a nationalist movement and a movement hostile to the 'Marxist' Left. It offered the chance of 'conquering the streets' and wresting them from the Left. It contained many young people with the right ideas about the need to restore German greatness and who, apart from anything else, would provide excellent recruits for the Army. It was essential therefore to harness this movement for a new regime of the Right. If Hitler were brought into the Government in a subordinate capacity, he would be forced to become more 'responsible'. While power would continue to lie in the hands of the conservative establishment, Hitler would use his gifts as a propagandist to sell the policies of the Government to the masses. There was also another factor. If Hitler were not brought into the Government, there was a danger that the Nazis might attempt to come to power by force. This would lead to a civil war between Right and Left which would destroy the social order and ruin Germany's chances of regaining her military strength. The radical elements in the Nazi movement might get the upper hand and make common cause with the Communists against the conservative Right, and the Army might well find it impossible to deal with such a combined front. Such considerations lay behind attempts to persuade Hitler to join the Government or at least give it his support.

Hitler, on the other hand, was determined to avoid being harnessed in this way. He was not prepared to come into a Conservative Government in a subordinate capacity—if he was to bear the responsibility he wanted to have the power as well. Initially, he insisted on a government dominated by Nazis. By the end of 1932, however, the crisis in the Party caused largely by the failure to achieve office persuaded him to settle for less. Provided he had the Chancellorship and one or two key ministries, he was prepared for a government dominated by the Conservatives. Banking on their majority in the Cabinet, on their influence with the President, and on their greater political experience, the Conservatives assumed that they had managed to harness him to their cause. Hitler was content with the compromise, confident that it would not take him long to break out of the frame within which they had tried to fetter him.

(i) The Path of Legality and the Problem of the SA

Success in the 1930 election apparently justified the policy of 'legality' followed since 1925. Yet the Party's substantial representation in the Reichstag raised the question of its revolutionary aims and the reconciliation of its contempt for parliamentary democracy with participation in the parliamentary process.

In September 1930, three Army lieutenants accused of working for the Nazi Party were tried before the Supreme Court at Leipzig on a charge of subversion. Hitler, called as a witness, made the following statement in which he carefully distinguished between means and ends:

63

The National Socialist movement will try to achieve its aim with constitutional means in this state. The constitution prescribes only the methods, not the aim. In this constitutional way we shall try to gain decisive majorities in the legislative bodies so that the moment we succeed we can give the state the form that corresponds to our ideas.

The chairman of the court summed up the statement to the effect that the setting up of the Third Reich was being worked for in a constitutional way...

This important statement helped forestall a possible prohibition of the Party, enabled the State authorities and the Army to rationalise their unwillingness to take action against the movement, however wild its excesses, and convinced them that cooperation with the Party was possible.

There were, however, those in the Party, particularly in the SA, who resented the limitations imposed by the tactics of legality. Before 1930, most Party members were in the SA and the Party and SA had formed a fringe group of zealots whose isolation in a hostile environment welded them together in comradeship. They were crudely anti-capitalist in their hostility to big business and banks and suspicious of and hostile towards 'bosses' of all kinds. They despised conventional parliamentary politics and politicians seeing the Reichstag as a sink of corruption. It was an aggressively male world, formed through service in the military and the Free Corps, whose supreme values were physical courage, comradeship and loyalty to a leader who had won their respect. After September 1930, the SA was faced with the need to move within the world of conventional politics, where a new kind of party—no longer a collection of like-minded individuals but a huge organisation in which bureaucracy proliferated— would give them orders through Party officials whose sole claim to importance seemed to be ability at paper work. Many bitterly resented these changes. They resented doing all the dirty work, risking injury or even their lives fighting political opponents, spending long hours in arduous marches and parades while the political wing of the Party monopolised influence and even the 'perks' such as a majority of the Reichstag seats in the 1930 elections. For their contempt for Parliament did not stop them wanting seats in it and the salaries that went with them.

Hitler was obliged to move carefully between alienating the conservative pressure groups by appearing to conciliate the military and revolutionary ambitions of the SA and alienating the SA by appearing to renege upon the revolutionary goals of the movement through a compromise with the conservative establishment. The former danger had been dealt with temporarily by the Leipzig oath. This was given official recognition, in January 1931, when the Army removed the ban on the employment of Nazis in Army installations and on Nazi enlistment. But the other danger remained. Just before the elections in September 1930, the Berlin SA had mutinied and it had required all Hitler's powers of persuasion and a promise of a higher subsidy to pacify them. After the elections the danger recurred. On 20 February 1931, as an earnest of the sincerity of his policy of legality, Hitler forbade the SA to take part in street fighting. But, for many this was a typical instance of the way in which the ideals of the movement were being compromised. In April 1931, the leader of the SA in east Germany, Walter Stennes, who wished Hitler to return to the revolutionary path, was dismissed. Some SA units, however, remained loyal to him and tried to resist, including the one in Berlin which distributed the following pamphlet:

64

National Socialists of Berlin!

The Munich party leadership of the NSDAP yesterday ordered the dissolution of the Berlin SA and dismissed the supreme SA leader, Captain Stennes, whom Hitler had repeatedly assured of his trust.

The news has provoked indignation, embitterment and a deep feeling of shock in the Berlin SA and beyond that in SA sections throughout the Reich.

What is at stake?

Is it only a conflict of personalities, a leadership struggle?

No, the cause of National Socialism is at stake!

In the person of Captain Stennes the whole SA is being attacked. Munich has forgotten that readiness for sacrifice and simplicity once created the Party and made it strong. Today they build the 'Brown House' in Munich at a cost of millions whereas the individual SA men have not a penny with which to repair their torn boots.

In the face of the emergency decree, in the face of daily sacrifices of blood by the SA, while the fight against the movement and the terror have reached their peak, a Munich clique brings fratricidal warfare into the ranks of the Party.

The SA has helped the Party in its struggle to gain thousands of seats in the Reich, states and communes

Now the SA have done their duty, they can go. They are now a cumbersome conscience, reminding people of the betrayed Party programme and demanding the fight for the old ideals of National Socialism, in contrast to the opportunistic policy of interests in Munich.

This is not illegal putschism, as the Jewish press wants to represent it, but only in order to prevent the Party's betrayal of the SA and of National Socialism.

The SA leadership has no intention of letting their SA comrades be misused for the financing of the Brown House and as a pawn in political bargains. With a sense of deep responsibility towards every single SA man and towards the whole German people, it acts according to the great fundamental law of National Socialism:

The common welfare comes before individual welfare and according to the deepest law of comradeship, loyalty for loyalty.

'With our flag held high and our ranks tightly closed'.

The SA marches.

Stennes takes over command.

Significantly in their appeal to the SA in Silesia the rebels insisted that 'our struggle is not directed against Adolf Hitler but against those round him whom he has not yet recognised for what they are'. Hitler moved quickly and made a strong personal appeal to the SA, demanding declarations of loyalty from each of its leaders. The affair brought a decisive victory for the political leadership and some important reforms in organisation, including tighter control over the membership and activities of local branches, the introduction of training schools for SA leaders, and the further centralising of administration in the SA, begun after Röhm's appointment as SA chief of staff at the beginning of 1931.

Conflict between the political organisation and the SA, however, remained endemic at all levels of the Party, and was most commonly expressed in rivalry over finance.

(ii) Relations between Nazis and Nationalists in 1931-32

During 1931 the Brüning Government appeared to be firmly established as a result of its toleration by the moderate Left and Right in the Reichstag. Hitler had the difficult task of maintaining some contact with the reactionary Nationalists and of cultivating powerful interest groups such as industry—all of whom had growing political influence in the vacuum left by the breakdown of the parliamentary system—without at the same time alienating his activist and radical followers and without allowing himself to be used as a pawn by reactionaries bent on counter-revolution.

In the summer of 1931 Hitler and Hugenberg, the leader of the Nationalists, made tentative moves towards reviving the cooperation begun with the Young Plan campaign of 1929. In July they announced their decision to work together to overthrow the existing 'system'. This led to a big demonstration of the extreme Right at Bad Harzburg on 11 October, dominated however by the reactionaries, with whom Hitler basically had little sympathy. He demonstrated the · Nazi Party's determination to preserve its independence by leaving the rostrum after the SA march past and before the nationalist ex-servicemen's association, the Stahlhelm, had arrived. Sir Horace Rumbold, the British ambassador in Berlin, commented on the Harzburg meeting in his report of 14 October:

65

The Harzburg meeting, which has been a theme of conversation in political circles for many weeks, was expected to mark a turning-point in the political history of Germany. For the first time all the parties of the Right were to join forces, and it was expected that the outcome would be a spectacular reconciliation between the Nazis and Nationalists, followed by the issue of a joint programme on which all the parties of the Right had agreed to unite. This was counted upon to win over the small wavering parties of Right tendency. So far, however, as one can gather from the reports of the meeting, little in the way of unity was achieved beyond the outward show, and it remains to be seen whether any real working agreement can be established between the two main Opposition parties. It is true that a joint resolution was passed to the effect that the parties of the Right were ready to take over the responsibility of governing the Reich and Prussia and the other federal states. Implacable opposition to the present Brüning Government constituted, so far as one can ascertain, the main plank of the political platform on which the groups and parties present agreed to unite. The National Socialist press publishes the speeches of the Nazi leaders as well as the text of the joint resolution in many columns, but devotes only half a column to Herr Hugenberg's speech, while the Stahlhelm are scarcely mentioned as participating. The Nationalist press returns the compliment, and is at pains to emphasise the leading part played by Hugenberg.

There is nothing in Herr Hitler's speech to suggest that he has sacrificed any part
of the Socialist section of his programme in order to fall into line with Herr
Hugenberg and the big industrialists.

There appears to have been no settled programme at Harzburg. Hitler issued the
address summarised above to a gathering of his own followers before noon. It was
prefaced by a cynical speech on the part of Herr Frick, who sought to allay 'the very
comprehensible misgivings of his party friends' by assuring them that the Nazi
leaders were merely using the Nationalists as a convenient ladder to office.
Mussolini, he asserted, had done the same thing before assuming sole control of the
Government of Italy.

Although Hitler insisted on retaining his Party's independence from the
other sections of the Right, he was also anxious to win the sympathy of
powerful interests, necessary to acquire finance for the elaborate Party
organisation and propaganda. Hitler cultivated relations with industrialists
and financiers in the Rhineland in an endeavour to remove the radical
image of the Party. Most notable was the speech he made to the influential
Industry Club in Düsseldorf in January 1932, on an invitation by Fritz
Thyssen, a major Ruhr industrialist and keen Nazi supporter:

66

...People say to me so often: 'You are only the drummer of national Germany'.
And supposing that I were only the dummer? It would, today be a far more
statesmanlike achievement to drum once more into this German people a new faith
than gradually to squander the only faith they have... . The more you bring a
people back into the sphere of faith, of ideals, the more will it cease to regard
material distress as the one and only thing that counts. And the weightiest evidence
for the truth of that statement is our own German people. We will never forget that
the German people waged wars of religion for 150 years with prodigious devotion,
that hundreds of thousands of men once left their plot of land, their property, and
their belongings simply for an ideal, simply for a conviction. We will never forget
that during those 150 years there was no trace of even an ounce of material interest.
Then you will understand how mighty is the force of an idea, of an ideal. Only so
can you comprehend how it is that in our movement today hundreds of thousands
of young men are prepared to risk their lives to withstand our opponents. I know
quite well, gentlemen, that when National Socialists march through the streets and
suddenly in the evening there arises a tumult and a commotion, then the bourgeois
draws back the window-curtain, looks out, and says: 'Once again my night's rest is
disturbed: no more sleep for me. Why must these Nazis always be so provocative
and run about the place at night?' Gentlemen, if everyone thought like that, then,
true enough, no one's sleep at night would be disturbed, but then also the
bourgeois today would not be able to venture into the street. If everyone thought in
that way, if these young folk had no ideal to move them and drive them forward,
then certainly they would gladly be rid of these nightly fights. But remember that it

means sacrifice when today many hundreds of thousands of SA and SS men of the National Socialist movement have every day to mount on their lorries, protect meetings, undertake marches, sacrifice themselves night after night and then come back in the grey dawn to workshop and factory, or as unemployed to take the pittance of the dole: it means sacrifice when from the little they possess they have further to buy their uniforms, their shirts, their badges, yes and even pay their own fares. Believe me, there is already in all this the force of an ideal—a great ideal! And if the whole German nation today had the same faith in its vocation as these hundreds of thousands, if the whole nation possessed this idealism, Germany would stand in the eyes of the world otherwise than she stands now! (*loud applause*). For our situation in the world in its fatal effects is but the result of our own underestimate of German strength. (*'Very true!'*) Only when we have once more changed this fatal undervaluation of ourselves can Germany take advantage of the political possibilities which, if we look far enough into the future, can place German life once more upon a natural and secure basis—and that means either new living space [*Lebensraum*] and the development of a great internal market or protection of German economic life against the world without and utilisation of all the concentrated strength of Germany. The labour resources of our people, the capacities, we have them already: no one can deny that we are industrious. But we must first refashion the political preconditions: without that, industry and capacity, diligence and economy are in the last resort of no avail; an oppressed nation will not be able to spend on its own welfare even the fruits of its own economy but must sacrifice them on the altar of exactions and of tribute.

And so in contrast to our own official Government I see no hope for the resurrection of Germany if we regard the foreign politics of Germany as the primary factor: our primary need is the restoration of a sound national German body politic armed to strike. In order to realise this end I founded thirteen years ago the National Socialist movement: that movement I have led during the last twelve years and I hope that one day it will accomplish this task and that, as the fairest result of its struggle, it will leave behind it a German body politic completely renewed internally, intolerant of anyone who sins against the nation and its interests, intolerant of anyone who will not acknowledge its vital interests or who opposes them, intolerant of and pitiless towards anyone who shall attempt once more to destroy or undermine this body politic, and yet ready for friendship and peace with anyone who has a wish for peace and friendship (*long and tumultuous applause*).

In fact the response to Hitler's speech was disappointing. And, although the Party acquired some finance from big business, the sums were smaller than those provided for other bourgeois parties. Before 1933, only a minority of major industrialists actively supported them; more important were contributions from smaller businessmen at local level. The Party was, however, largely self-financing from membership dues, entry fees, etc.

The main task remained convincing the President. Hindenburg was persuaded to see Hitler in October 1931 but the interview was not a success. Earlier, in a meeting with the Nationalists' leader, Hugenberg, on 1 August 1931, Hindenburg had expressed his scepticism about the Nazis:

67

The Reich President referred to the cooperation of the German Nationalists with the National Socialists who, he feared, were more socialist than nationalist and whose behaviour in the country he could not approve. He, the Field-Marshal and liberator of East Prussia, had during his East Prussian journey, particularly on the drive across the battlefield of Tannenberg, been repeatedly insulted by scandalous demonstrations of National Socialists and had had to comment very unfavourably on these young people who had been misled. He did not regard them as a reliable national party.

To this Privy Councillor Dr Hugenberg replied that it was for this very reason—to bind the National Socialists to the nationalist side and prevent their slipping towards socialism or communism—that he had decided to work with the Nazis over the past one-and-a-half years and he took credit for this. He believed also that the National Socialists had been politically educated thereby. The demonstrations which the Reich President deplored had probably not been meant so badly. Meetings held by him, Hugenberg, were also often accompanied by National Socialist demonstrations and the shout of 'Germany, awake!' He could not stop these demonstrations either. To a suggestion by the Reich President that Hugenberg should use his press to oppose these demonstrations which were particularly embarrassing in view of the age and standing of the Reich President, he gave us no definite reply.

In the spring of 1932 Hindenburg's seven-year term as President came to an end. Brüning and the parties of the Centre and moderate Left wished to extend it for a year or two to keep Hitler from the presidency and provide more time to solve the crisis and thereby undermine the Nazi Party. Under the Constitution an extension required a two-thirds majority in the Reichstag and for this the agreement of the Nazis would be necessary. It was hoped to persuade Hitler by a hint that he could replace Brüning as Chancellor in a year or two and by the difficulty of defeating Hindenburg in an election. The Nazi leadership was divided on the issue. Röhm, and Goebbels wanted to reject the plan and try and defeat Hindenburg in the election, while Gregor Strasser, the head of the Party's organisation, argued that Hitler would not be able to defeat Hindenburg and that they should therefore accept the plan. Hitler hesitated and negotiated with General Groener who was both Minister of the Interior and Minister of Defence. But when Hugenberg rejected the idea in the name of the Nationalists, Hitler felt obliged to follow suit in order not to be outflanked. He counterattacked, however, by offering to support Hindenburg if he would replace Brüning with a right-wing government comprising Nazis and Nationalists and to hold new elections for the Reichstag and Prussian Landtag. When Hindenburg refused, Hitler had to decide whether or not to enter the election, knowing that he would almost certainly lose.

Although he hesitated for a month, in fact he had little choice. Refusal would have been widely interpreted as cowardice, something Hitler could afford even less than defeat.

In the Presidential elections of March–April 1932 Goebbels surpassed all previous Nazi propaganda campaigns, to no avail. In the first ballot on 13 March Hindenburg polled 18,661,736 votes (49.45 per cent) against Hitler's 11,338,571 votes (30.23 per cent). The remaining votes were divided between the Stahlhelm leader, Düsterberg, the candidate of the Nationalists (6.81 per cent), and Thälmann, the Communist leader (13.23 per cent). Since Hindenburg had just failed to win the absolute majority needed, a second ballot was held on 10 April in which Hindenburg gained 52.9 per cent and Hitler 36.6 per cent. Düsterberg did not run and his votes were divided between Hitler and Hindenburg, the majority of them going to Hitler. Thälmann too appears to have lost votes to Hitler, slipping back to 10.1 per cent.

(iii) From Brüning to Papen

With their direct assault on the citadel of power thwarted by Hindenburg's re-election, the Nazis concentrated on Brüning. Brüning and his supporters had reason to believe that for the time being their position was secure. Brüning's entire dependence on the President's support was, however, to prove fatal. For Hindenburg, though relieved at his re-election, had resented its being achieved by Social Democrats, Catholic Centre, and Democrats who had opposed his first election in 1925, while the Right, to which he had first owed his election and with whom he had far more in common, had opposed his re-election. Instead of being grateful to Brüning, he tended to blame him and increasingly lent his ear to conservative pressure groups urging the replacement of Brüning by an uncompromisingly right-wing government not reliant on the toleration of the Centre and moderate Left, but counting on the support of the Nazis.

The Government's decision to ban the SA opened the breach between Hindenburg and Brüning. Pressure from the state governments for action against the SA had been mounting. After the first ballot in the Reich presidential election, Prussian police, acting on instructions from Severing, the Social Democrat Prussian Minister of the Interior, had raided Nazi headquarters throughout the state and found evidence that the SA had planned to carry out a coup in the event of Hitler's securing a majority. The evidence was forwarded to the Supreme Court in Leipzig and as a result pressure on the Reich Government increased. The decision whether or not to impose such a ban lay with General Wilhelm Groener, Reich Minister of the Interior, with overall responsibility for internal security in

the Reich. Groener, however, relied heavily upon the advice of his chief
political adviser, General von Schleicher. Schleicher had played a significant part in the appointment of Brüning, but had become increasingly
disillusioned with the Chancellor's dependence on the Left. He had
already established contact with the Nazis and in particular with the SA,
which he was anxious to harness by integrating it into a new state
organisation for pre-military training. He also believed it possible to win
the support of the Nazis for a more right-wing government which would
then be able to dispense with the Left. Schleicher, therefore, was furious at
Severing's move against the SA, which, as he told Groener on 23 March,
he saw as an attempt to force the Reich Government to come out against
the Right in the Prussian elections fixed for 24 April:

68

...Basically their aim is to win Your Excellency for the struggle against the Right in
the Prussian elections so that you will be branded as a faithful ally of the Socialists.
To achieve this end they regard any means as permissible, such as mysterious hints
about the Border Guard to French correspondents [i.e. that Germany was evading
the Versailles restrictions] and naked threats by the SPD party headquarters and by
the Prussian Ministry of the Interior that they will not vote for Hindenburg on 10
April if your Excellency does not take up the struggle against the SA... After the
events of the past few days, I am quite glad that a counterweight exists in the shape
of the Nazis though they too are naughty boys and must be handled with extreme
care. If they did not exist one would really have to invent them. The course which
your Excellency is following—no one's friend and no one's enemy—is, I believe, in
these circumstances the only correct one...

Groener however, feared if he did not act, the states would go ahead
with their own separate bans. Moreover, he envisaged a ban on the SA as
a means of taming the Nazi Party as he explained in a letter to a friend,
Alarich von Gleich, on 2 April 1932:

69

On Monday or Tuesday, the Ministers of the Interior of the states are coming to a
meeting about the SA. I have no doubt that we will master it—one way or the
other. I think we have already drawn its poisonous fangs. One can made good
tactical use of the endless declarations of legality made by the SA leaders, which
they have handed to me in thick volumes. The SA is thereby undermining its
credibility. But there are still difficult weeks of political manoeuvring until the
various Landtag elections are over. Then, one will have to start working towards
making the Nazis acceptable as participants in a government because the move-

ment, which will certainly grow, can no longer be suppressed by force. Of course the Nazis must not be allowed to form a government of their own anywhere, let alone in the Reich. But in the states an attempt wil have to be made here and there to harness them in a coalition and to cure them of their utopias by constructive government work. I can see no better way, for the idea of trying to destroy the Party through an anti-Nazi law on the lines of the old anti-Socialist law I would regard as a very unfortunate undertaking. With the SA of course it is different. They must be eliminated in any event, and ideally the so-called Iron Front[22] as well... .

The conference with the Ministers of the states on 5 April finally persuaded Groener to go ahead with a ban. He now came up against opposition from Schleicher, however, anxious to avoid a confrontation with the Nazi Party. Schleicher suggested the idea of first sending an ultimatum to demand changes in the SA; only if these were rejected would it be necessary to go ahead with the ban. When Hindenburg rejected this idea and accepted an immediate ban, Schleicher intrigued to have the decision reversed. Groener noted down at the time what followed:

70

In the afternoon of the 10th, State Secretary Zweigert rang me up to inform me that State Secretary Meissner of the Reich President's Office had told him while at breakfast with Reich Minister of Transport Treviranus that the President had changed his mind under the influence of General von Schleicher brought to bear on him by his own son... .

12 April.... I met Col. von Hindenburg who was in a state of great agitation about the fact that once again his father was expected to sign a decree, although he had only just been appointed Reich President. His father would only have dirt thrown at him again by the Right. They might at least wait a little. He did not bring up any objective reasons, in fact he emphasised that he was not interested in the SA. In view of his excitement, it was impossible to have an objective discussion with him. But I was in no doubt about the fact that his opinion was based purely on naïve and sentimental feelings... .

At five o'clock in the afternoon, the Reich Chancellor and I went to see the Reich President. State Secretary Meissner was present at the interview. The Chancellor gave a lengthy explanation of why the ban was necessary. I supplemented it by slowly reading out the official explanation which was later released. The Reich President made no substantial objections; in fact his attitude was in no way one of fundamental opposition... . At the end, the Reich President stated that it should not be held against his son if he tried to protect his father. He was prepared to sign the decree if the Chancellor and the Reich Minister of the Interior considered it necessary.

---

[22] The Iron Front was a propaganda organisation formed by the Social Democrats and the Reichsbanner at the end of 1931.

The decree banning the SA and the SS was issued on 13 April. The intrigue, however, continued; as Groener later reflected:

71

My hands were tied as regards these manoeuvres because any attempt to get the Reich President to take action against these officers would have met with such resistance that there would have been nothing left but immediate resignation. But this would have also brought about the fall of the Brüning Government even before the Prussian elections, before the Reichstag had convened, and in the middle of the Geneva negotiations on disarmament.... I knew very well that the intention was to bring down the Chancellor. In the course of the winter, the Reich President had twice mentioned to me that Dr Brüning did not quite represent his ideal as Reich Chancellor. He did not accept my comment that at the moment he would not find a better one. General von Schleicher had also made no bones about the fact that he was thinking in terms of a change of Chancellor. In view of his connexions with the Reich President's entourage, it can be assumed that he took part in the removal of Dr Brüning as Chancellor. During the absence of the Reich President in Neudeck, his country estate, where Brüning's fall was decided upon, General von Schleicher was in continual contact by telephone with Hindenburg's son.

Schleicher succeeded in bringing about Groener's fall on 13 May. It was only a preliminary move towards the main objective, the dismissal of Brüning, particularly vulnerable because of his total dependence on the President. He had failed to win popular support because he had consistently subordinated domestic politics to foreign affairs. Although initially under pressure to fulfil reparations obligations, Brüning's position was relieved by the moratorium declared on 20 June 1931 by President Hoover. Nevertheless, Brüning continued his rigid deflationary policies because of his determination to secure the complete ending of reparations by demonstrating Germany's inability to pay. This would then free Germany's hands for a more aggressive foreign policy, in particular challenging French and British influence in South East Europe. He assumed such diplomatic gains would secure his position with public opinion at home and, in particular, against his right-wing critics. In fact, however, his deflationary economic policies only resulted in the growing alienation of many not only from his own government but from the political system itself, while the fruits of his foreign policy were to be garnered by his successors. In addition, after his failure in 1930 to secure a new right-wing majority he had neglected the Reichstag. The increasingly presidential regime associated with rule by decree accorded with his own sympathy for the pre-war system of a government ruling 'above the parties' under the direction of the emperor.

By the spring of 1932, however, he had lost the support of the President.

In addition to the elements of intrigue a final factor emerged. Junker landowners were bitterly hostile to the Government's plans to take over bankrupt Junker estates and divide them up among landless peasants. The Junkers could now claim Hindenburg's particular sympathy because they had recently presented him with his old family estate, bought with funds subscribed by industrialists. But before Hindenburg could be persuaded to dismiss Brüning an acceptable alternative had to be provided. Schleicher proposed Franz von Papen, a Catholic aristocrat from Westphalia who had been a member of the same regiment as Hindenburg's son. Although a member of the Centre Party on account of his Catholicism, his political views had far more in common with those of the Nationalists than with even the right wing of his own party. Papen's aristocratic manner appealed to Hindenburg, while Schleicher assumed he would be pliable.

Before engineering the replacement of Brüning by Papen, Schleicher had conducted extensive negotiations with the Nazis in an attempt to secure their toleration of the new government. In return he had promised Papen would lift the ban on the SA and call an election. Without committing himself on paper, Hitler succeeded in conveying the impression he would be sympathetic to such a bargain. Goebbels's diary provides an insight into the atmosphere of intrigue which preceded Brüning's fall:

72

8 May 1932. On Saturday the delegates come and give us some information. The Führer has an important interview with Schleicher in the presence of a few gentlemen of the President's immediate circle.

All goes well. The Führer has spoken decisively. Brüning's fall is expected shortly. The President of the Reich will withdraw his confidence from him. The plan is to constitute a Presidential Cabinet. The Reichstag will be dissolved. Repressive enactments are to be cancelled. We shall be free to go ahead as we like, and mean to outdo ourselves in propaganda.

11 May 1932. The Reichstag drags on. Groener's position is shaken; the Army no longer supports him. Even those with most to do with him urge his downfall.

This is the beginning; once one of these men falls, the whole Cabinet, and with it the system, will crash. Brüning is trying to salvage what he can. He speaks in the Reichstag, and cleverly beats a retreat on foreign politics. There he becomes aggressive. He believes himself within sight of the goal. He does not mention Groener at all. So he too has given him up!

The whole debate turns on the lifting of the ban on the SA. Groener strongly objects to this. It will be his undoing. I proceed as if the Reichstag were already dissolved. Our preparations are being made on quite a large scale... .

The ban on the SA has suddenly become the pivot upon which home affairs would seem to turn... .

24 May 1932. The Prussian Diet is convened. Through our confidential agents we are assured that we stand a good chance. Saturday will see the end of Brüning.

Secretary of State Meissner leaves for Neudeck. Now we must hope for the best.
The list of Ministers is more or less settled: von Papen, Chancellor; von Neurath,
Minister of Foreign Affairs, and then a list of unfamiliar names. The main point as
far as we are concerned is to ensure that the Reichstag is dissolved. Everything else
can be arranged. The Prussian question can only be solved in this way... .
30 May 1932. The bomb has exploded. Brüning has presented the resignation of the
entire Cabinet to the President, at noon. The system has begun to crumble. The
President has accepted the resignation. I at once ring up the Führer. Now he must
return to Berlin at once... .
    Meet the Führer at Nauen. The President wishes to see him in the course of the
afternoon. I get into his car and give him a good all-round summary. We are
tremendously delighted... . Pay our SA at Wilmersdorf a short visit. The Führer is
already waiting for me at home. The conference with the President went off well.
The SA prohibition is going to be cancelled. Uniforms are to be allowed again. The
Reichstag is going to be dissolved. That is of the first importance.
    Von Papen is likely to be appointed Chancellor, but that is neither here nor
there. The Poll! the Poll! It's the people we want. We are all entirely satisfied.
2 June 1932. All through the morning and afternoon we wait for news from Berlin.
It arrives at four. The Opposition demands a written undertaking from the Führer
that he will work smoothly with von Papen even after the election. Such a
statement cannot be made... .
    After the meetings we have long consultations with the Führer. He has no
intention of writing either letter or memorandum. The main things is dissolution
and re-election.
    If the election is not to miscarry, we must contest it unhampered by any such
pledges.
    On the opposite side also there are men who need to be tackled with
circumspection. Intrigues are everywhere afoot. We are playing a risky game. So
much the more must the dissolution of the Reichstag be a *sine qua non.*
    The Führer estimates his opponents very exactly. He is very logical and an
amazingly quick worker.
4 June 1932. Friday. The Führer has nevertheless dictated a memorandum on the
question of dissolution of the Reichstag. Résumé: it must come off, otherwise
further development is impossible. The Führer meets Schleicher on a neighbouring
estate. He wants me to go through the note again. It is then sent after him by
express. The motor-cyclist gets there too late. The conference is already over, so
that it is impossible to deliver it.
    When the Führer gets back, he is beaming with contentment. Everything went
off well. The Reichstag is going to be dissolved and the SA prohibition cancelled.
(But not until 16th.)

New Reichstag elections were called for 31 July and Hitler's confidence
in success was confirmed by results in the June state elections. For
Goebbels, the new Papen Cabinet, with its strong aristocratic image,
presented a new quandary—how to campaign as a party of opposition
without losing support from conservative bourgeois circles and alienating
the President and his entourage. His answer was to ignore the new
Government and concentrate on attacking the political system in general:

73

Reich Propaganda Department   *4 June 1932*
To all Party Offices for their confidential information

During this *Reichstag* election no judgement is to be passed on the actions of the von Papen Cabinet but instead on the acts of those governments and parties responsible for the crime of November 1918 [i.e. the revolution] and who from then until now have as a system to bear the responsibility for the greatest historical collapse of recent centuries. This election will be the moment for dealing with the people responsible for the thirteen years behind us, but not, as the propaganda of our opponents wants to pretend, for the few bridging weeks of the von Papen Cabinet. All our party offices must refrain from any discussion of the von Papen Cabinet during this campaign and any attempt by our opponents to discuss it must be rejected right from the start.

Papen was bent on replacing the democratic system of Weimar with an authoritarian dictatorship as soon as possible. On 20 July 1932, he took the first major step by using the President's emergency powers to depose the Prussian Government, a coalition of Social Democrats and Catholic Centre and long a target of right-wing hostility. He appointed himself as Reich Commissioner for Prussia, and Bracht, the Mayor of Essen and a National- ist, as his deputy and Prussian Minister of the Interior. A purge of the Prussian administration replaced civil servants who were loyal to the Republic with Nationalists. Since Prussia formed three-fifths of the Reich, this devastating blow to the Republic helped to prepare the way for the Nazi take-over of power in 1933.

Its extremely narrow basis of support made Papen's Government vulnerable. The Cabinet contained so many aristocrats that it was dubbed by its opponents 'the Cabinet of the Barons'. Papen hoped, as did his mentor Schleicher, the Nazis would provide a basis of mass support for the regime. They were to be disappointed. Initially the Nazis did exercise some restraint towards the Government. But after the SA ban had been lifted and the election held on 31 July, the Party refused to become lobby fodder for Papen. The election brought a big advance. The Nazis won 37 per cent of the vote as against 18 per cent in September 1930. With 230 seats as against 107 they were now by far the largest party in the Reichstag, but still did not possess an overall majority. Could this increased vote be turned into concrete political power? Hitler felt in a strong position, particularly as the parties supporting the Government—the Nationalists and some of the People's Party—had lost heavily to the Nazis and now held only 44 seats beteen them out of 608. At a meeting with Schleicher on 5 August he demanded the Chancellorship for himself and other key posts for Nazis. Papen, however, failed to react. Once again because Hitler could not form a government with a majority in the Reichstag power still lay with the

President who had the use of Article 48 and the right to appoint the
Chancellor. At an interview in the morning of 13 August, Papen rejected
Hitler's demands and Hindenburg confirmed this in the afternoon. Unlike
Brüning in the last months of his Chancellorship, Papen still had the full
confidence of the President. On 13 August, Hindenburg listened calmly to
Hitler's case for forming a government but refused to be swayed. Hitler's
hope that his large popular following would convince the President proved
incorrect. The meeting was a personal disaster for Hitler and ended with
his threatening more uncompromising opposition to the Papen Government. Otto Meissner, head of the Presidential Chancellery, took minutes
of the second meeting between Hitler and Hindenburg:

74

The President of the Reich opened the discussion by declaring to Hitler that he was
ready to let the National Socialist Party and their leader Hitler participate in the
Reich Government and would welcome their cooperation. He then put the
question to Hitler whether he was prepared to participate in the present government of von Papen. Herr Hitler declared that, for reasons which he had explained
in detail to the Reich President that morning, his taking any part in cooperation
with the existing government was out of the question. Considering the importance
of the National Socialist movement he must demand the full and complete
leadership of government and state for himself and his party.
        The Reich President in reply said firmly that he must answer this demand with a
clear, unyielding No. He could not justify before God, before his conscience or
before the fatherland the transfer of the whole authority of government to a single
party, especially to a party that was biased against people who had different views
from their own. There were a number of other reasons against it upon which he did
not wish to enlarge in detail, such as fear of increased unrest, the effect on foreign
countries, etc.
        Herr Hitler repeated that any other solution was unacceptable to him.
        To this the Reich President replied: 'So you will go into opposition?'
        Hitler: ' I have now no alternative.'
        The Reich President: 'In that case the only advice I can give you is to engage in
this opposition in a chivalrous way and to remain conscious of your responsibility
and duty towards the fatherland. I have had no doubts about your love for the
fatherland. I shall intervene sharply against any acts of terrorism or violence such as
have been committed by members of the SA sections. We are both old comrades
and we want to remain so, since the course of events may bring us together again
later on. Therefore, I shall shake hands with you now in a comradely way.'
        This discussion was followed by a short conversation in the corridor between the
Reich Chancellor and me, and Herr Hitler and his companions, in which Herr
Hitler expressed the view that future developments would lead to the solution
suggested by him and to the overthrow of the Reich President. The Government

would get into a difficult position; the opposition would become very sharp and he could assume no responsibility for the consequences.
The conversation lasted for about twenty minutes.

Goebbels commented in his diary:

75

...The Führer is back in under half an hour. So it has ended in failure. He has gained nothing. Papen is to remain Chancellor and the Führer has to content himself with the position of Vice-Chancellor!
A solution leading to no result! It is out of the question to accept such a proposal. There is no alternative but to refuse. The Führer did so immediately. Like the rest of us, he is fully aware of the consequences. It will mean a hard struggle, but we shall triumph in the end... .
In the back room the SA leaders assemble at the command of the Chief of Staff. The Führer and he give them a fairly full outline of events. Their task is the most difficult of all. Who knows if their units will be able to hold together? Nothing is harder than to tell a troop with victory already in their grasp that their assignment has come to nothing!
A grim task, but we have to go through with it. There is no other way. The idea of the Führer as Vice-Chancellor of a bourgeois Cabinet is too ludicrous to be treated seriously. Rather go on struggling for another ten years than accept that offer.
The Führer maintains an admirable calm. He stands above all vacillations, hopes, vague ideas, and conjectures; a point of rest in a world of unrest.
The first game is lost.
Well, the fight goes on! In the end the Wilhelmstrasse will give in. There is no Cromwell in the Cabinet, and in the long run, despite everything, strength and tenacity will win the day... .

(iv) The crisis months, August–December 1932

Hindenburg's refusal to appoint Hitler Chancellor was, as Goebbels recognised, a serious blow to the Party. After waging an incessant and exhausting propaganda campaign for nearly three years, the whole movement had assumed they had at last reached their goal. The shock of disappointment had very damaging effects on Party morale and particularly on its most active members in the SA. It appeared the policy of legality, pursued since 1925 had led to a cul-de-sac. Gregor Strasser advocated a coalition with the Catholic Centre Party, some of whose members believed that the Nazi Party should be brought into the government either to make

it 'responsible' or to discredit it with the masses. Hitler agreed to
negotiations but primarily to put pressure on Papen. These contacts bore
fruit in the election of Göring to the Reichstag presidency with Centre
support. Meanwhile, Papen, aware of the decline in Nazi morale, decided
to apply pressure by calling another election. He hoped they would lose
votes and would then be in a mood for cooperation. On 12 September,
therefore, he dissolved Parliament. The Nazis could only retaliate rather
futilely by holding up the dissolution until a motion of 'no confidence'
proposed by the Communists had been passed by 513 votes to 32.

  Since Papen had captured the conservative ground, Goebbels decided to
launch a radical campaign against the reactionary nature of the Papen
regime, a line to which he himself was most sympathetic. On the day of the
dissolution, therefore, he issued the following instructions:

76

Reich Propaganda Department   *12 September 1932*
To all Gauleiters and Gau *Propaganda Directors:*

As we have already stated in our express circular, dated 3 September, the struggle
against the Papen Cabinet and the reactionary circles behind it must now begin all
along the line... . We have no reason to defend ourselves against Herr von Papen
and his policy. On the contrary, in accordance with old National Socialist tactics we
are now going over to the attack... , The aim is to isolate the Papen regime from
the people and prove to the world that it is only a small feudal clique with no other
aim than to isolate the National Socialist movement and thereby make its impact
ineffectual. The struggle which is now beginning must be carried out ruthlessly and
is restricted only by the existing laws and not by any tactical considerations. The
NSDAP has no reason whatsoever to spare the Papen regime in any way... .

There were dangers that this would alienate the middle class, hitherto
the Party's main support, without capturing the working class. It might also
alienate the influential elites who held part of the key to the appointment
of Hitler as Chancellor. Hess, possibly acting for Hitler, pointed out some
of these dangers in a memorandum:

77

*It is inexpedient to gear the campaign to the slogan: 'Against the rule of the barons',
as has already happened in some cases in the Party's propaganda and press.* This
slogan is welcome ammunition to the Government, the German Nationalists, and
other opponents who can, with some appearance of justification, maintain that the
NSDAP, having already 'given up the fight against the Centre', having 'stood by

parliamentary methods',[23] is now 'showing class war tendencies'... .
The electoral damage produced by this would be greater than any advantage gained. A large number of voters on the Right will undoubtedly be impressed by the partly justified claim that the NSDAP is going over to class-war slogans. We cannot expect to make up for this by extra votes from the Left. For the majority of those who are impressed by this slogan will gravitate towards or stay with the party which expresses it in the most radical way. And that means now, as before, the Marxist parties, for class war is one of the basic points in their programme... .
The [Nazi] movement has now won over just about all the voters it can by the methods of propaganda pursued hitherto, that is to say, by means of its general ideological line and propaganda based on general aims. In addition, in this election campaign we are confronted by a government that has succeeded in creating the impression among part of the electorate, and no doubt among some of our former supporters, that it is they who are now putting into practice, or in some cases have already carried out, the things which the National Socialists aimed for but were not themselves in a position to carry out. They claim that the National Socialists have no clear and practical goals and that in so far as their aims are known, they represent dangerous experiments; the Nazis can certainly damn the measures taken by the Government but they do not explain how they propose to do better... .
Criticism of the Government, therefore, must above all not be phrased in too general terms such as 'Government of the Barons', 'reactionary legacy hunters', but must always be supported with concrete examples... .

Whether or not as a result of this memorandum, Goebbels was obliged to tone down the radical campaign slightly:

78

Reich Propaganda Department

Strictly Confidential Information No. 8, valid 12–14 October

IMPORTANT!

Through the attempt of the Papen Government to exclude Adolf Hitler from power, we have come into sharp conflict with a certain kind of anti-social and therefore capitalistic concept of economics. This opposition is justified and must be carried out with all our strength.
But it must not lead to a complete condemnation of all employers as such and thereby get into the deep waters of Marxist class war. For instance, it is wrong to equate, as Marxism does, employers with exploiters, just as it is wrong to spread details of the unjustifiable salaries of leading industrial figures... .
It is also wrong to make industry as a whole responsible for the deficiency of the Papen agrarian programme, as has happened now and then... .
In every political situation we must adhere to the old, tried guidelines of National

---

[23] This refers to the Nazis' cooperation with the Centre Party in the Reichstag against the Papen Government.

Socialism; not treating all business alike in the Marxist way, but distinguishing strictly between healthy business leadership, which is indispensable to the economy, and exploiters. To talk of the expropriation of all industrial concerns is, of course, a direct contravention of National Socialist principles.

Moreover, the fight against the Papen Cabinet must not develop into a fight against the aristocracy as such. We must always be aware of the fact that the best part of the German aristocracy fights in our own ranks and therefore does not deserve to be demoted from the German front just because of a few black sheep.

Nevertheless, during the last few weeks of the campaign, the radical line culminated in cooperation with the Communists in support of the Berlin transport workers' strike, which had broken out in protest against the wages policy of the Government.

The extent to which the radical campaign against Papen had alienated the upper and lower middle classes, who had hitherto supported or at least been sympathetic to the Nazis, is apparent in the following document. In her diary Frau Luise Solmitz gives an insight into the attitude of many of the upper middle class during the autumn of 1932:

79

13.viii.32....Goebbels in the National Socialist *Angriff!*[24] We know this language only too well from Socialist and Communist papers; we don't want to hear it from Goebbels! This is just what deters many; these are the objections which bourgeois-orientated Hitler supporters have to fight again and again. Perhaps this language is necessary to bring in the masses who tend to the Left, but it alienates the valuable bourgeois element; to embrace them all becomes impossible. Hitler, remain master in your own house!

29.ix.32. The trade unions are no longer Marxist enough for the Nazis; they demand that the trade unions should call a strike against the underbidding of wage agreements—and thus against the re-employment of the unemployed. And they want to expel every employer from their ranks who lowers wages in order to enlarge the number of employees. Can an employer remain a Nazi at all?!....

3.xi.32. E.M. said, shaking his head, 'One can't possibly vote for Hitler.' He met a Herr von S., whom he knows from the war: 'I voted for Hitler twice; it's no longer the thing to do.' Our old carrier: 'Hitler? He is far to the Left! I have always voted for Hugenberg.' Old Professor H. persists in voting for his stale old *Volkspartei*,[25] his daughter is fanatically pro-Hitler....

If only one could summon up some enthusiasm for the German Nationalist Party and Hugenberg! With the National Socialist Party we had a love match. The German Nationalist marriage which we are about to enter is a marriage of convenience and without passion [*Schwung*].

---

[24] *Der Angriff*, the daily paper of Goebbels's *Gau*, Berlin.
[25] The *Deutsche Volkspartei* (German People's Party), the right-wing liberal party.

31.xii.32. This year has robbed us of a great hope—this *year*, not death. Adolf Hitler. Our reviver and great leader towards national unity...and the man who in the end turns out to be the leader of a party sliding more and more into a dubious future. I still cannot come to terms with this bitter disappointment... .

Hampered by the decline in morale and by shortage of money now that the Party had alienated the upper classes with its radical line, the Party's propaganda machine found the going hard. In October, Goebbels noted in his diary that 'the organisation has naturally become a bit on edge through these everlasting elections. It is as jaded as a battalion which has been too long in the front trenches, and just as nervy'. The election held on 6 November was indeed a setback for the Nazis. Their vote fell from 37 per cent to 33 per cent and their seats from 230 to 196. Even more important than the number of votes lost was that for the first time they had actually lost votes. The myth of invincibility, projected so successfully hitherto, which had played a substantial part in their appeal had been broken. Nothing could disguise the fact that they were in trouble.

Yet although his gamble had paid off, Papen had not really solved his problems. While the Nationalists had gained slightly, the Government still rested on an extremely narrow basis. Moreover, contrary to Papen's hopes, Hitler was still not prepared to join the Government in a subordinate capacity nor was he prepared to become Chancellor except with a Cabinet dominated by his party and with full freedom to use the powers contained in Article 48. This, however, was unacceptable to President Hindenburg.

Frustrated in his attempt to acquire a mass base, Papen contemplated a coup, replacing the Weimar Constitution by an authoritarian presidential dictatorship. This plan, however, would require the elimination of both the Nazis and the Communists, both bound to resist this development by force. President Hindenburg, wishing to retain Papen for whom he had developed considerable affection, was prepared to acquiesce. General von Schleicher, however, now Minister of Defence, did not believe the Army capable of dealing with the SA and the Communists simultaneously, particularly as the junior officer corps was permeated with Nazi ideas. Furthermore, he was not a simple reactionary like Papen. He was aware that in an advanced industrial society it is impossible to rule without some degree of mass support, however acquired. This was essential if Germany's armed strength was to be fully restored. Schleicher was influenced by a group of young right-wing intellectuals associated with the journal, *Die Tat*, who attacked both liberal capitalism and Marxist socialism. They advocated an organic authoritarian state based on *Stände* (estates) which, by combining social and nationalist principles, would offer Germany a 'third way' between the capitalist West and the Communist East. Schleicher believed mass support could be won for a rightist regime sympathetic to rearmament if such a regime pursued social and economic policies more attractive to the masses than those of the reactionary Papen Government, such as a more vigorous attempt to solve the unemployment problem, if necessary by public expenditure. He also believed he could acquire support by splitting the mass movement of the Right, winning over elements within the Nazi Party, most notably Gregor Strasser, primarily interested in a practical contribution to solving the economic and political crises, especially unemployment. They feared the opportunity to make it might be jeopardised by Hitler's stubborn insistence on all or nothing. He also thought he could split the Left, winning over the Trade Unions and the Reichsbanner for whom the solution of the unemployment problem would be more important than doctrinaire principles. That his government would be more socially concerned than that of either Papen or Hitler and would avoid the danger of either Papen or Hitler establishing a dictatorship would be sufficient to commend it to these groups.

Of the alternatives offered by Papen and Schleicher, Hindenburg preferred the former and, after Papen had formally resigned following the election, the President asked him to form another government. Schleicher now intervened and declared the Army could not support the *coup* envisaged by Papen. Regretfully, the President was forced to accept Papen's resignation and to appoint Schleicher to see if his solution would work. Schleicher at once tried to put his plan into operation. In a broadcast on 15 December he announced that his government's programme would concentrate above all on 'creating work' and he appointed a special Reich Commissioner for Employment to carry it out. He also announced that he was not a dogmatic supporter of either capitalism or Socialism. He then repealed the deflationary measures such as wage and benefit cuts introduced by Papen on 4 September.

Schleicher's attempts to win support from a section of the Left and to split the Nazis were, however, both abortive. The trade unions were forced to end the negotiations under pressure from Social Democrats suspicious of Schleicher. His previous role as an intriguer made this understandable, but nonetheless short-sighted. On 3 December, Schleicher offered Strasser the Vice-Chancellorship which he was anxious to accept, enjoying the sympathy of some of the Nazi deputies including their leader Frick. Göring and Goebbels, however, were strongly opposed and Hitler, though agreeing to continue negotiations with Schleicher, took them out of Strasser's hands. After a stormy interview on 7 December, Strasser wrote Hitler a letter of resignation and, on the morning of the 8th, called a meeting of the Party's regional inspectors—the senior Gauleiters—in the Reichstag building. To this group Strasser announced his resignation and, according to a post-war account by Hinrich Lohse, Gauleiter of Schleswig-Holstein, gave the following explanation of his action:

80

For some time I have been aware of a development which affects not so much the programme or the final goal but rather the way of achieving this goal, and which I can no longer go along with. At least since August, since the time of his first meeting with Papen, Schleicher and Hindenburg, the Führer has not been following a clear line of policy in his endeavour to achieve power. He is only clear about one thing—he wishes to become Reich Chancellor. He should, however, have become aware of the fact that he is being consistently refused this post by everybody and that in the foreseeable future there is no prospect of his attaining this goal. As a result of this situation, the movement is being put under considerable stress which is undermining its unity and may expose it to splits and disintegration. In view of the appalling distress of our supporters, we cannot let our SA men and our ordinary Party comrades wait for ever or they will become impatient and in the end leave the movement in a mood of disappointment. There is no doubt that our enemies have been waiting for this moment, not just recently but for a long time. The Party must, therefore, come to a decision one way or the other.

There are two paths which can lead to a solution of this serious crisis and if the collapse of the movement is to be avoided one of them must be followed: the legal or the illegal path. I would be prepared to follow either path. But I refuse to wait until the Führer is made Reich Chancellor, for by then the collapse will have occurred. If the legal path was to be followed, the Führer should have accepted Hindenburg's offer in August to make him Vice-Chancellor. From this basis the attempt should have been made to secure new positions. The Vice-Chancellor should have made it clear to the coalition Cabinet in which the National Socialists were participating that without the carrying out of National Socialist ideas there could be no recovery for Germany. The same thing should have happened in a Prussian coalition government and in other state governments.

Had Vice-Chancellor Hitler not succeeded in this task, he would have been weighed and found wanting; his departure from the political stage and the collapse of the government would have been deserved. History does not concern itself with methods but only with success.

The second method is the illegal path. I would have been prepared to follow this path as well. The National Socialist stormtroops of the SA and SS are still intact; they are prepared for the final march and will be at the ready the moment the order comes. This conquest of power by force would also have had a chance of success even if it had been bloody and confronted by serious resistance from the State. For who could withstand this well-organised army which has a firm ideological commitment, which has already passed the half-million mark, and the whole of which is under the leadership of front-line officers and soldiers? But this path has also been rejected and for my part I no longer see any possibility of future activity.

So far as the personal aspect of the problem is concerned, I am aware of an increasingly prevalent game of intrigue within the entourage of the Führer and of personal insults and slights which I am simply no longer able to put up with. I also naturally want to see and speak with the Füher occasionally—both for personal and for official reasons. If I go to the Kaiserhof or to the Brown House in Munich, I always find the same people there. During such visits I usually learn little, at any rate nothing detailed about the current issues of the day, about political meetings or the current state of discussions being carried on with individuals or with groups and parties.

I have no desire to take second place to Göring, Goebbels, Röhm, and others. If they are invited, I expect also to be honoured with an invitation. This the Führer has never done. I regard this as a slight, as a personal humiliation which I have not deserved and which I am no longer prepared to tolerate. Apart from this, I am at the end of my strength and nerves. I have resigned from the Party and am now going to the mountains to recuperate. I ask you all not to draw any conclusions for yourselves from my action but rather to continue to carry out your duties.

Strasser's speech caused consternation among his audience. Gauleiter Rust, the regional inspector of Lower Saxony, reported to Hitler what had happened. Hitler immediately called a meeting in the Kaiserhof at twelve o'clock for those who had been present at the Strasser meeting.

Dr Ley gave an account of what Strasser had said to the Regional Inspectors and Hitler made the following comments:

81

'I thought Gregor Strasser was much cleverer than that; I am shocked by the position he adopts and even more by the fact that, after twelve years' acquaintanceship and comradeship in the Party, he did not consider it necessary to let me know about these things and discuss them with me. I find it very difficult to accept this account as an adequate explanation for his momentous decision.

'I will answer you point by point:

'1. The path to the conquest of power depends upon imponderables which Strasser, according to his own account, either completely ignores or does not wish to see, or is simply not aware of. With a man of his calibre one would have thought that was impossible. He spoke to you about the legal path to the conquest of power and declared that it was my duty in August to accept the office of Vice-Chancellor. Herr Strasser knows quite well that Herr von Papen and Herr von Schleicher are not National Socialists and therefore are not willing to follow National Socialist policies. Judging by the measures introduced by and the results of the policy of Reich Chancellor von Papen, as Vice-Chancellor I would have had serious differences with him within the first week. If I did not want to abdicate all influence, betray my movement and make my position in the eyes of the public impossible, I would have had to protest against his policies. I would have had to make demands concerning a whole range of burning issues in economics and the administration, in social, labour and financial policies, demands which would have been turned down flat. Herr von Papen would have declared to me with a smile, "Forgive me, Herr Hitler, but I am Chancellor and head of the Cabinet. If my political course and the measures which result from it do not suit you, I am not forcing you to stay. You can resign your office. But in any case I reject your demands and proposals."

Gentlemen, can you imagine the effect of such a conclusion to my Vice-Chancellorship on the Party and on public opinion? Herr von Papen and his backers, on the other hand, would have achieved their goal—the proof of the incapacity of Hitler and his subordinates would have apparently been provided. The Party comrades and the electorate would have turned their backs on me in fury, the movement would have collapsed, and in the end over its body not Herr von Papen but, as the last elections show, Bolshevism would have triumphed. I reject this path and intend to wait until I am offered the post of Chancellor. That day will come—it is probably nearer than we think.

'Whether or not the movement disintegrates does not depend on the Party comrades and is not encouraged by them. It lies entirely in our own hands; it depends on our unity and on our unshakeable faith in victory; it depends on our leadership.

'2. The illegal path to the conquest of power is even more dangerous and more fatal. It cannot be said that I do not have the courage to carry out a *coup* by force and, if necessary, by a bloody revolution. I tried it once in Munich in 1923. Herr Strasser knows that; he was there.

'But what was the result and what would the result be now? Our formations are without weapons and, if there are some which have been kept hidden here and there against my wishes and without my knowledge, they would have no effect against the united action of the police and the Reichswehr which are armed with the most modern weapons. You surely do not believe that they would stand by. The police will shoot at the command of Herr von Papen and the Reichswehr at the command of its Supreme Commander, Reich President Hindenburg, for they have taken their oath to him and not to me.

'In the past the police have invariably obeyed the existing political power in the State completely irrespective of the political tendency within the State.

'General [*sic*] von Reichenau[26] said to me recently: "Herr Hitler, you have wonderful troops whose discipline is voluntary. The fact that it is not based on the law and that the leaders do not possess any State authority makes it even more worthy of recognition. The Reichswehr is different. It is under oath and is subordinate to the Field-Marshal as Reich President. If your columns march against the law, the Reichswehr would be compelled to shoot and would carry out the order even though its heart would bleed to do so. If you were Reich President and the Reichwehr was under oath to you, we would obey your orders in just the same way and shoot at the enemies of your State if you gave the order. We are unpolitical, obey the law, obey orders and keep the oath we have given. I urge you to keep within the law. One day power will inevitably fall into your lap."

'Gentlemen, I am not irresponsible enough to drive German youth and the generation of front-line soldiers who are the best representatives of the nation's manhood into the machine guns of the police and the Reichswehr. Gregor Strasser will not see that happening!

'3. I distribute political tasks to my closest colleagues according to specific

[26] Colonel von Reichenau was Chief of Staff of the Wehrkreis I (East Prussia). An ambitious man, he was already pro-Nazi, and with the appointment of his Commanding Officer, General von Blomberg, as Minister of Defence in Hitler's Cabinet he came to play an influential role in politics, notably in the so-called Röhm 'putsch' of June 1934.

principles. The nearer we come to the decision, the more attempts are made by our opponents to create divisions within our own camp and to break us. Whether or not they have already succeeded with Gregor Strasser is a subject I will not go into. 'If I am here in the Reich capital I carry out the most important discussions with ministers, generals, and party and pressure group [*Verband*] leaders myself. If I am not here, we cannot have a situation in which one moment Strasser is negotiating with the Centre in a certain direction, while tomorrow Goebbels is negotiating with Hindenburg in another direction, and the day after Göring is negotiating with the Reichswehr in a completely opposite direction. During my absence from Berlin, my authorised representative is Reichstag President Göring, who knows my intentions, who knows where I am, who can therefore inform me at once about any important discussions and to whom I can if necessary give an immediate counter-order.... .

'Furthermore, I do not like the reorganisation of the Party leadership and their spheres of operation put forward by Strasser, although I approved it in order to avoid a dispute.[27] It is completely wrong that you as Regional Inspectors have given up your office as Gauleiters and are left hanging completely in the air. You are the oldest and most experienced Gauleiters. You must remain rooted in the soil in which you have grown and developed through the fulfilment of your assignment. I shall cancel the order in order to avoid upheaval and damage to the movement.... .

'4. ...I do not issue invitations to any particular Party comrades. Anyone who visits me is welcome. I receive, as soon as I am available, anyone who wishes to and has to speak to me. Naturally I feel closer to some than to others. But is this not normal in human life?

'For some time I have noticed that Gregor Strasser has been avoiding me and when we see each other he is reserved, serious and uncommunicative. Is that my fault? Am I to blame for the fact that Göring and Goebbels visit me uninvited more often that Strasser? Did I not receive you when you wanted to speak to me? Did I not ask you to dine with me if you were with me and I had time for you? Is that sufficient reason for one of my closest and oldest colleagues to turn his back on the movement?'

Hitler became quieter and more personal, more amiable and appealing. At the end of the two-hour-long interview he had found that comradely tone which those present knew and found completely convincing. Now he was their friend, their comrade, their leader, who had shown them the way out of the hopeless situation which Strasser had portrayed, who had won them over both emotionally and intellectually....He, Hitler, triumphed and proved to his indispensable comrades, who in the most serious crisis of the movement first wavered and then recovered their nerve, that he was the master and Strasser the journeyman... . Those present once more sealed their old bond with him with a handshake... .

Strasser's unwillingness to lead a revolt against Hitler together with the total commitment of the Party leadership to Hitler as Führer ensured that the crisis was contained. The loss of confidence throughout the Party continued, however, and on 15 December Goebbels noted in his diary that

---

[27] Strasser had recently appointed some of the more senior Gauleiters to new posts as 'Regional Inspectors' who were intended to supervise the *Gaue* in their regions.

it was 'very difficult to hold the stormtroopers and the departmental officials on a straight course. It is high time we attained power and at the moment there is no sign of it.'

(v) The appointment of Hitler as Chancellor, 30 January 1933

At the lowest point in the Party's fortunes the tide turned. Papen had not overcome his resentment at being elbowed aside by Schleicher. He was determined to bring down Schleicher and return to office himself, even if not as Chancellor. To achieve this he would have to prove to the President that he could secure the mass support his previous government had lacked and which Schleicher had promised but failed to get. Without support from the Left or from the Catholic Centre Party, the only possibility was the Nazis. Their decline implied both the danger that the crisis would pass without having been used to change the regime and the likelihood of the Nazis' now proving more cooperative and amenable. During December, therefore, Papen opened negotiations with Hitler through various contacts, including Wilhelm Keppler, Hitler's economic adviser and a liaison with industry, Schacht, the former President of the Reichsbank, and Kurt von Schroeder, a Cologne banker and member of the Party.

As a result of these contacts, Hitler agreed to meet Papen on 4 January at Schroeder's house in Cologne. After the war Schroeder gave an account to the Nuremberg Tribunal of the background to the meeting and of what transpired at it:

82

On 4 January 1933 Hitler, von Papen, Hess, Himmler and Keppler arrived at my house in Cologne. Hitler, von Papen and I went into my study where a two-hour discussion took place. Hess, Himmler and Keppler did not take part but were in the adjoining room…The negotiations took place exclusively between Hitler and Papen. …Papen went on to say that he thought it best to form a government in which the conservative and nationalist elements that had supported him were represented together with the Nazis. He suggested that this new government should, if possible, be led by Hitler and himself together Then Hitler made a long speech in which he said that, if he were to be elected Chancellor, Papen's followers could participate in his (Hitler's) Government as Ministers if they were willing to support his policy which was planning many alterations in the existing state of affairs. He outlined these alterations, including the removal of all Social Democrats, Communists and Jews from leading positions in Germany and the restoration of order in public life. Von Papen and Hitler reached agreement in principle whereby many of the disagreements between them could be removed and cooperation might be possible. It was agreed that further details could be worked out later either in Berlin or some other suitable place. This happened, as I learned later, at a meeting with Ribbentrop.

This meeting between Hitler and Papen on 4 January 1933 in my house in Cologne was arranged by me after Papen had asked me for it on about 10 December 1932. Before I took this step I talked to a number of businessmen and informed myself generally on how the business world viewed a collaboration between the two men. The general desire of businessmen was to see a strong man come to power in Germany who would form a government that would stay in power for a long time...

Business was in fact divided in its attitude to the political possibilities. Although Schleicher's policies evoked sympathy from sections of export- and consumer-oriented industries, they met with bitter opposition from heavy industry and, in general, industry was suspicious of his wooing of the trade unions. In their concern to replace Schleicher Hitler now appeared a more attractive ally, although Papen remained their first choice.

To demonstrate that his party was not yet finished Hitler decided to stake his prestige on the outcome of the state elections in Lippe-Detmold on 15 January. Although the electorate was only 90,000, Hitler needed an election victory to dispel the defeatist mood which still affected the Party and to convince the President and his advisers it was not a spent force. He, therefore, concentrated all his propaganda resources there during the week before polling and his efforts brought an increase in the vote for the NSDAP (39,000 votes compared with 33,000 in November). This result deprived his opponents of an excuse to block his ambition.

Papen now concentrated on trying to win over the President to a Hitler Government of which he himself would be Vice-Chancellor. In order to achieve this, the President's camarilla and, in particular, his son Oskar had to be persuaded to work on Hindenburg. One important factor influencing Hindenburg against Schleicher was the pressure from agriculture organised in the Nazi-influenced *Reichslandbund*. Agriculture had long been demanding a moratorium on debt repayments and protective tariffs. On 11 January 1933, the *Reichslandbund* publicly accused Schleicher's Government of discriminating against agriculture and in favour of export industries: 'the plundering of agriculture in favour of the all-powerful money-bags interests of the internationally-oriented export industry and its satellites continues'. The Junker landowners of East Elbia also feared Schleicher's plans to settle agricultural workers on bankrupt estates in the East. As a Junker himself, Hindenburg was particularly sensitive to this kind of pressure. Moreover, this sensitivity must have become particularly acute when the Centre Party and SPD Reichstag deputies succeeded in setting up an enquiry by the Public Accounts Office into the misuse of government money provided for the Eastern Aid Programme to bail out bankrupt Junker estates. There were even rumours that Oskar von Hindenburg was involved in the corruption. It has been suggested that Hitler offered to prevent such an investigation in the event of his becoming Chancellor. Certainly these events formed the background to the fall of Schleicher and Hitler's appointment as Chancellor. Otto Meissner, the State Secretary in the Reich President's office gave the Nuremberg Tribunal an account of the developments leading to Hitler's appointment:

83

...Papen was dismissed because he wanted to fight the National Socialists and did not find in the Reichswehr the necessary support for such a policy, and...Schleicher came to power because he believed he could form a government which would have the support of the National Socialists. When it became clear that Hitler was not willing to enter Schleicher's Cabinet and that Schleicher on his part was unable to split the National Socialist Party, as he had hoped to do with the help of Gregor Strasser, the policy for which Schleicher had been appointed Chancellor was shipwrecked. Schleicher was aware that Hitler was particularly embittered against him because of his attempt to break up the Party, and would never agree to cooperate with him. So he now changed his mind and decided to fight against the Nazis—which meant that he now wanted to pursue the policy which he had sharply opposed when Papen had suggested it a few weeks before. Schleicher came to Hindeburg therefore with a demand for emergency powers as a prerequisite of action against the Nazis. Furthermore, he believed it to be necessary to dissolve, and even temporarily eliminate, the Reichstag, and this was to be done by Presidential decrees on the basis of Article 48—the transformation of his government into a military dictatorship, and government to be carried on generally on the basis of Article 48.

Schleicher first made these suggestions to Hindenburg in the middle of January 1933, but Hindenburg at once evinced grave doubts as to its constitutionality. In the meantime Papen had returned to Berlin, and by an arrangement with Hindenburg's son had had several interviews with the President. When Schleicher renewed his demand for emergency powers, Hindenburg declared that he was unable to give him such a blank cheque and must reserve to himself decisions on every individual case. Schleicher for his part said that under these circumstances he was unable to stay in office and tendered his resignation on 28 January.

In the middle of January, when Schleicher was first asking for emergency powers, Hindenburg was not aware of the contact between Papen and Hitler—particularly, of the meeting which had taken place in the house of the Cologne banker, Kurt von Schroeder. In the latter part of January, Papen played an increasingly important role in the house of the Reich President, but despite Papen's persuasions, Hindenburg was extremely hesitant, until the end of January, to make Hitler Chancellor. He wanted to have Papen again as Chancellor. Papen finally won him over to Hitler with the argument that the representatives of the other right-wing parties which would belong to the Government would restrict Hitler's freedom of action. In addition Papen expressed his misgivings that, if the present opportunity were again missed, a revolt of the National Socialists and civil war were likely. Many of Hindenburg's personal friends, such as Oldenburg-Januschau,[28] worked in the same direction as Papen, also General von Blomberg.[29] The President's son and adjutant, Oskar von Hindenburg, was opposed to the Nazis up to the last moment. The turning-point at which his views changed came at the end of January. At Papen's suggestion, a meeting had been arranged between Hitler and Oskar von Hindenburg in the house of Ribbentrop. Oskar von Hindenburg asked me to accompany him; we took a taxi, in order to keep the appointment secret, and drove out to Ribbentrop's home. On our arrival we found a large company assembled; among those present were Göring and Frick.

Oskar von Hindenburg was told that Hitler wanted to talk to him *tête à tête*; as Hindeburg had asked me to accompany him, I was somewhat surprised at his accepting this suggestion and vanishing into another room for a talk which lasted quite a while—about an hour. What Hitler and Oskar von Hindenburg discussed during this talk I do not know.

In the taxi on the way back Oskar von Hindenburg was very silent; the only remark he made was that there was no help for it, the Nazis had to be taken into the Government. My impression was that Hitler had succeeded in getting him under his spell...

Joachim von Ribbentrop, who had married into a large German champagne business, had become a member of the Party in 1931. It was in his villa in Dahlem, a fashionable Berlin suburb, that many of the crucial negotiations were held. His wife dictated the following notes of these meetings at the time:

84

Wednesday, 18th January: In Dahlem at noon: Hitler, Röhm, Himmler, Papen. Hitler insists on being Chancellor. Papen again considers this impossible. His influence with Hindenburg was not strong enough to effect this. Hitler makes no further arrangements for talks. Joachim tentatively suggests a meeting between Hitler and Hindenburg's son.

Thursday, 19th January: Long talk between Joachim and Papen.

Friday, 20th January: In the evening long talk at Papen's house. He says that young Hindenburg and Meissner will come to Dahlem on Sunday.

Saturday, 21st January: Joachim reports to Hitler, who explains why he will not invite Schleicher. Hitler wants to bring Göring and Epp.

Sunday, 22nd January: Meeting at Dahlem at 10 p.m. Papen arrives alone at nine o'clock. Present: Hitler, Frick, Göring, Körner, Meissner, young Hindenburg,

---

[28] A leading and ultra-reactionary Prussian Junker.

[29] The district commander in East Prussia, who had come into contact with Hitler during 1932 through the Protestant Chaplain Müller, who was an ardent Nazi. As a result, Blomberg had become very sympathetic to Nazism.

Papen and Joachim. Hitler talks alone to young Hindenburg for two hours, followed by Hitler-Papen talk. Papen will now press for Hitler as Chancellor, but tells Hitler that he will withdraw from these negotiations forthwith if Hitler has no confidence in him.

Monday, 23rd January: In the morning Papen saw Hindenburg, who refused everything. Joachim goes to Hitler to explain this. Long talk about the possibility of a Schacht Cabinet. Hitler rejects everything.

Tuesday, 24th January: Tea in Dahlem: Frick, Göring, Papen, Joachim. Resolved to form national front which is to support Papen *vis-à-vis* old Hindenburg.

Wednesday, 25th January: Again tea in Dahlem: Joachim sees young Hindenburg alone. Hitler's Chancellorship under the auspices of a national front does not appear quite hopeless. Young Hindenburg promises to talk to Joachim again before his father makes final decision.

Thursday, 26th January: Long talk with Frick and Göring in the Reichstag. Negotiations with German Nationals. In the evening at Prince [*sic*] Oskar's house in Potsdam, letter to Hugenburg.

Friday, 27th January: Hitler back in Berlin. Long talk with him at Göring's flat. Hitler wants to leave Berlin forthwith. Joachim proposes link-up with Hugenberg for a national front. New meeting with old Hindenburg arranged. Hitler declares that he has said all there is to say to the Field Marshal, and does not know what to add. Joachim persuades Hitler that this last attempt should be made, and that the situation is by no means hopeless. Joachim suggests that the national front should be formed as soon as possible and that Hitler should meet Papen in Dahlem at 10 p.m. Hitler agrees to negotiate with Papen and Hugenberg in the evening. Followed long talk with Göring to discuss further tactics. Late in the afternoon Göring telephones to say that Joachim should go to the Reichstag President's house immediately. There talk with Hugenberg, Hitler and Göring (two names illegible), broken off because of impossible demands by German Nationals. Hitler very indignant, wants to leave for Munich immediately. Göring persuades him to stay or at least to go only as far as Weimar. Gradually Göring and Joachim calm Hitler down, but all his suspicions are revived. Situation very critical. Hitler declares he cannot meet Papen in Dahlem that evening, because he is not in a position to talk freely.'

The remainder of the notes were dictated by Ribbentrop personally:

'I have never seen Hitler in such a state; I proposed to him and Göring that I should see Papen alone that evening and explain the whole situation to him. In the evening I saw Papen and convinced him eventually that the only thing that made sense was Hitler's Chancellorship, and that he must do what he can to bring this about. Papen declared that the matter of Hugenberg was of secondary importance, and that he was now absolutely in favour of Hitler becoming Chancellor; this was the decisive change in Papen's attitude. Papen has become conscious of his responsibility—three possibilities: a Presidential Cabinet, followed by (illegible), return of Marxism under Schleicher, or Hindenburg's resignation. As opposed to these the one and only clear solution: Hitler's Chancellorship. Papen is now absolutely certain that he must achieve Hitler's Chancellorship at all costs, and that he must abandon his belief that it is his duty to remain at Hindenburg's disposal.

This recognition by Papen is, I believe, the turning point. Papen has an appointment with Hindenburg for Saturday at 10 a.m.

Saturday, 28th January: About 11 a.m. I went to see Papen who received me with the question: 'Where is Hitler?' I told him that he had probably left, but could perhaps be contacted in Weimar. Papen said that he had to be got back without delay, because a turning point had been reached; after a long talk with Hindenburg he, Papen, considered Hitler's Chancellorship possible. I went to see Göring immediately and heard that Hitler was still at the Kaiserhof. Göring telephoned him, Hitler will remain in Berlin. Then a new difficulty arose: the question of Prussia. Long argument with Göring. I declared that I would withdraw from the negotiations immediately if suspicions of Papen were revived. Göring gave in and expressed his complete agreement with me; he promised to do what he could to bring the matter to a satisfactory conclusion together with Hitler. Göring promised to persuade Hitler to accept the Prussian settlement proposed by Papen. Göring and I then went to see Hitler. Long talk with Hitler alone, explaining that a solution depended entirely on trust and that his Chancellorship did not now appear to be impossible. I asked Hitler to see Papen that very afternoon. But Hitler first wanted to think over the question of Prussia, and see Papen on Sunday morning. This I reported to Papen, who was again very worried. He said: "I know the Prussians." Then we arranged a Hitler-Papen meeting for 11 a.m. on Sunday morning.

Sunday, 29th January: At 11 a.m. long Hitler-Papen talk. Hitler declared that on the whole everything was clear. But there would have to be general elections and an Enabling Law. Papen saw Hindenburg immediately. I lunched with Hitler at the Kaiserhof. We discussed the elections. As Hindenburg does not want these, Hitler asked me to tell the President that these would be the last elections. In the afternoon Göring and I went to Papen. Papen declared that all obstacles are removed and that Hindenburg expects Hitler to-morrow at 11 a.m.

Monday, 30th January: Hitler appointed Chancellor.'

To sum up, the following factors were involved in the winning over of the President: firstly, Schleicher's economic policies, geared to winning mass support, were alienating powerful interests. Industry, in particular heavy industry, objected to his labour policies as inflationary and too favourable to the workers; the Junkers resented his policy of encouraging export industry—as they saw it at their expense—and bitterly opposed his attempt to revive Brüning's plan of breaking up bankrupt Junker estates and settling them with peasants. These interests pressed their views vigorously with the President. Secondly, Hindenburg had never really forgiven Schleicher for forcing Papen's resignation. He wanted 'Fränzchen' back in the Government. Finally, Schleicher had patently failed in his objective of acquiring a mass base for his government. He had no alternative to offer other than another election, action against the Nazis and a dictatorship through Article 48. This had been not far from the policy he had prevented Papen from carrying out and the President did not see why he should allow Schleicher to do what Papen had been prevented from doing. Hindenburg's refusal to grant a dissolution of the Reichstag forced Schleicher to resign on 28 January.

Yet, despite his growing disenchantment with Schleicher, Hindenburg was still not happy about the idea of Hitler as Chancellor. As late as 26 January, he told the Army generals that they surely did not believe he would make this 'Austrian corporal' Reich Chancellor. Hindenburg was finally persuaded by the structure of the proposed government and by the fact that it promised to secure a parliamentary majority and so relieve him of the responsibility of governing. In the first place, Papen had persuaded Hitler that the Nazis should have only two ministries in the Cabinet apart from the Chancellorship—the Reich Ministry of the Interior (Frick) and a Minister without Portfolio (Göring) who was also Prussian Minister of the Interior; secondly, Papen became Reich Commissioner in Prussia, i.e. Göring's superior, and had the right of being present at Hitler's audiences with the President; thirdly, the Ministry of Defence was given to a general acceptable to Hindenburg (Blomberg); and finally, Papen persuaded both the Nationalists and the right-wing ex-servicemen's organisation, the Stahlhelm, of which Hindenburg was the honorary head, to cooperate in forming the Government. The Nationalist leader, Hugenberg, was won over by the offer of the Ministries of Economics and Agriculture, refused him by Schleicher and which he though would make him virtually economic dictator; the Stahlhelm leader, Seldte, was made Minister of Labour. In short, Hindenburg believed that, as Papen put it, Hitler would be 'framed' within the Cabinet by Conservatives who would be able to control the policies which Hitler would 'sell' to the country through his Party and propaganda machine. To a doubter, Papen remarked: 'Don't worry, we've hired him.'

Hitler, however, was content with this solution. He himself, as Chancellor, had the supreme position in the Government; Göring, as Prussian Minister of the Interior, controlled the police in three-fifths of the Reich; and General von Blomberg, unbeknown to Hindenburg, was a pro-Nazi. Finally, as one of his conditions for taking office, he had insisted that the new Cabinet and the President should agree to an immediate dissolution. These were, he believed, adequate weapons for the consolidation of power. Time was to prove him right.

The composition of Hitler's first Reich Cabinet was as follows:

Reich Chancellor	Adolf Hitler (NSDAP)
Vice-Chancellor and Reich Commissioner for Prussia	Franz von Papen (DNVP)
*†Reich Foreign Minister	Constantin von Neurath

Reich Minister of the Interior	Dr Wilhelm Frick (NSDAP)
Reich Minister of Defence	General Werner von Blomberg
*†Reich Finance Minister	Count Schwerin von Krosigk
Reich Minister of Economics Food and Agriculture	Dr Alfred Hugenberg (DNVP)
Reich Minister of Labour	Franz Seldte
*†Reich Minister of Posts and Transport	Paul von Eltz-Rübenach
Reich Minister without Portfolio, Reich Air Commissioner, and acting Prussian Minister of the Interior	Hermann Göring (NSDAP)
*†Reich Commissioner of Employment	Dr Günther Gereke
*†Reich Minister of Justice	Dr Franz Gürtner (DNVP)

*Member of the previous administration.
†Conservative civil servant.

NOTE. Goebbels became a Cabinet Minister as Minister of Propaganda on 13 March 1933. Hess was named Deputy Führer on 21 April, and as such was given the power of independent decision on all Party questions; but neither he nor Röhm was nominated to the Cabinet, as Reich Minister, until 1 December. Hugenberg resigned on 27 June 1933 and was replaced by Walter Darré as Minister of Agriculture and Kurt Schmitt as Minister of Economics.

CHAPTER 5

The 'Seizure of Power' 1933–1934

Though now Chancellor, Hitler had not yet achieved absolute power. Only three Cabinet members were Nazis, his Party had not a majority in the Reichstag, and he could be dismissed at any time by the Reich President. On the other hand, he had a number of important advantages. Göring as Prussian Minister of the Interior controlled the internal administration, including the police, in three-fifths of the Reich; Frick as Reich Minister of the Interior had certain limited powers of supervision over the remainder. With General Von Blomberg as Minister of Defence he had little to fear from the Amy. But, above all, there was no obvious alternative candidate to represent the forces of the Right. The years 1930–32 had seen several attempts by it to establish a government at once effective, amenable to the right-wing pressure groups—the Army, the Junkers, and Industry—and able to command a degree of mass support. None had managed to fulfil all these requirements, certainly not the last. That Hitler could provide the Right with mass support had led to his appointment; and the other right-wing politicians' awareness of their lack of a popular following gave them a sense of inferiority in regard to the Nazis which helped to paralyse their will. The alternative to Hitler would be a right-wing dictatorship against both the NSDAP and the Left—an unattractive prospect. Moreover, Hitler offered the German establishment not only a way out of the political impasse but also the possibility of reviving the economy without having to make concessions to labour. Profits rather than wages would reap the main benefits of the recovery.

Hitler had no blueprint or timetable for the take-over of power. It took the form of a complex and dynamic process involving both initiatives from above as well as pressures from below, some of which were orchestrated but many of which were spontaneous and uncoordinated. There was a struggle for power among the various elements within the regime itself as well as against the previous incumbents. Hitler, however, had certain broad objectives. During his first weeks in office he sought to build up his mass support in the country in order to legitimise his own position with direct democratic sanction independent of the indirect form provided by the Constitution. This would increase his leverage not only against the right-wing politicians and pressure groups, who could command no such popular support, but against the President himself. Since Hitler's electoral support had consistently been shown to be less than 40 per cent, he now used the propaganda machine provided by his Party, assisted by the resources of the State, to project the idea that the new Government represented a 'national uprising' in which the nation was united behind a Government determined to end the crisis and to lead Germany towards a new and glorious future. In this way, he could create the myth of overwhelming support for the new regime even in the face of hard fact.

Once this myth was established, opposition to the regime wore the appearance of treason. Added weight was given to this impression by Governmental exploitation of the alleged threat of Bolshevism. To many this appeared real. The Nazis, however, used the 'Marxists' and the Jews as 'outgroups' in order to solidify the 'national community'. Here the Nazis were building on a tradition which went back fifty years to Bismarck's division of Germans into 'friends' and 'enemies' of the Reich, the latter including Left-Liberals, Catholics and Socialists, and later the Jews. The Weimar Republic, born out of defeat and revolution, had represented in the eyes of the Right the triumph of Bismarck's *Reichsfeinde* (enemies of the Reich). Thus to many it appeared as if Hitler was now restoring the situation which obtained before November 1918.

The psychological pressure on individuals created by this myth of a 'national uprising', particularly in the context of a desperate national crisis, was considerable: individuals and groups tended to 'coordinate' them-selves, sometimes with enthusiasm, sometimes with a sense of resignation. This pressure towards conformity was increased by the knowledge that overt opposition would be mercilessly crushed. Those whom their political background marked out as unlikely to conform were intimidated into silence by the strong-arm methods of the SA and SS.

The degree of violence and intimidation exercised by the Nazi organisa-tions has sometimes been underestimated in those accounts of the Nazi seizure of power which have stressed its pseudo-legality. The maintenance of an appearance of legality was undoubtedly an important element in Hitler's strategy. However, it was only one aspect of the situation; it was not always the one most evident at the time. The 'seizure of power' was in fact anything but peaceful. There was of course no fighting in the streets because the Left offered no resistance. During March, however, there began a 'revolution from below' on the part of the local Nazi organisations who interfered in a totally arbitrary manner with the State administration, with the course of justice and with commercial life; and this interference continued to a lesser extent throughout 1933.

It is as contrasted with the violence against individuals and the arbitrary interference on the part of the local Party organisations that the importance of this aspect of legality is most clearly seen. Hitler, appointed Chancellor by the President acting under Article 48 of the Weimar Constitution, headed a government which was legal in the narrow definition of that word. Once in office, he used the power to issue emergency decrees vested in the Reich President under Article 48 to strip the Constitution of its guarantees for civil liberties. In doing so he could claim to be merely taking a stage further the emergency powers used by his three predecessors. He was keeping to the letter of the Constitution even if he flouted its spirit. Moreover, maintaining the appearance of legality, he removed any qualms which might otherwise have been felt by the State officials obliged to carry out his policies. Indeed, for the civil servants and businessmen, faced with the 'revolution from below', the fact that Hitler was keeping to the letter of the law was an incentive to cooperate with the regime in the hope that this would encourage the 'moderate' Hitler to keep his local militants in check.

The fact that Hitler moved first against the Left lulled the Right into a sense of security. In the myth of the 'national uprising' Nationalists saw a reassertion of the conservative and nationalist values to which they adhered. By the time they became fully aware that Nazism was a totalitarian not a conservative movement, it was too late. In cooperating with the Nazis in projecting the image of a 'national uprising' and in identifying it with Hitler's rule, they had fatally undermined their own position and became now isolated. The only centres of power to which they could look for help were the President and the Army. The President by now senile was unwilling to face the upheaval which would be caused by dismissing Hitler. In any case, he appears to have been fed carefully selected information by his entourage. The Army was under a Minister of Defence who sympathised with the Nazi movement, its numbers were too small in comparison to those of the SA to guarantee success, and its younger officers were increasingly falling under Nazi influence.

Nevertheless, although Hitler was not prepared to tolerate a rival political organisation representing the conservative nationalists, he appreciated that he could not do without the traditional elites such as the Civil Service, Industry and the Army if he was to achieve his major goal of territorial expansion. He was therefore obliged to allow them to remain largely intact for the time being. Some of his rank-and-file followers in the SA and the Party, however, having provided the mass support and the drive to bring him to power and having then helped him to consolidate his power by terrorising their opponents, now wished to depose these elites, take over or destroy their organisations and introduce economic policies reflecting their hostility to big business. This would clearly jeopardise Hitler's major goal of rearmament, and he was prepared, if necessary, to use drastic methods to prevent such a development.

Instead of producing a thorough-going social and economic revolution, therefore, the Nazi take-over represented a compromise between the Nazi leadership who had acquired political power, and the traditional elites who retained their positions but put themselves at the service of the new regime. They were encouraged to do so by the fact that Hitler's initial objectives—the repression of the Left, rearmament, and the revision of various parts of the Versailles treaties—reflected their own wishes. But by assisting Hitler during these early years they increased his power and prestige and rendered themselves progressively superfluous. As the regime later moved towards its final goals of unbridled conquest and racial extermination, the Conservatives were replaced by technocrats or racialist fanatics who did not share their qualms at such revolutionary policies. The bravest of the Conservatives tried to make amends for their previous collaboration by going into active opposition, but once again it was too late.

(i) The 'NATIONAL UPRISING'—The Election Campaign of February–March 1933

On his appointment as Chancellor, Hitler's first objective was the elimina-tion of the Reichstag as an effective organ either of legislation or of opposition, achievable only by passing an Enabling Act requiring a two-thirds majority. The first Cabinet meetings, therefore, were concerned with securing this majority. One possibility was an alliance with the Catholic Centre Party. Though negotiations were begun, neither Nazis nor Nationalists wanted success because the Centre would demand concessions limiting their freedom of action. Hitler, therefore, soon broke off negotia-tions arguing that the Centre's demands were too high. Other possibilities were the suppression of the Communist Party and the confiscation of their seats, or new elections. A condition for Hitler's acceptance of the Chancellorship had been the dissolution of the Reichstag. He favoured new elections, for an increased Nazi vote would add an aura of democratic legitimacy to his gradual assumption of power, and would correspondingly undermine the position of the Nationalists. Hugenberg, the Nationalist leader, conscious that the Nazis now had the full power of the state behind them, demurred, but on receiving Hitler's promise not to alter the composition of the Cabinet after the election irrespective of the outcome, acquiesced. Indeed, he went further. According to the Cabinet minutes of 31 January 1933, the initiative for the abolition of the parliamentary system and for the deposition of the Social Democratic Government of Otto Braun in Prussia came from the non-Nazis Papen and Hugenberg. The Nazis, far from being restrained by their 'conservative' colleagues, merely had to acquiesce in their requests. The election was scheduled for 5 March. It was made clear that the coalition would continue after the election but Nazis and Nationalists fought as separate groups:

85

...(2) Political Situation
The Reich Chancellor reported on his conversation held on the morning of 31 January with representatives of the Centre Party, Dr Kaas and Dr Perlitius. The representatives had told him that they did not wish to join the Government at this time, although the Centre Party might abstain from opposition to the Cabinet.
The Reich Chancellor had immediately asked them whether they would consent to an extended adjournment of the Reichstag, perhaps for a year. He had received the reply that the Centre Party could not immediately consent to an adjournment for a whole year, but at the most for two months at a time. In any event, it was not inconceivable that in this way an adjournment for a whole year might be obtainable. But such an attitude on the part of the Centre Party would depend on the replies to a series of questions which Mgr Kaas wanted to send the Reich Chancellor today in writing. As Dr Kaas further stated, the Centre Party would consider a coalition only if this would include Prussia. The Centre Party representatives had been unable to deny during the conversation that a very large part of the German people stood behind the present Government.
He would sum up the result of the conversation with the representatives of the Centre Party to the effect that a year's adjournment could not be obtained with certainty. Perhaps he could talk again about the course of the conversation and the further development of the political situation with Reich Minister Dr Hugenberg, personally.
The Reich Minister of Economics, Food and Agriculture stated he would be very glad to have such a talk.
The Reich Chancellor further stated that if a new election were held he thought that 51 per cent of the Reichstag might be found backing the present Government. He had talked on the morning of 31 January with a number of Gauleiters of the NSDAP, who had confirmed this. In his opinion, further negotiations with the Centre Party were useless; there was no alternative to a new election.
The Vice-Chancellor and Reich Commissioner of Prussia stated that it would be best to decide now that the coming election of the Reichstag would be the last one and that a return to the parliamentary system was to be avoided permanently.
The Reich Chancellor declared that he would make the following binding promises:

(a) The outcome of the new election of the Reichstag is to have no influence on the composition of the present Government;

(b) The forthcoming election of the Reichstag is to be the last election. Any return to the parliamentary system is to be absolutely avoided.

The Reich Minister of Finance pointed out that the votes in the committees of the Reichstag were gradually bringing the Reich Government into some impossible situations. The Government parties must immediately declare that, in view of the political situation, they demanded the adjournment of the committees. If an adjournment could not be obtained, the representatives of the Government parties must dissolve the committees of the Reichstag and in this way prevent them from passing resolutions.

No objections were made to this proposal of the Reich Minister of Finance.

The Reich Chancellor then read a letter received in the meantime from Dr Kaas, containing the questions to the Reich Government promised by him. The Reich Chancellor declared that it was not possible to go into the details at this time. To deal with the individual questions satisfactorily, if it was really desirable, would mean several weeks' work. In his opinion, a detailed substantive reply could not be given.

The Reich Minister of Economics, Food and Agriculture pointed out that it was urgently necessary to depose the so-called sovereign Braun Government[30] in Prussia as soon as possible. Otherwise, the civil servants in Prussia would get into an intolerable situation.

The Chancellor agreed in principle to this point of view. He then turned to the future work of the Reich Government and stated that an extension of the protection against distraint was urgently needed in the interest of the German farmer.[31] In his view, distraint proceedings against farming property must be suspended, with great respect to all claims that had arisen prior to the appointment of the present Cabinet... .

State Secretary Meissner pointed out that it was possible to dissolve the Prussian Diet by a decree based on Article 48 of the Reich Constitution. Such a decree will have to be based on the decision of the Supreme Court for Constitutional Questions that unity in the leadership of the State, the Reich, and Prussia, was required.

The Vice-Chancellor and Reich Commissioner of Prussia stated that in his opinion it would be best if the President were to appoint himself State President in Prussia.

State Secretary Meissner expressed certain objections to this proposal and said it would be best to obtain a voluntary dissolution of the Prussian Diet. If such a voluntary dissolution could not be obtained, a dissolution on the basis of Article 48 of the Reich Constitution could then be considered. In any case it would be

---

[30] The German Supreme Court had ruled on 25 October 1932 that the Presidential Decree of 20 July 1932, appointing a Reich Commissioner for Prussia and removing Prussian Minister-President Otto Braun and his Cabinet from office, was constitutional, but that the Decree could not deprive the Prussian Cabinet of the power to represent Prussia in her relations with the Reich, the Prussian Diet and other German States.

[31] As a result of the depression large numbers of farmers were being foreclosed for debt.

necessary for the so-called Braun Government to disappear soon.
The Cabinet approved these statements.

The attitude of many of the upper middle class to Hitler's appointment is
well summed up in the following extracts from the diary of Frau Solmitz:

86

30.i.33
And what did Dr H. bring us? The news that his double, Hitler, is Chancellor of
the Reich! And what a Cabinet!!! One we didn't dare dream of in July. Hitler,
Hugenberg, Seldte, Papen!!!
On each one of them depends part of Germany's hopes. National Socialist drive,
German National reason, the non-political Stahlhelm, not to forget Papen. It is so
incredibly marvellous that I am writing it down quickly before the first discordant
note comes, for when has Germany ever experienced a blessed summer after a
wonderful spring? Probably only under Bismarck. What a great thing Hindenburg
has achieved! How well he neutralised Hammerstein[32] who was presumptuous
enough to bring politics into the Reichswehr!
Huge torchlight procession in the presence of Hindenburg and Hitler by National
Socialists and Stahlhelm, who at long last are collaborating again. This is a
memorable 30 January!
6.ii.33
Torchlight procession of National Socialists and Stahlhelm! A wonderfully
elevating experience for all of us. Göring says the day of Hitler's and the nationalist
Cabinet's appointment was something like 1914, and this too was something like
1914; after Dr H. had only recently remarked that damned little of this spirit had
survived on the way from Berlin to Hamburg between 30 January and 3 February.
On Sunday, the Reds waded through relentless rain—Gisela saw them—with
wives and children to make the procession longer. The Socialists and Reds will
inevitably have to give in now.
But now the weather was beautiful. Dry and calm, a few degrees above freezing.
At 9.30 p.m. we took up our position, Gisela with us. I said she should stay till the
end for the sake of the children. So far the impressions they had had of politics had
been so deplorable that they should now have a really strong impression of
nationhood, as we had once, and store it in their memories. And so they did. It was
10 p.m. by the time the first torchlights came, and then 20,000 brown shirts
followed one another like waves in the sea, their faces shone with enthusiasm in the
light of the torches. 'Three cheers for our Führer, our Chancellor Adolf Hitler....'
They sang 'The Republic is shit' and called the colours 'black-red-mustard'[33] and
'The murderous reds have bloody hands and we won't forget the murder at the

---

[32] It had been rumoured (erroneously) that General von Hammerstein had been preparing to
use the Army to avert a Nazi take-over.
[33] Black-red-gold were the colours of the Republican flag. 'Mustard' is particularly derogatory
since the German word can be used colloquially to mean 'nonsense'.

Sternschanz.' Dreckmann was murdered there and I happened to spot his name on one of the flags, probably the one of the section he had belonged to. The military standards are much too Roman in appearance.

Now came the Stahlhelm, a grey stream; quieter, more spiritual perhaps. On their beautiful flags they carried our old colours black-white-red,[34] with mourning crêpe at the top... How wonderful and uplifting it is that the quarrels between brothers that once so depressed us have been settled! It should always be like tonight. But between the SA and the Stahlhelm there was marching a delegation of nationalist students. And they won the hearts of Hamburg. The women at the greengrocery stalls and their customers, all the women there were saying the same thing: 'Those students! Simply charming. They were the best, weren't they?'

And it was a magnificent picture, the snow-white, scarlet, moss-green and black colours, the fantastic berets, boots and gauntlets in the dancing light of the torches, the swords, the flags. They were followed by the Stahlhelm with shining Schellenbaum,[35] playing the old Prussian army marches.

The SS brought up the rear of the procession.

We were drunk with enthusiasm, blinded by the light of the torches right in our faces, and always enveloped in their vapour as in a cloud of sweet incense. And in front of us men, men, men, brightly coloured, grey, brown, a torrent lasting an hour and 20 minutes. In the wavering light of the torches one seemed to see only a few types recurring again and again, but there were between twenty-two and twenty-five thousand different faces!

Nest to us a little boy of three kept raising his tiny hand: 'Heil Hitler, Heil Hitlerman!'

An SA man said to Gisela that morning: 'One doesn't say Heil Hitler any more, one says Heil Germany.' 'Death to the Jews' was also sometimes called out and they sang of the blood of the Jews which would squirt from their knives. (subsequent addition: Who took that seriously then?)

Opposite the Eimsbüttel Sports Hall (what a pity we could not see it) stood the leader of the Hamburg National Socialists—and beside him with his hand touching his hat, the leader of the Hamburg Stahlhelm, Lieutenant-Commander Lauenstein, who a few months before had been stabbed by SA men (ten minutes from where he now stood) and now saluted the procession of the SA, just as the SA leader saluted that of the Stahlhelm. What moments! What a marvellous thought

The National Socialists have much more new blood and young people than the Stahlhelm. Good looking, fresh, gay youths in the procession.

When everyting was over, it was actually not yet over, for the last SS men were joined by a crowd of gay people with left-over torches, who made their own procession, happy to join in the occasion.

Finally, the torches were thrown together at the Kaiser Frederich embankment, after a march from the Lübeck Gate. It was 11.30 p.m. before all was over.

Unity at last, at long last, but for how long? We are after all Germans.

What must Hitler feel when he sees the hundred thousand people whom he

---

34 The colours of the old imperial flag.
35 A musical instrument.

THE 'SEIZURE OF POWER' 1933–1934

summoned, to whom he gave a national soul, people who are ready to die for him. Not only metaphorically speaking but in bitter earnest...

And these floods of people in Hamburg are only a small fraction of Hitler's support in the whole Reich... .

The following 'Appeal to the German People' of 31 January 1933 formed part of this attempt to project the image of a 'national uprising' by creating the impression of national unity and a determined Government and by describing the previous epoch as one of unmitigated disaster. By sticking to vague generalities the Government avoided specific commitments which might have alienated certain sections of the population and limited its freedom of manoeuvre. It also disguised the fact that at this stage the Government had few specific plans.

87

Over fourteen years have passed since that unhappy day when the German people, blinded by promises made by those at home and abroad, forgot the highest values of our past, of the Reich, of its honour and its freedom, and thereby lost everything. Since those days of treason, the Almighty has withdrawn his blessing from our nation. Discord and hatred have moved in. Filled with the deepest distress, millions of the best German men and women from all walks of life see the unity of the nation disintegrating in a welter of egoistical political opinions, economic interests, and ideological conflicts.

As so often in our history, Germany, since the day the revolution broke out, presents a picture of heartbreaking disunity. We did not receive the equality and fraternity which was promised us; instead we lost our freedom. The breakdown of the unity of mind and will of our nation at home was followed by the collapse of its political position abroad.

We have a burning conviction that the German people in 1914 went into the great battle without any thought of personal guilt and weighed down only by the burden of having to defend the Reich from attack, to defend the freedom and material existence of the German people. In the appalling fate that has dogged us since November 1918 we see only the consequence of our inward collapse. But the rest of the world is no less shaken by great crises. The historical balance of power, which at one time contributed not a little to the understanding of the necessity for solidarity among the nations, with all the economic advantages resulting therefrom, has been destroyed.

The delusion that some are the conquerors and others the conquered destroys the trust between nations and thereby also destroys the world economy. But the misery of our people is terrible! The starving industrial proletariat have become unemployed in their millions, while the whole middle and artisan class have been made paupers. If the German farmer also is involved in this collapse we shall be faced with a catastrophe of vast proportions. For in that case, there will collapse not only a Reich, but also a 2000-year-old inheritance of the highest works of human culture and civilisation.

All around us are symptoms portending this breakdown. With an unparalleled effort of will and of brute force the Communist method of madness is trying as a last resort to poison and undermine an inwardly shaken and uprooted nation. They seek to drive it towards an epoch which would correspond even less to the promises of the Communist speakers of today than did the epoch now drawing to a close to the promises of the same emissaries in November 1918.

Starting with the family, and including all notions of honour and loyalty, nation and fatherland, culture and economy, even the eternal foundations of our morals and our faith—nothing is spared by this negative, totally destructive ideology. Fourteen years of Marxism have undermined Germany. One year of Bolshevism would destroy Germany. The richest and most beautiful areas of world civilisation would be transformed into chaos and a heap of ruins. Even the misery of the past decade and a half could not be compared with the affliction of a Europe in whose heart the red flag of destruction had been planted. The thousands of injured, the countless dead which this battle has already cost Germany may stand as a presage of the disaster.

In these hours of overwhelming concern for the existence and the future of the German nation, the venerable World War leader [Hindenburg] appealed to us men of the nationalist parties and associations to fight under him again as once we did at the front, but now loyally united for the salvation of the Reich at home. The revered President of the Reich having with such generosity joined hands with us in a common pledge, we nationalist leaders would vow before God, our conscience and our people that we shall doggedly and with determination fulfil the mission entrusted to us as the National Government.

It is an appalling inheritance which we are taking over.

The task before us is the most difficult which has faced German statesmen in living memory. But we all have unbounded confidence, for we believe in our nation and in its eternal values. Farmers, workers, and the middle class must unite to contribute the bricks wherewith to build the new Reich.

The National Government will therefore regard it as its first and supreme task to restore to the German people unity of mind and will. It will preserve and defend the foundations on which the strength of our nation rests. It will take under its firm protection Christianity as the basis of our morality, and the family as the nucleus of our nation and our state. Standing above estates and classes, it will bring back to our people the consciousness of its racial and political unity and the obligations arising therefrom. It wishes to base the education of German youth on respect for our great past and pride in our old traditions. It will therefore declare merciless war on spiritual, political and cultural nihilism. Germany must not and will not sink into Communist anarchy.

In place of our turbulent instincts, it will make national discipline govern our life. In the process it will take into account all the institutions which are the true safeguards of the strength and power of our nation.

The National Government will carry out the great task of reorganising our national economy with two big Four-Year Plans:

saving the German farmer so that the nation's food supply and thus the life of the nation shall be secured.

saving the German worker by a massive and comprehensive attack on unemployment.

In fourteen years the November parties have ruined the German farmer.
In fourteen years they created an army of millions of unemployed.
The National Government will carry out the following plan with iron resolution and dogged perseverance.
Within four years the German farmer must be saved from pauperism.
Within four years unemployment must be completely overcome.
Parallel with this, there emerge the prerequisites for the recovery of the economy.
The National Government will combine this gigantic project of restoring our economy with the task of putting the administration and the finances of the Reich, the states, and the communes on a sound basis.
Only by doing this can the idea of preserving the Reich as a federation acquire flesh and blood.
The idea of labour service and of settlement policy are among the main pillars of this programme.
Our concern to provide daily bread will be equally a concern for the fulfilment of the responsibilities of society to those who are old and sick.
The best safeguard against any experiment which might endanger the currency lies in economical administration, the promotion of work, and the preservation of agriculture, as well as in the use of individual initiative.
In foreign policy, the National Government will see its highest mission in the preservation of our people's right to an independent life and in the regaining thereby of their freedom. The determination of this Government to put an end to the chaotic conditions in Germany is a step towards the integration into the community of nations of a state having equal status and therefore equal rights with the rest. In so doing, the Government is aware of its great obligation to support, as the Government of a free and equal nation, that maintenance and consolidation of peace which the world needs today more than ever before.
May all others understand our position and so help to ensure that this sincere desire for the welfare of Europe and of the whole world shall find fulfilment.
Despite our love for our Army as the bearer of our arms and the symbol of our great past, we should be happy if the world, by restricting its armaments, made unnecessary any increase in our own weapons.
But if Germany is to experience this political and economic revival and conscientiously to fulfil its duties towards other nations, a decisive act is required: *We must overcome the demoralisation of Germany by the Communists.*
We, men of this Government, feel responsible to German history for the reconstitution of a proper national body so that we may finally overcome the insanity of class and class warfare. We do not recognise classes, but only the German people, its millions of farmers, citizens and workers who together will either overcome this time of distress or succumb to it.
With resolution and fidelity to our oath, seeing the powerlessness of the present Reichstag to shoulder the task we advocate, we wish to commit it to the whole German people.
We therefore appeal now to the German people to sign this act of mutual reconciliation.
The Government of the National Uprising wishes to set to work, and it will work.
It has not for fourteen years brought ruin to the German nation; it wants to lead

it to the summit.

It is determined to make amends in four years for the liabilities of fourteen years. But it cannot subject the work of reconstruction to the will of those who were responsible for the breakdown.

The Marxist parties and their followers had fourteen years to prove their abilities.

The result is a heap of ruins.

Now, German people, give us four years and then judge us.

Let us begin, loyal to the command of the Field-Marshal. May Almighty God favour our work, shape our will in the right way, bless our vision and bless us with the trust of our people. We have no desire to fight for ourselves; only for Germany.

The patronizing reaction of Frau Solmitz is probably typical of many of the educated middle class:

88

7.ii.33

...His [Hitler's] appeal, signed by the whole Government, contains too many words of foreign derivation used in an uneducated way. But I say: let him act first, and then later we shall teach Hitler good, pure German.

19.ii.33

Unfortunately, I must say that the political scales do not come to rest....I see Hitler exchanging bureaucrats [Bonzen] for bureaucrats, party book for party book. I hear him talk of Socialism....

The black-white-red battle front represents responsibility, represents the solid citizens, morality, protection of individuality, property, free enterprise, without experiments, without the use of force—it is a powerless little group outside Hitler's mighty shadow. What can be done?

Although the Nazis could command the radio and the police for their campaign, to avoid accusations of corruption, Hitler insisted the election campaign be not financed by the State. Instead, industry was requested to subsidise it. On 20 February 1933, Hitler addressed a small gathering of some twenty industrialists as follows:

89

...Private enterprise cannot be maintained in the age of democracy; it is conceivable only if the people have a sound idea of authority and personality. Everything positive, good and valuable, which has been achieved in the world in the field of economics and culture, is solely attributable to the importance of personality. When, however, the defence of the existing order, its political administration, is left to a majority, it will go under irretrievably. All the worldly goods which we possess we owe to the struggle of the chosen. Had we had the present conditions in the Middle Ages, the foundations of our German Reich would never have been laid. The same mentality that was the basis for obtaining these values must be used to preserve these values....It is, however, not enough to say: We do not want Communism in our economy. If we continue on our old political course, then we shall perish. We have fully experienced in the past years that economics and politics cannot be separated. The political conduct of the struggle is the primary, decisive factor. Therefore, politically clear conditions must be reached. As economics alone has not made the German Reich, so politics did not make economics. But each one built steadily higher upon the other. Just as politics and economics working hand in hand brought us to the top, so the working of one against the other, as we experienced it after the revolution, meant our continuous decline. As I lay in hospital in 1918, I went through the revolution in Bavaria. From the very beginning I saw it as a crisis in the development of the German people, as a period of transition. Life always tears humanity apart. It is, therefore, the noblest task of a leader to find ideals that are stronger than the factors which pull people apart. I recognised, even while in hospital, that new ideas must be sought conducive to reconstruction. I found them in Nationalism, in the value of personality, in the denial of reconciliation between nations, in the strength and power of individual personality... .

Now we are facing the last election. No matter what the outcome, there will be no retreat, even if the coming election does not bring about a decision. If the election does not decide, the decision must be brought about in one way or another by other means. I have intervened in order to give the people once more the chance of deciding their fate for themselves. This determination is a strong asset for whatever may happen later. If the election brings no result, well, Germany will not be ruined. Today, as never before, everyone is under an obligation to pledge themselves to success. The need to make sacrifices has never been greater than now. As for the economy, I have only one wish—that together with the internal political structure it may look forward to a calm future. The question of the restoration of the armed forces will not be decided at Geneva but in Germany, when we have gained internal strength through internal peace. There will, however, be no internal peace until Marxism is eliminated. Here lies the decision which we must face up to, hard as the struggle may be. I put my life into this struggle day after day as do all those who have joined me in it. There are only two possibilities: either to resist the opponent by constitutional means, and for this purpose, once again, the election is necessary; or the struggle will be conducted with other weapons, which may demand greater sacrifices. I would like to see them avoided. I hope therefore that the German people recognize the greatness of the hour. It will be decisive for the next ten or probably even the next hundred years. It will prove a turning-point in German history, to which I pledge myself with burning energy.

Göring concluded the meeting by pointing out that 'the sacrifices asked for would be the easier for industry to bear if it was realised that the election of 5 March would certainly be the last for the next ten years, probably even for the next hundred years'. Industry responded generously.

In the meantime, Göring through his control of the Prussian administration and police, had taken the initiative against the Nazis' opponents. A purge was carried out among the numerous SPD, Centre and Liberal police chiefs, and in the provincial administration in general. Even those who were not immediately affected were clearly intimidated. Moreover, on 17 February Göring issued the following order to the police throughout Prussia:

90

I assume that it is unnecessary to point out especially that the police must in all circumstances avoid giving even the appearance of a hostile attitude, still less the impression of persecuting the patriotic associations [the Nazi Storm Detachments and the Stahlhelm]. I expect all police authorities to maintain the best relations with these organisations which comprise the most important constructive forces of the State. Patriotic activities and propaganda are to be supported by every means. Police restrictions and impositions must be used only in the most urgent cases.

The activities of subversive organisations are on the contrary to be combated with the most drastic methods. Communist terrorist acts and attacks are to be proceeded against with all severity, and weapons must be used ruthlessly when necessary. Police officers who in the execution of this duty use their firearms will be supported by me without regard to the effect of their shots; on the other hand, officers who fail from a false sense of consideration may expect disciplinary measures.

The protection of the patriotic population, which has been continually hampered in its activities, demands the most drastic application of the legal regulations against banned demonstrations, illegal assemblies, looting, instigation to treason and sedition, mass strikes, risings, press offences, and the other punishable acts of the disturbers of order. Every official must constantly bear in mind that failure to act is more serious than errors committed in acting. I expect and hope that all officers feel themselves at one with me in the aim of saving our fatherland from the ruin which threatens it by strengthening and unifying the patriotic forces.

On 22 February, he authorised the employment of SA and SS men and Stahlhelmers as auxiliary police, to give them official status, to put pressure on the police, and also as a means of controlling them. They were issued with armbands and firearms and were officially placed under the authority of the police. But since they were employed as units rather than individuals, they were in fact able to act to a large extent independently, particularly since they could claim to be the true representatives of the new regime.

The Left was uncertain how to respond to the new developments. It was bedevilled by the split between Communists and Social Democrats. The Trade Unions had been undermined by three or more years of mass unemployment so that the prospects for a general strike along the lines of that which had helped defeat the Kapp putsch in 1920 were not encouraging. The Left had no previous experience of a totalitarian dictatorship and many underestimated the repression it would involve; they assumed the party would survive as it had during Bismarck's anti-Socialist Law of 1878-1890. Many believed that the regime would be dominated by Hugenberg and the reactionaries rather than the Nazis and saw it as a sign of the death throes of the capitalist system. They thought it would not last long and by sharpening class tension would bring forward the revolution. Also, there was the problem of choosing the right moment to resist. The Government had, after all, been installed according to the letter of the Constitution and, during its first phase, it operated under the appearance of legality. The SPD leadership were anxious not to be provoked into unconstitutional actions which would give the Government the excuse to crush the movement. Finally, although some among the rank and file were keen to resist the regime by violence if necessary, the SPD leadership had long become accustomed to working along peaceful and constitutional lines. They were temperamentally unsuited to lead a campaign of violent resistance, particularly after the demoralising political experience of the previous three years, a campaign which was in any case unlikely to succeed and would spill much blood.

Some of these considerations emerged in the discussions of a meeting of the SPD Executive Committee and representatives of the Free Trade Unions held on 5 February:

91

Wels [SPD] declares that he summoned the meeting with representatives of the Trade Unions to discuss what measures of defence should be taken. There were repeated enquiries from the factories as to when they should stop work. The comrades had been calmed down but there had been a lot of discussion in the factories about a united front [with the Communists]. Arrests and newspaper bans were increasing and there was the danger that some particular incident might start the ball rolling...We knew that we were far from being anxious and from acting rashly, but we had to come to an agreement about what might have to be done. If there was a general strike then there would be no question of elections. If the avalanche starts we must try and guide it into our channels...

Leipart [Trade Union leader]...He had to raise the question of what our aim would be in a general strike. Those workers who were now in employment would be afraid of losing their jobs. There would, therefore, not be much enthusiasm for a general strike. They would probably follow our call.

Then one should bear in mind that the Nazis were in a strong position with their SA which would probably occupy the factories in the event of a strike. If the only goal we could proclaim was: We're calling a general strike to re-establish constitutional conditions that would probably not be enough and it is questionable whether we would have any other slogans.

And even if the Communist workers joined in, there would still be a certain split in the movement because we would be fighting for the Constitution and the Communists against it...He came...to the conclusion that we should still wait until an open breach of the Constitution has occurred.

Stampfer [SPD]...He is not so opposed to a limited general strike of about a day. But that will only be possible if there is a prior agreement with the Communists. We will then have to tell them straight out that our aim is not the establishment of a Soviet Germany.

Grassmann [SPD] considers that if we were to follow Stampfer's advice we might as well pack up. Nothing at all would come of a discussion with the Communists...

Wels: The discussion has shown that our views are in complete agreement and that everyone is of the opinion that we must put ourselves at the head of the movement.

The Nazis' increasing intimidation of their opponents, particularly of the Left had its effects:

92

24.ii.33: Grzesinski (former SPD Police-President in Berlin) to the SPD Secretaries Franz Klupsch (Dortmund), Paul Röhle (Frankfurt am Main), Paul Bugdahn (Altona) and Richard Hansen (Kiel) on the need to cancel meetings.

Dear Comrade,

The incidents of the past few days in the meetings of those comrades who might be called prominent have prompted the Party committee this morning to examine the question whether, in the interests of our audiences, it would not be better to withdraw these speakers, of which I am one, for the time being. Several of my meetings have been disrupted and a considerable section of the audience had to be taken away badly injured. In agreement with the Party committee, I therefore request the cancellation of meetings with me as speaker. As things are, there is obviously no longer any police protection sufficient to check the aggressive actions of the SA and SS at my meetings... .

The following letters were from members of the SPD in Hanover: *17 February 1933*

93

I hereby return my membership card and signify my resignation from the Party.

I am and remain a 'religious socialist'. Under the pressure of circumstances the SPD, even against its will, will be pushed aside and into the methods of left-wing radicalism. On the other hand, pressure from the opposite side will grow. The only thing left for me to do in all conscience as a teacher, a Christian, and a German is to try to evade the double pressure and, as ten years ago, try to live for my job, my family and my books, without being a member of a party.

Yours faithfully, GEORGE M.

9 March 1933
In accordance with Paragraph 9 of the organisation statutes, I hereby signify my resignation and that of my wife with immediate effect... .

As a civil servant I have to make a choice. On the one hand, I see how the tendency is growing on the part of my employer, the Reich, not to tolerate those employees belonging to anti-Government associations. On the other hand, there is my loyalty to the Party. Unfortunately, I see no other solution but my resignation. The existence of my family is at stake. If the fate of unemployment, which in my experience can be *very, very* hard, is unavoidable, I need not reproach myself for not have done everything in the interests of my wife and child.

HANS J.

Then, on 27 February, a week before the election, the Reichstag building was set on fire and a young Dutch Communist named van der Lubbe was caught apparently red-handed in the building. The fire came very conveniently for the Nazis who could use it to claim the Communists were plotting revolution and so justify wholesale arrests. So convenient was it that many have thought it probable that the Nazis themselves started the fire and blamed it on the Communist van der Lubbe whom they used as a dupe. Other historians, however, have denied this and argued that van der Lubbe acted alone. The controversy continues and will probably never be satisfactorily resolved. One contemporary witness was the police chief in charge of the investigation, Rudolf Diels, the head of the Prussian political police soon to become known as the Gestapo. Looking back after the war he wrote:

94

...When I pushed my way into the burning building with Schneider, we had to climb over the bulging hoses of the Berlin fire brigade, although, as yet, there were few onlookers. A few officers of my department were already engaged in interrogating Marinus van der Lubbe. Naked from the waist upwards, smeared with dirt and sweating, he sat in front of them, breathing heavily. He panted as if he had completed a tremendous task. There was a wild triumphant gleam in the burning eyes of his pale, haggard young face. I sat opposite him in the police headquarters several times that night and listened to his confused stories. I read the Communist pamphlets he carried in his trouser pockets. They were of the kind which in those days were publicly distributed everywhere. And from the primitive hieroglyphics of his diary I tried to follow his trips down to the Balkans.

The voluntary confessions of Marinus van der Lubbe prevented me from thinking that an arsonist who was such an expert in his folly needed any helpers. Why should not a single match be enough to set fire to the cold yet inflammable splendour of the Chamber, the old upholstered furniture, the heavy curtains, and the bone-dry wooden panelling! But this specialist had used a whole knapsack full of inflammable material. He had been so active that he had laid several dozen fires. With a firelighter, the 'Industrious Housewife', he had set the Chamber aflame. Then he had rushed through the big corridors with his burning shirt which he brandished in his right hand like a torch to lay more fires under the old leather sofas. During this hectic activity he was overpowered by Reichstag officials.

He also confessed to several smaller arson attacks in Berlin, the mysterious cause of which had aroused the attention of the Criminal Investigation Department. Several details suggested that Communist arsonists who had helped him in Neukölln and the Berlin Town Hall might have helped him with the Reichstag. The interrogating officers had pointed their investigations in this direction. But meanwhile things of a quite different nature had happened.

Shortly after my arrival in the burning Reichstag, the National Socialist elite had arrived. Hitler and Goebbels had driven up in their large cars; Göring, Frick and Helldorf[36] arrived; Daluege, the police chief, was not there.

One of Hitler's chief adjutants came to look for me in the maze of corridors, now alive with the fire brigade and the police. He passed me Göring's order to appear in the select circle. On a balcony jutting out into the Chamber, Hitler and his trusty followers were assembled. Hitler stood leaning his arms on the stone parapet of the balcony and stared silently into the red sea of flames. The first hysterics were already over. As I entered, Göring came towards me. His voice was heavy with the emotion of the dramatic moment: 'This is the beginning of the Communist revolt, they will start their attack now! Not a moment must be lost!'

Göring could not continue. Hitler turned to the assembled company. Now I saw that his face was purple with agitation and with the heat gathering in the dome. He shouted uncontrollably, as I had never seen him do before, as if he was going to burst: 'There will be no mercy now. Anyone who stands in our way will be cut down. The German people will not tolerate leniency. Every Communist official will be shot where he is found. The Communist deputies must be hanged this very night. Everybody in league with the Communists must be arrested. There will no longer by any leniency for Social Democrats either.'

I reported on the results of the first interrogations of Marinus van der Lubbe—that in my opinion he was a maniac. But with this opinion I had come to the wrong man; Hitler ridiculed my childish view: 'That is something really cunning, prepared a long time ago. The criminals have thought all this out beautifully; but they've miscalculated, haven't they, Comrades! These gangsters have no idea to what extent the people are on our side. They don't hear the rejoicing of the crowds in their rat holes, from which they now want to emerge', and so it went on.

I pulled Göring aside; but he did not let me start. 'Police on an emergency footing; shoot to kill; and any other emergency regulations which might be

---

[36] Count Wolf von Helldorf, the Berlin SA Chief.

appropriate in such a case.' I said again that a police radio message would be sent to all police stations in his name, putting the police in a state of alert and ordering the arrest of those Communist officials whose imprisonment had been intended for some time in the event of a ban on the Party. Göring was not listening: 'No Communist and no Social Democrat traitor must be allowed to escape us' were his last words. When I met Schneider again I tried to collect my thoughts: 'This is a mad-house, Schneider, but apart from that the time has come: all Communist and Social Democrat officials are to be arrested, big raids, a state of alert and all that goes with it!'

Schneider forgot the Social Democrats when he passed on Göring's order as a radio message. When I returned to the 'Alex'[37] after midnight it was buzzing like a beehive. The alerted operational battalions of the police stood lined up in long rows in the entrance drives with steel helmets and rifles. While squad vans arrived and whole troops of detectives with registers prepared many years before jumped on the ramps, joined by uniformed officers, the first cars were arriving back at the entrance of the building with dazed prisoners who had been woken up from their sleep...

Whoever was responsible, the Nazis exploited their opportunity to the full. Yet it appears the measures which followed were not carefully planned and coordinated but were rather spontaneous and largely irrational responses to an imagined threat of a Communist uprising. The arrests of the Communists, for example, were carried out on the basis of lists drawn up by the political police before 1933 and they were not as successful as was subsequently claimed. In fact, the Nazis had hoped to postpone the elimination of the Communists until after the election when they would be in a stronger position to deal with them. But their fear of an uprising prompted them to take precipitate and drastic action which resulted not only in these arrests, but in the most important single legislative act of the Third Reich, the Decree of the Reich President for the Protection of People and State, of 28 February 1933.

The origins of this decree are not entirely clear. It appears the original impulse came from a German Nationalist, Ludwig Grauert, a top official in the Prussian Ministry of the Interior. During the night of the 27th, wishing to legalise the arrests, Grauert suggested an 'emergency decree against arson and terrorist acts'. Hitler accepted and put it on the agenda of the Reich Cabinet meeting to be held the following day. Both Grauert and Hitler probably conceived the decree as a purely defensive measure directed specifically against the Communists. Before the Cabinet meeting, however, the Reich Minister of the Interior, Frick, redrafted the measure. Under the Weimar Constitution the powers of the Reich Minister of the Interior were restricted as the state governments had direct authority over the police and internal administration. Frick decided to use the opportun-

---

[37] The police headquarters in the Alexanderplatz.

ity presented by this decree to strengthen his control over the states, basing the new decree on the Prussian decree of 20 July 1932 which had legalised the *coup* against the Social Democrat/Centre Party Government and thereby giving it a far wider scope than originally intended. Article 2 enabled Frick, as Reich Minister of the Interior, to take over power in the states and, unlike Papen's Prussian decree of July 1932, the Reich Government, not the Reich President decided when Article 2 should be applied. This Article was to be of crucial importance in the seizure of power in the states during the first half of March. No less important was Article 1. This represented 'a kind of *coup d'état*' (Mommsen) and the suspension of civil rights which it contained provided a quasi-legal foundation for the regime of terror and intimidation which was to follow. In particular, it provided the legal warrant for the expedient of 'protective custody' used by the Gestapo to imprison without trial:

95

By the authority of Section 48 (2) of the German Constitution the following is decreed as a defensive measure against Communist acts of violence endangering the State:
  1. Sections 114, 115, 117, 118, 123, 124 and 153 of the Constitution of the German Reich are suspended until further notice. Thus restrictions on personal liberty, on the right of free expression of opinion, including freedom of the press, on the right of assembly and association, and violations of the privacy of postal, telegraphic and telephonic communications, and warrants for house-searches, orders for confiscations as well as restrictions on property rights are permissible beyond the legal limits otherwise prescribed.
  2. If in any German state the measures necessary for the restoration of public security and order are not taken, the Reich Government may temporarily take over the powers of the supreme authority in such a state in order to restore security.
  3. States and local authorities have to comply to the limits of their responsibilities with the orders issued by the Government of the Reich under the powers conferred on it by Paragraph 2... .

Although the Government failed to produce any concrete evidence of a Communist plot, its propaganda had a receptive audience among the middle class. Frau Solmitz recorded in her diary:

96

1.iii.33
...The Reich Government spoke....Göring, like an old greying civil servant, reported dryly and very gravely the dreadful murder plans of the Communists—

who have withdrawn into the stronghold of Hamburg. It started with the going over of the Karl Liebknecht House, where a whole system of underground tunnels was discovered, as well as galleries above ground....Proof was brought to light by the hundredweight. Hostages from bourgeois circles, wives and children of police officers were to be taken and used as shields, all cultural monuments were to be destroyed as in Russia: palaces, museums, churches. They started with the Reichstag. Fire broke out in twenty-eight places. All the Communist Party leaders have been taken into custody. Thälmann has fled to Copenhagen. They wanted to send armed gangs to murder and start fires in the villages; in the meantime terrorism was to take over the big cities stripped of their police forces. Poison, boiling water, every tool from the most refined to the most primitive, were to be used as weapons. It would sound like a fairy tale of robbers—if it wasn't for Russia having experienced methods and orgies of torture which a German mind, even when sick, is incapable of devising, and, when healthy, is unable to believe.

If Italy, America and England were wise, they should send us money to fight Bolshevism—our ruin will be their ruin!

Göring said he had not lost his nerve nor would he lose it. I hope the voters won't lose their nerve and stay away from the polling booths out of fright. The streets really are dangerous these days.

In the Reichstag election on 5 March 1933 the Nazis won 288 seats compared with 196 in the November 1932 election and increased their percentage of the vote from 33.1 to 43.9. They had still failed to win an absolute majority. The Nationalists had gained only one seat, winning 52, and their percentage of the heavy poll of 88 per cent had declined slightly. Although the Government coalition between Nazis and Nationalists had a bare overall majority of 51.7 per cent, this was insufficient to pass an Enabling Act for which a two-thirds majority was necessary.

The opposition parties maintained their position remarkably well, particularly in view of such difficult circumstances. The Catholic Centre actually gained three seats, winning 73, and its percentage of the larger poll declined only slightly. The SPD lost only one seat, still retaining 120, and their proportion of the poll declined by only 2 per cent. It was significant that in Prussia, where the impact of the new regime had had most effect as a result of Göring's ruthless measures, Nazi success was more limited. In the State Diet election which took place on the same day as the Reichstag election the Nazis only managed to increase their vote from 36.3 per cent to 43.2 per cent and to win 49 additional seats. Here the Nationalists managed to win 12 more seats, which suggests that some people hoped to strengthen the Conservative wing of the coalition in the light of their experience with Göring and the Nazis. In the south German states Nazi electoral success was most striking notably in Bavaria. Here the anti-Bolshevist campaign paid dividends with conservative rural voters. This breakthrough allowed the Nazis to demand that the south German states adjust their politics to the new regime.

(ii) The Seizure of Power in the States and the SA/Party 'Revolution from Below' of March 1933

On 21 February 1933, while covering the election campaign, *The Times* correspondent in Germany had remarked on 'the starkness of the contrast between conditions in Prussia and in states where the Reich Government have not yet taken charge of the State affairs, or where the Nazis have not yet obtained local control'. The majority of the federal states were not yet controlled by the Nazis, and here the authorities which had responsibility for the police and for public order in general endeavoured to maintain an attitude of neutrality towards the various conflicting forces and to preserve the basic liberties.

The Nazis, determined to remove this contrast between Prussia and the other states, proceeded to exploit the momentum created by the election campaign to seize power in the states. They combined intimidation from below by mass action on the part of the Party and the SA with pressure from above by Frick and the Reich Ministry of the Interior. The SA created disorder, usually culminating in the hoisting of the swastika on the town hall. The local Party leadership then requested the Reich Ministry of the Interior to intervene as the existing state authorities were incapable of maintaining order and showed insufficient sympathy with the new Reich Government. The Reich Minister of the Interior then appointed a leading local Nazi as a Reich Police Commissioner as explicitly provided for in the Presidential Decree of 28 February and local Nazis could then intimidate the state governments into resignation and form Nazi governments.

The first state to experience this technique was Hamburg, where it occurred just before the election. The process began with Frick's demand for a ban on the SPD newspaper, the *Hamburg Echo*. A Nationalist senator, Paul de Chapeaurouge, wrote in complaint to Papen on 9 March:

97

...On the morning of 3 March, the Social Democrat senators resigned from the Senate because they did not want to consent to the ban on the *Echo* contemplated by the Reich Government. The remaining bourgeois senators pronounced this ban, which was undoubtedly permissible by law, as their first official act.

After the resignation of the Social Democrat senators, I, as the previous deputy police chief, had to take over the police. I knew that I had taken on a very difficult office. But I had no idea that my administration would prove as difficult as it at once became owing to the activities of the Reich Ministry of the Interior....

After the resignation of the Social Democrat senators, the Senate's first duty was to continue to carry out its functions in accordance with a strict observance of the Constitution and the laws until the new election, and to try its best to achieve an early election [of the senate]. This I was determined to do.

The Reich Government had the clear duty of supporting the Senate as the official organ of legal power. In my opinion, the Reich Ministry of the Interior, which is mainly responsible for relations with the states, failed in its task. To a large extent it bears the responsibility for the developments in Hamburg. The city was quite calm; according to absolutely reliable information given to the police, no serious disturbance of public order was to be expected from the Left. The course of events has proved the correctness of this opinion held by the police authorities.

Unrest occurred in Hamburg only because a few authorities, especially the *Gau* leadership of the NSDAP, sent alarmist reports to Berlin and caused the Reich Minister of the Interior to ask the Senate officially to transfer the command of the police to the former police lieutenant, Richter.[38] This suggestion was apparently passed on from Berlin simultaneously to the NSDAP and the press. In Hamburg it was underlined by wild press articles and by pressure on the members of the Senate in personal discussions in a most questionable way, and thus the situation was aggravated.

The course which the Senate should have followed was laid down in the Constitution. According to the Constitution and the law, it was unable to meet the request which had been made. In my opinion, since the election to the Senate was obviously to take place shortly, it was the Reich Minister's duty to urge the *Gau* leadership of the NSDAP, which prided itself on its constant contact with the Ministry, to maintain law and order so that the Constitution and the law would not be broken before the forthcoming election. But, so far as I could observe events, there were no such attempts at persuasion. Despite the alarmist press articles, Hamburg remained completely peaceful; only the police, among whom the NSDAP had begun an active propaganda campaign some time before, began to waver.[39]...

...The Hamburg events were, in my opinion, determined by the NSDAP's intention, known to me since 3 March, of gaining control of the police before the election of the Senate. This aim could not be achieved owing to the present legal position in Hamburg. Therefore, the NSDAP tried to reach their goal via the Reich. Owing to the fact that the NSDAP did not want to wait over the police question, circumstances have developed in Hamburg which are very regrettable from the point of view of police discipline and public order in the future.

The fact was noted that the final order of the Reich Minister of the Interior to the Senate to give the command of the police to Police Lieutenant Richter apparently reached the *Gau* headquarters of the NSDAP before it reached the Senate. Furthermore, the way in which Gauleiter Kaufman and Harry Hennigsen, [NSDAP] member of the city council, conveyed the order of the Reich Ministry of the Interior to the Senate was in no way appropriate to the importance and gravity of the moment.

It is my firm conviction that, if the Reich Ministry of the Interior had used its full authority to persuade the NSDAP to keep the peace, Hamburg would have been spared the events of 5 March, so constitutionally and politically unsatisfactory. The

---

[38] An SA leader.

[39] A section of the police sympathetic to the Nazis hoisted the swastika on the town hall.

situation now is that, contrary to the solemn promises of the Reich Government, an interference in Hamburg's sovereignty has taken place which could have been avoided and is undesirable from the point of view of the initial work on the Reich reform... .

I must add a few personal remarks: I regard the procedure of the Reich Ministry of the Interior towards Hamburg as at the same time an injustice towards myself. The Reich Ministry knows who I am and where I stand politically and as a soldier. I met State Secretary Pfundtner only a few weeks ago at a dinner of the local Nationalist Club, of which I have been a member since its foundation, given in honour of the presence of His Royal Highness the Duke of Coburg-Gotha. In former times there was a way by which a German officer, a German graduate could take the law into his own hands. Today, unfortunately, I have to confine myself to asking you, Vice-Chancellor, to inform the Reich Government of my letter in the hope that they will then adopt the correct attitude towards me... .

During the next few days, all the other states were taken over in a similar fashion. The most important state, Prussia, was already effectively under the control of the new regime. The administration had already been purged of Social Democrats and Democrats after Papen's *coup* in July 1932. Although Papen as Reich Commissioner for Prussia was theoretically superior to Göring as Minister of the Interior, in practice Papen did not interfere because at this stage Göring's activities were directed against the Left. Furthermore, immediately after the appointment of Hitler as Chancellor, on 6 February, all the representative bodies within Prussia were dissolved and new elections were ordered; on 5 March for the Landtag, on 13 March for the provincial and local councils.

The 'coordination' completed, the Nazis proceeded to provide more solid legal foundations for their power in the states. They ensured themselves a majority in the other state assemblies through a law of 31 March and, by a law of 7 April, appointed special Reich Governors (*Reichsstatthalter*) to the states, nearly all chosen from the senior Gauleiters in the area.

The pressure from below erupted into an orgy of violence against the Party's opponents, particularly those on the Left. This violence may have been initiated from above or largely spontaneous, but it rapidly began to get out of control. It represented the unleashing of all the frustration of the SA and local Party organisations during the pre-1933 period caused by the need to follow a policy of strict legality. The Party's rank and file saw at last the possibility of taking revenge on their opponents and of acquiring the prizes of power. As far as they were concerned, it was now their state and they were not in a mood for compromise or half measures. During the following weeks trade union offices were smashed and Social Democrat officials were 'arrested' by SA men, cruelly beaten up and dragged off to hastily improvised concentration camps. The SA and local Party officials also seized the opportunity to exploit their position by intimidating Business into giving them employment in one form or another. A kind of protection racket developed. The following account by the first head of the Gestapo, Rudolf Diels, gives a good impression of the confusion and violence which characterised the first months of the allegedly peaceful national uprising:

98

The uprising of the Berlin SA electrified the remotest parts of the country. Around many big cities in which the authority of the police had been transferred to the local SA leaders, revolutionary activities took place beyond the periphery of these cities throughout the whole area of their regiments [*Standarten*] and groups. The higher the rank of these police-presidents, the farther afield extended the noisy abuses of these parhelions of the revolution. In Lower Silesia, the SA Gruppenführer [Edmund Heines] carried on a regime of violence from Breslau. In the North Rhineland, SS Gruppenführer Weitzel, the newly appointed police president of Düsseldorf, displayed violent radicalism together with the SA leader Lobek; in Essen and the cities of the Ruhr area, the SA of Terboven[40] held sway.

In East Prussia, Gauleiter Koch had allowed neither the SA nor the SS to come to power. Here the political leaders ruled. They were opposed to the 'reactionary' elements. The country was in a sort of state of war in which the aristocracy, as the imagined enemy, had to put up with a flood of arrests. From Stettin, the example of the SS Standartenführer, Engel, encouraged the Pomeranian SA to terrorise the country. From the cities of Rostock, Stargard and Greifswald, cases of beatings up were reported in which Communists and Social Democrats had been subjected to mock drownings and hangings. The torments had cost some victims their lives. In Silesia, the Rhineland, Westphalia and the Ruhr area unauthorised arrests, insubordination to the police, forcible entry into public buildings, disturbance of the work of the authorities, the smashing up of dwellings and nightly raids had begun before the Reichstag fire at the end of February... .

It was no longer possible to tell which public or private spheres had been penetrated by the SA, and scarcely possible to guess the purposes for which it allowed itself to be hired and employed. There was hardly a single business undertaking which had not employed an 'old fighter' of the SA for protection against the dangers of coordination, denunciation and threats. They were present everywhere as self-appointed directors, special commissars and SA delegates... .

...No order and no instruction exists for the establishment of the concentration camps; they were not established, one day they were simply there. The SA leaders put up 'their' camps because they did not want to trust the police with their prisoners or because the prisons were overcrowded. No information about many of these *ad hoc* camps ever got as far as Berlin. Years after my departure from Berlin I heard of the existence of some camps of which I had no knowledge in 1933. We first heard of a camp in Kemma in the Ruhr area through the foreign press. It was the

40 Josef Terboven, Gauleiter of Essen 1928-45.

American journalist Lochner who informed the state police office that the [SA] group leader Heines had established a concentration camp near Dürrgoy in Silesia... .

In the state of Brunswick, where the Nazis had formed a coalition government with the Nationalists since 1930, relations between the Nazis and their opponents had always been particularly bad. The Nazis now took their revenge, as the following account published by the SPD in exile indicates:

99

From 3 March 1933 the atmosphere in the town and the countryside became unbearable. One brawl after another. There were growing rumours that the *Volksfreund*—the [SPD] Party, trade union and publishing house building of the workers—was to be raided by National Socialists. All demonstrations were banned. On 9 March at 11 a.m. a fight started between an SS member, obviously sent out for the purpose of provocation, and a member of the *Reichsbanner*. At about 12 noon a small police car appeared in front of the *Volksfreund* building with about ten policemen and the SS man who was alleged to have been beaten up. They searched the *Volksfreund* for the member of the *Reichsbanner* who had taken part in the fight and who, according to them, was in the building. The search of course was fruitless.

At about 3 p.m. the [SPD] parliamentary group of the provincial diet held a meeting. Meanwhile the SA and the SS continued their activities of the previous day; under the eyes of the authorities they hoisted swastika flags on public buildings. The Nazis also tore a large poster off the boathouse of the *Reichsbanner* in the presence of the police and carried it through the town, heading for the *Volksfreund.*

There, lorries with SA and SS had driven up at 4.05 p.m. The porter promptly closed the doors. But the Nazis broke the big display windows and pushed into the building through the holes. They opened fire inside the building with a number of rifles and revolvers. During this, the 28-year-old salesman, Hans Saile, the advertising manager of the Advertising Union, Berlin, was killed by a shot in the stomach. He had received an order from his superiors to leave the threatened district of Brunswick and to travel to Saarbrücken on the same day... .

The intruders rushed up the stairs and smashed in the locked doors with their rifle butts. Union secretaries, employees, typists, Co-op salesgirls were all driven together with cudgels, rifles, revolvers and daggers. Then, with the order 'Hands up!', they were locked up for hours, before being released with kicks and slaps.

Although the leadership of the organisation had endeavoured for weeks to remove important and valuable material and funds from the building, they did not succeed in securing all the money, books and documents in time. So several thousand Reichsmarks were confiscated by the intruders on their own authority. The whole building was searched for valuables. Then the swastika flag was hoisted. A certain worker, A.P., had hidden behind a cupboard as the Nazis broke in. He had seen from there how the account books had been destroyed in childish vandalism. He had heard the men grumbling that their booty of money and valuables had been far too small. A.P. was discovered, badly beaten up and then thrown out of the building.

The former police lieutenant, Richard Neuenfeldt, now a driver with the *Volksfreund*, who lived in the *Volksfreund* apartment building, Oelschlägern 27 in Brunswick, was busy doing car repairs in the yard at the outset of the occupation. He was recognised and beaten on his head and face with cudgels, steel pipes, revolver butts and metal tools until he collapsed unconscious. Even then he was kicked, dragged across the yard and thrown out. Neuenfeldt is an ex-serviceman, who served at the front and fought right through the war. Those who beat him up—a typical case that was repeated countless times—were 20-year-old boys. As a result of this beating up, Neuenfeldt is a broken man, physically and mentally.

During the course of the action, the private tenants of the *Volksfreund* building were raided in their flats, abused, threatened with weapons and beaten up.

The regular police had meanwhile blocked off the surrounding streets with a strong force. The Nazis looted the building in front of their very eyes. They destroyed the furniture and equipment. Anything that was movable they dragged out into the yard. Documents, pieces of furniture, valuable administrative material, the book supplies of the *Volksfreund* bookshop, many hundredweight of expensive propaganda film, records, account books, and flags were heaped up on a pyre and set alight. The fire burned for three days and nights.

Immediately after the raid on the building, Comrade Dr Heinrich Jasper, the former Minister-President of Brunswick, rang up the Police-President from the diet and informed him of what had happened. He accused the solicitor and deputy, Alpers, leader of the SS in Brunswick, of armed riot, unlawful assembly, housebreaking and disturbance of public order.

Police-President Lieff replied that these actions were completely legal. Deputy Alpers had been provided with a police warrant for this action.

After this phone call, the regular police units were withdrawn from the *Volksfreund*, so Alpers's hordes had a free hand.

After that, Comrade Dr Jasper got in touch with Nazi Minister Klagges and sought redress. Klagges replied that he knew nothing of these events. Jasper should file a written complaint in the usual way. He refused to intervene before the complaint had been dealt with.

There was of course no redress. On the contrary, Alpers became Minister of Justice [in Brunswick] under the Hitler regime.[41]

In the evening of this eventful day the city of Brunswick resembled a military camp. Hundreds of heavily armed Nazi patrols marched through the town, chased passers-by and beat up members of the public. In the course of this a member of the National Air Association was shot dead. The young man had allegedly raised only one hand on being told to put his hands up... .

The bourgeois papers in Brunswick reported the occupation the following morning. According to them it had been carried out quite legally, for the building had been a centre of unrest for a long time. Moreover, it was alleged that masses of

---

[41]Dr Jasper was soon afterwards arrested and sent to Dachau concentration camp where he later died of ill-treatment.

treasonable material and ammunition had been found. Not one of these statements is true... .

Such violence was not peculiar to Brunswick. It occurred throughout Germany, thogh not uniformly. Many towns escaped it. State violence in the form of police arrests and party violence in the form of SA thuggery directed largely at the Left proved a lethal combination, destroying its organisations, intimidating its members and thereby undermining both the ability and the will to resist.

In the course of this violence, a number of foreigners, particular Jews, were molested, producing protests from their diplomatic representatives. The Government became concerned about the excesses of the 'revolution from below' over which they appeared to have little control. Hitler in particular seemed torn between loyalty to his followers, with whose actions against their opponents he entirely sympathised, and the need not to alienate the conservative elites and in particular the President. On 10 March he appealed for an end to the violence, distinguishing between 'legitimate' and 'illegitimate' violence, as a gesture to demonstrate to conservative opinion at home and to foreign opinion the good intentions of the Government.

100

Comrades, SA and SS men! A revolution has taken place in Germany. It is the result of hard struggles, the greatest tenacity, but also the tightest discipline. Unscrupulous characters, mainly Communist spies, are trying to compromise the Party by individual actions which have no relation to the great work of the national uprising, but could discredit and detract from the achievements of our movement. In particular, they try to bring the Party or Germany into conflict with foreign countries by molesting foreigners and cars with foreign flags. SA and SS men, you yourselves must immediately stop such creatures and take them to task. Furthermore, you must hand them over to the police, whoever they may be.

From this day onwards the National Government has executive power throughout Germany. The further progress of the national uprising will therefore be guided and planned from the top. Only where these orders are resisted or where individuals or marching columns are ambushed must this resistance be crushed, as before, thoroughly and immediately. The molesting of individuals, the obstruction or disturbance of business life, must cease on principle. You, Comrades, must see to it that the national revolution of 1933 cannot be compared in history with the revolution of the knapsack Spartacists in 1918. Apart from this, do not be deterred for a second from our watchword. It is: The extermination of Marxism.

Its effect was to a large extent neutralised by a speech made by Göring on the same day in Essen in which he declared: 'For years past we have told the people: 'You can settle accounts with the traitors.' We stand by our word. Accounts are being settled'. Hitler was obliged to reaffirm his appeal in a broadcast on the 12th which appears to have had some effect. The situation remained confused. As Rudolf Diels indicates, the SA and SS continued to act as independent powers with complete disregard for the police and the administration under Göring, confident that in the last resort the Führer would protect them against proceedings:

101

At the beginning of October we heard that in Esterwegen and Papenburg prisoners had been shot while escaping....I was refused access to the Esterwegen camp by the SS. I had announced my visit to the camp a week before. But Göring's order, which I had to show, had not impressed the SS. When I appeared at the entrance of the camp, as far as they were concerned I was a civilian without position or rank in their mighty organisation. Only when Weitzel, the SS group leader in Düsseldorf, had given the commandant permission by telephone was I allowed to enter the camp.

The Papenburg camp granted me admission. But what can an 'inspection' of such an institution reveal? The prisoners' replies to the questions put by the inspector are determined by the fear of displeasing their tormentors in whose power the prisoners remain. The food is always adequate and the shining cleanliness of floors and barracks and the scrupulous tidiness of the beds do not tell that they are a means of tormenting the inmates. Nobody can see in the ridiculous straightness of the freshly raked expanses of sand that a violation of such orderliness means 'bunker' and corporal punishment. In Papenburg the unusual happened; a few of the prisoners' spokesmen 'let themselves go'. They not only complained of the food, but they made it clear that they had been subjected to ill-treatment.

In Papenburg, the mayor too had told me of the excesses of the SS towards the population. SS men roamed through the district pillaging like the Swedes in the Thirty Years War. They 'confiscated' arrested people who had incurred their displeasure and started brawls with the youths of the surrounding villages.

My visit had also encouraged the *Regierungspräsident*[42] in Osnabrück to inform me of the misdeeds of the SS in the camp.

Then, just at the right time, came a serious complaint by a Cologne lawyer, Dr Pünder, made to the Reich Minister of the Interior, Frick, on behalf of his brother, State Secretary Pünder, who was in the hands of the SS thugs in Papenburg. Frick had Pünder's complaint passed on to me and Gürtner[43] by *Oberregierungsrat* Erbe. Erbe promised me his support and Hanfstaengl[44] promised to work on Hitler. At the same time, the Chief Prosecutor Halm of Osnabrück had reported that investigations in the camps which he had wanted to undertake because of the ill-treatment of the innkeeper, Hillig, by SS men in Papenburg had been refused

---

[42]The senior government official for the area.
[43]The Minister of Justice.
[44]A German–American friend of Hitler's.

with severe threats. By-passing SS and Police Chief Daluege, I went with Joel, the public prosecutor, to Göring's representative, State Secretary Grauert. He gave us fifty Berlin police officers armed with carbines with whom Joel set off for Papenburg. A delegate sent by Joel was told that if the police approached the camp they would be received with machine guns. When Joel attempted to get into the camp, bullets flew round his ears. On his informing Grauert of this state of affairs, he was told to wait for further instructions. Meanwhile, Himmler had protested to Göring against the use of the police against the SS. Göring would have given in, had Joel not informed him that the SS were fraternising with the prisoners in the camp and were going to arm them. This brought a new element into the revolutionary situation. Mention of the mutinous SS put all other arguments in the shade. Göring asked me to report to Hitler in his presence on what had happened. Hitler ordered the 'take-over' of the camps by the police. When I had informed Grauert, he sent 200 Osnabrück police off to the Dutch border. But they had to make ready to lay siege, as it were, to the camps, especially as a representative of SS Group Leader Weitzel appeared on the scene and tried to intimidate the police officers with threats from Himmler. I now went to ask Hitler straight whether the police could not use force of arms against the SS. Hitler let me see him and after my renewed account of the excesses in the camps, he interrupted me in a military voice of command and ordered me to ask the Reich Defence Minister for army artillery, and to shoot up the camps, the SS and their prisoners without mercy. My colleagues were horrified when I arrived with this order from the Führer. It was clear to me that I could not take it seriously.

I asked my superior, *Ministerialdirektor* Fischer in the Ministry of the Interior, to negotiate with the mutinous SS about their 'demands' which, like freebooters, they had made the conditions of their departure. They had demanded coats, blankets, and back pay. After he had informed the SS, through an SS leader of Weitzel's, of the fulfilment of their demands, Joel took possession of the camps without bloodshed. He then spent some time in Papenburg to begin investigations into the violence of the SS guards.

...At this time Joel also went to Kemma near Wuppertal at Grauert's and my instigation. The SA had tortured the Communists there in a particularly 'original' way. They were forced to drink salty herring solution and then left to pant in vain for a sip of water throughout the hot summer days. One of my officers who had accompanied Joel reported that the SA there had also played the 'joke' of getting their prisoners to climb trees; they had to hang on in the treetops for hours on end and at certain intervals cry 'cuckoo'. The public prosecutor Winckler in Wuppertal, who proposed to act against the SA, had to flee with his wife and child from their threats. The *Regierungspräsident* Schmidt in Düsseldorf poured out his heart to me about the atrocities. With Joel, I succeeded in getting Göring to have the 'responsible' SA Group Leader relieved of his office, to ensure that Joel had a free hand in the prosecution of the SA guards. After a few months, Joel succeeded, despite the opposition of the Gauleiter Florian, in starting proceedings against the guilty SA men. But the struggle against Hitler, who finally terminated the proceedings, he was bound to lose... In reality, there were neither commands nor prohibitions. Before or after my reports to Göring and Hitler on acts of violence in the country, SA and SS leaders talked about the bravery of their men on the field of revolution. These acts were approved of and laughed over just as they were disapproved of when I represented them as excesses against the authority of the new state.... Already, the SA were breaking into the police prisons, to get hold of the Communist leaders who had been arrested after the Reichstag fire, and who, they intended, should be the victims of their special revenge. From the police headquarters they took the files which could incriminate their leaders; the frightened officials handed over what they were asked for.

This violence, directed primarily against the Left and mostly behind closed doors, was overlooked or rationalised by the middle class which referred to the crisis of the moment. Many were prepared to accept Göring's explanation that 'Where planing is going on there are bound to be shavings', the German equivalent of 'You can't make an omelette without breaking eggs'. Many felt the Left had it coming to them anyway. Even so, the official version of the take-over contrasted the 'bloodless national uprising' of 1933 with the allegedly 'bloody revolution' of November 1918. The image of a glorious and bloodless national revolution was reinforced by the spectacle staged on 21 March in the garrison church at Potsdam, a Prussian shrine, to celebrate the opening of the new Reichstag session. Erich Ebermeyer, a dramatist and the son of the former chief public prosecutor at the Supreme Court in Leipzig, describes the scene and its impact on himself and his family. Their response is particularly significant because their general outlook was liberal and unsympathetic to Nazism:

102

The 'Day of Potsdam'. A sea of flags in all the streets. We too couldn't opt out. So I get the old black-white-red flag from the World War down from the loft and hoist it. The black-red-gold one, the good old disgraced, betrayed, and never properly respected thing has to go up to the loft in its place...

In the morning a broadcast of the ceremonies in Potsdam. All cleverly done, impressive, spell-binding even, at any rate for the masses. But we too cannot and must not shut our eyes in the face of what is going on. Today and here, the marriage took place, if not for ever then at least for a time, between the masses led by Hitler and the 'Spirit of Potsdam', Prussian values, represented by Hindenburg.

How marvellously it's been staged by that master producer Goebbels. The procession of Hindenburg, the Government, and the deputies goes from Berlin to Potsdam past a solid line of cheering millions. The whole of Berlin seems to be on the streets. Government and deputies walk from St Nicholas' Church to the Garrison Church together. The radio announcer almost weeps with emotion.

Then Hindenburg reads his speech. Plain, strong, coming from a simple heart and so presumably speaking to simple hearts. The very fact that there stands a man, who unites in himself generations of German history, who fought in 66, who was there at the Imperial Coronation in 71 in Versailles, who became a national hero

TRTP–K

between 14 and 18, from whom no lost battle and no lost world war can reduce his popularity among our peculiar people, whom, on the contrary, the defeat itself raised to a mythical state of glorification, who then as an old man once more took over the leadership of the Reich and even did so for a second time, and not out of vanity or a hunger for power but undoubtedly from a Prussian sense of duty—he now, soon to die, presides over the marriage of his world with the new rising one which the Austrian corporal, Hitler, represents.

Then Hitler speaks. It cannot be denied. He has grown in stature. Out of the demagogue and party leader, the fanatic and agitator—for his opponents surprisingly enough—a true statesman seems to be developing. So he is a genius in whose enigmatic soul lie unsuspected and unprecedented possibilities? The Government's declaration is marked by notable moderation. Not a word of hatred for the opposition, not a word of racial ideology, no threat aimed at home or abroad. Hitler says only what they want: the maintenance of the great traditions of our nation, firmness of government instead of eternal wavering, consideration for all the experiences of individual and human life which have proved useful for the welfare of mankind over thousands of years.

Hindenburg lays wreaths on the graves of the Prussian kings. The old Field Marshal shakes hands with the World War corporal. The corporal makes a deep bow over the hand of the Field Marshal. Cannons thunder over Potsdam—over Germany.

No-one can escape the emotion of the moment. Father too is deeply impressed. Mother has tears in her eyes... .

In the evening a quiet hour with M. He is completely unmoved by the day's events as if he was surrounded by a thick protective skin. He considers the whole thing simply a put up job, doesn't waver for one moment from his instinctive dislike. 'You've got it coming to you', says the 21 year old.

I remain silent, ashamed and torn.

(iii) The 'Coordination' of the Reichstag and of the Political Parties, March–June 1933

After coordinating the states, Hitler returned to his initial objectives of the destruction of the Reichstag as an effective institution, and the elimination of rival political parties. An Enabling Law would enable the Government to introduce legislative measures independently of the legislature, including alterations to the Constitution. This was not an entirely new concept in German politics. Enabling Laws had been introduced during the Weimar Republic, notably those of 13 October and 8 December 1923 which dealt with the crisis caused by the inflation and the Ruhr invasion. Moreover, during the years 1930–33 laws passed by the Reichstag had increasingly been replaced by Government decrees issued by the Reich President under Article 48 of the Weimar Constitution. In 1932, for example, there were sixty emergency decrees compared with only five Reichstag laws, and an increasing number of these emergency decrees empowered the Government to issue supplementary regulations with the force of law.

Initially, the Enabling Law was drawn up along the lines of the Weimar laws and was intended to permit the issuing of Government decrees with the force of law without the need for prior approval from the Reichstag or the Reich President. Some time between 15 and 20 March, however, the draft was modified to empower the Government to issue not merely 'decrees' (*Verordnungen*) but also 'laws' (*Gesetze*), and even laws which deviated from the 1919 Constitution and had therefore hitherto required a two-thirds Reichstag majority. The distinction between a 'law' and a 'decree' was not clear-cut, but the Weimar Constitution had imputed somewhat greater significance to laws than to decrees by restricting certain legislation (e.g. the taking up of loans by the Government) to laws. In the final draft of the Enabling Law the Reichstag surrendered its powers over the budget and over the taking up of loans.

Since this Enabling Law involved a change in the Constitution, a two-thirds majority in the Reichstag was necessary. After the election of 5 March, the two largest parties after the NSDAP—the Social Democrats (SPD) and the Centre Party—still possessed between them over one-third of the seats. If the SPD and the Centre had boycotted the debate this would have represented an effective veto, since a quorum of two-thirds of the Reichstag membership was necessary for changes in the Constitution. This danger was averted by a change in the Reichstag standing orders suggested by Frick. The new regulation, accepted by all save the SPD, provided that those members absent without leave or excluded would count as being present, the decision lying with the President of the Reichstag (Göring).

At the Cabinet meeting of 7 March 1933, the Government, reconciled to the opposition of the Social Democrats, concentrated on trying to win over the Centre:

103

(1) *Political Situation*
The Reich Chancellor opened the meeting and stated that...he regarded the events of 5 March as a revolution. Ultimately Marxism would no longer exist in Germany.

What was needed was an Enabling Law passed by a two-thirds majority. He, the Reich Chancellor, was firmly convinced that the Reichstag would pass such a law. The deputies of the German Communist Party would not appear at the opening of the Reichstag because they were in jail... .

The Vice-Chancellor and Reich Commissioner of Prussia [Papen] expressed to the Reich Chancellor and the National Socialist Organisation the thanks of the Reich Cabinet for their admirable performance in the election... .

With regard to the internal political situation, the Vice-Chancellor stated that yesterday (6 March) Dr Kaas had been to see him. He had stated that he had come without previously consulting his party and was now prepared to let bygones be bygones. He had, moreover, offered the cooperation of the Centre Party... .

Reich Minister Göring stated that the Communist deputies would not take part in the sessions of the Reichstag because they were in jail. Serious charges were also to be made against a number of Marxist deputies. Forty persons of the Iron Front had carried out united action with the German Communist Party.

He was firmly convinced that the two-thirds majority in the Reichstag would be obtained for an Enabling Law. Deputies who left the session in order to make it impossible for the two-thirds majority to be present would have to forfeit their free travel passes and allowances for the duration of the legislative period. He wished to make a change in the rules to this effect. In his opinion, the duty of the Deputy to exercise his mandate also entailed that he must not absent himself from sessions without being excused.

Grass, the chairman of the parliamentary group of the Prussian Centre Party, had been to see him even before the election. Grass had made the offer that if no further changes in personnel were made before the election, then the Centre Party would be prepared to cooperate. According to the statements made by Grass, the collaboration of the German Nationalists could then be dispensed with. It was best to tell the Centre Party that all its civil servants would be removed from office if the Centre Party did not agree to the enabling law. For the rest, the tactics to be employed towards the Centre Party would have to consist in courteously ignoring it... .

The Catholic Church authorities, however, were still hostile to the Nazi Party and their influence with the Centre Party was considerable. On 19 March, Cardinal Bertram, the senior German Catholic bishop, issued a confidential statement to the Catholic bishops that 'as a result of biased announcements to the effect that the Church will revise its attitude to the National Socialists, Vice-Chancellor von Papen brought up this question during his visit yesterday. I replied that it is for the leader of the National Socialists to revise his attitude.'

To win over the Catholics and the Centre Party, Hitler promised in his Reichstag speech on 23 March to respect the rights of the Catholic Church and stressed the Government's recognition of the importance of the Churches:

104

...By its determination to carry through the political and moral purging of our public life, the Government is creating and ensuring the preconditions for a truly deep and inward religious life. The political advantages derivable from compromises with atheistic organisations come nowhere near outweighing the consequences to be seen in the destruction of our common religious and moral values. The National Government sees in both Christian denominations the most important factors for the maintenance of our society. It will respect the agreements concluded between them and the states; their rights will not be touched. It expects, however, that its task of the national and moral renewal of our people will meet with similar appreciation from their side. The Government will treat all other denominations with objective justice. It can never, however, condone the idea that membership of a given denomination or race can be regarded as absolving any person from common legal obligations or as a licence to commit or tolerate crimes without punishment. The National Government will permit and guarantee to the Christian denominations the enjoyment of their due influence in schools and education.[45] Its concern will be for the sincere cooperation of Church and State. The struggle against the materialist ideology and for the establishment of a real national community is in the interests of the German nation as much as of our Christian faith... .

Besides being wooed by promises, the Centre were also intimidated by the fear of what would happen, particularly to Catholic civil servants, if they refused. The distinguished historian of the Centre Party, Karl Bachem, summed up their uncertainty after the Party had supported the Bill. Particularly interesting is his hope that it would be possible to cooperate with and influence the NSDAP.

105

Was this vote right? This may be doubted, though only future developments will make a definite judgement possible. It was certainly in the spirit of the call for unity which Kaas had sent out weeks ago on 17 October 1932 in Münster. It may also be said that the law would have been passed even if the Centre had voted against it or abstained. If the Centre had voted against it, it would, given the current mood of the National Socialists, probably have been smashed at once just like the Social Democratic Party and the Italian Partito Popolare.[46] All civil servants belonging to the Centre would probably have been dismissed. There would have been a great fracas in the Reichstag, and the Centrists would probably have been beaten up and thrown out. The parliamentary group would have made an heroic exit, but with no benefit to the Catholic cause or to the cause of the Centre Party. The links between the Centre and National Socialism would have been completely cut, all collaboration with the National Socialists and every possibility of influencing their policy would have been out of the question. Perhaps, then, it was right to make the attempt to come to an understanding and cooperate with the National Socialists, in order to be able to participate in a practical way in the reshaping of the future.

---

[45] Significantly this sentence was omitted from the report of the speech in the *Völkischer Beobachter* and most other publications.
[46] The Catholic party in Italy.

Certainly all this can be said. But what if this attempt fails? What if the National Socialist wave, true to its basic ideological beliefs, wants to engulf our Catholic organisations, our Catholic youth clubs etc., as in Italy? Will not people then say that it was the fault of the Centre for giving the Hitler Government a blank cheque for four years? Will not the Centre be so discredited with its followers that it will lose all influence on them and be unable to achieve anything?

Then again, can it be morally and politically justifiable to grant the Government, whose instincts are so completely different from what we stand for, such far-reaching, unique authority? The Centre has always been the party of the law, of the Constitution, and also of freedom. What has now happened has nothing to do with law, freedom, and the Constitution. It is true that parliamentarism and with it the democratic idea have come to a dead end. Brüning tried up to the last minute to save parliamentarism as it was part of the Constitution; but in vain. It is Hugenberg's fault. But it has really proved impossible. So was it justified to try a new way? Certainly, Hitler has inserted several points in his speech which meet our wishes, to a far greater extent than would have been thought possible, and give us a certain security. But will he be able to stick to this line since many of his colleagues—Hugenberg, Göring—are strongly opposed to Catholicism?

In any case: as in 1919 we climbed calmly and deliberately into the Social Democrat boat, so, in the same way, we were able to enter the boat of the National Socialists in 1933 and to try to lend a hand with the steering. Between 1919 and 1933 this proved quite satisfactory: the Social Democrats, since they were not able to govern without the Centre, were unable to do anything particularly antireligious or dubiously socialistic. Will it be possible to exercise a similarly sobering influence on the National Socialists now?

Quod Deus bene vertat![47] It would indeed be a great thing, and if it turns out like that, everyone in our party will praise the present attitude of the parliamentary group. Just as after 1919, when the association with the Social Democrats saved us from Bolshevism. It is enough if cooperation with the National Socialists can protect us against Communists, Bolshevism and anarchy! The latter is very important now. One may say: *Prius vivere, deinde philosophari.*[48] First remove the danger of Communism; then everything will sort itself out.

In short: in this question too there is no obvious solution. As so often in politics. And in life too! The risk is great, but if one had not run it the danger would have been even greater.

Ergo: for the time being we go along with the new direction of the Centre. Whether it is right nobody can say yet. *Qui vivra, verra!*[49] All splits are dangerous now. As they were before.

Hitler's Reichstag speech had satisfied not only lay Catholics but also the Church authorities, above all concerned to protect their various organisa-tions, as the Fulda Conference of Bishops stated on 28 March 1933:

---

[47]'May God turn this to good effect!'
[48]'Live first, then philosophise.'
[49]'He who lives will see!'

106

During the last few years, the Bishops of the German dioceses, in their dutiful concern for the party of the Catholic faith and the protection of the tasks and rights of the Catholic Church, have adopted, for good reasons, towards the National Socialist movement a negative attitude, expressed through prohibitions and warnings, which were to remain in force for as long as and as far as those reasons remained valid.

It must now be recognised that public and solemn declarations have been issued by the highest representative of the Reich Government, who is simultaneously the authoritarian leader of that movement, which acknowledge the inviolability of the teachings of the Catholic faith and the immutable tasks and rights of the Church. Similarly, the full validity of the treaties concluded between the various German states and the Church is guaranteed.

Without revoking the condemnation contained in our previous statements of certain religious and ethical errors, the Episcopate nevertheless believes it can cherish the hope that those general warnings and prohibitions need no longer be regarded as necessary.

Catholic Christians, for whom the opinion of their Church is sacred, need no particular admonition to be loyal to the legally constituted authorities, to fulfil their civic duties conscientiously, and to reject absolutely any illegal or revolutionary activity.

The admonition which has so often been solemnly addressed to all Catholics, namely to stand up for peace and the social welfare of the nation, for the protection of Christian religion and morality, for the freedom and rights of the Catholic Church and the protection of the denominational school and the Catholic youth organisations, is still valid...

Only the SPD voted against the Bill. The courage this required can be judged from the following account of the atmosphere of the debate by a Bavarian SPD deputy:

107

...The wide square in front of the Kroll Opera House was crowded with dark masses of people. We were received with wild choruses: 'We want the Enabling Act!' Youths with swastikas on their chests eyed us insolently, blocked our way, in fact made us run the gauntlet, calling us names like 'Centre pig', 'Marxist sow'. The Kroll Opera House was crawling with armed SA and SS men. In the cloakroom we learned that Severing[50] had been arrested on entering the building. The assembly hall was decorated with swastikas and similar ornaments. The diplomats' boxes and the rows of seats for the audience were overcrowded. When we Social Democrats had taken our seats on the extreme left, SA and SS men lined up at the exits and

---

[50]An SPD Party leader and former Prussian Minister of the Interior.

along the walls behind us in a semicircle. Their expressions boded no good. Hitler read out his government declaration in a surprisingly calm voice. Only in a few places did he raise it to a fanatical frenzy: when he demanded the public execution of van der Lubbe and when, at the end of his speech, he uttered dark threats of what would happen if the Reichstag did not vote the Enabling Act he was demanding. I had not seen him for a long time. He did not resemble the ideal of the Germanic hero in any way. Instead of fair curls, a black strand of hair hung down over his sallow face. His voice gushed out of his throat in dark gurgling sounds. I have never understood how this speaker could carry away thousands of people with enthusiasm.

After the government declaration, there was an interval. The former Reich Chancellor, Dr Wirth, came over and said bitterly that in his group the only question had been whether they should also give Hitler the rope to hang them with. The majority of the Centre was willing to obey Monseigneur Dr Kaas and let Hitler have his Enabling Act. If they refused, they feared the outbreak of the Nazi revolution and bloody anarchy. Only a few, among them Dr Brüning, were against any concession to Hitler.

Otto Wels read out our reply to the government declaration. It was a masterpiece in form and content, a farewell to the fading epoch of human rights and humanity.[51] In concluding, Otto Wels, with his voice half choking, gave our good wishes to the persecuted and oppressed in the country who, though innocent, were already filling the prisons and concentration camps simply on account of their political creed.

This speech made a terrifying impression on all of us. Only a few hours before, we had heard that members of the SA had taken away the 45-year-old welfare worker, Maria Janovska of Köpenick, to a National Socialist barracks, stripped her completely, bound her on a table and flogged her body with leather whips. The female members of our group were in tears, some sobbed uncontrollably.

But Hitler jumped up furiously and launched into a passionate reply. When the Social Democrats were in power the National Socialists had been outlawed. Anyone who bowed down before an International could not criticise the National Socialists. If the National Socialists had not a sense of justice, the Social Democrats would not be here in the hall. But the National Socialists had resisted the temptation to turn against those who had tormented them for fourteen years. 'You are oversensitive, gentlemen, if you talk of persecution already. By God, the National Socialists would have had the courage to deal with the Social Democrats in a different way.... You, gentlemen, are no longer needed. I do not even want you to vote for the Enabling Act. Germany shall become free, but not throúgh you.'

There was no question of the National Socialists having been persecuted in the German Republic. On the contrary, the movement had frequently been furthered

---

[51]'At this historic hour, we German Social Democrats pledge ourselves to the principles of humanity and justice, of freedom and Socialism. No Enabling Law can give you the power to destroy ideas which are eternal and indestructible. You yourself have declared your commitment to Socialism. The Socialist Law [of 1878] did not succeed in destroying Social Democracy. From this new persecution too German Social Democracy can draw new strength. We send greetings to the persecuted and the oppressed. We greet our friends in the Reich. Their steadfastness and loyalty deserve admiration. The courage with which they maintain their convictions and their unbroken confidence guarantee a brighter future.'

by the State authorities. Only when its members broke the existing laws were they punished, in most cases very mildly. The Communists were made to feel the strong arm of the law in a very different way.

We tried to dam the flood of Hitler's unjust accusations with interruptions of 'No!', 'An error!', 'False!' But that did us no good. The SA and SS people, who surrounded us in a semicircle along the walls of the hall, hissed loudly and murmured: 'Shut up!', 'Traitors!', 'You'll be strung up today.'

The Enabling Law, passed by 444 votes to the 94 votes of the Social Democrats, was published on 24 March. It gave the destruction of parliamentary democracy an appearance of legality. This was important for the prestige of the regime abroad, among the middle class at home, and particularly with the Civil Service. The Reichstag became merely a sounding board for Hitler's major speeches. Only seven more laws were passed by the Reichstag. Moreover, despite the statement in Article 2 that 'the powers of the President remain unaffected', in fact the signature of the President was no longer necessary for legislation or decrees. Only three more presidential decrees were issued and they had already been prepared before the passage of the Enabling Law. From now onwards the legislation of the Third Reich took the form of 'government laws' and, increasingly, of Führer edicts (*Erlasse*).

108

The Reichstag has passed the following law, which is, with the approval of the Reichsrat,[52] herewith promulgated, after it has been established that it satisfies the requirements for legislation altering the Constitution.
Article 1. In addition to the procedure for the passage of legislation outlined in the Constitution, the Reich Cabinet is also authorised to enact Laws. This applies equally to the laws referred to in Article 85, paragraph 2, and Article 87 of the Constitution.[53] Article 2. The national laws enacted by the Reich Cabinet may deviate from the Constitution provided they do not affect the position of the Reichstag and the Reichsrat. The powers of the President remain unaffected.
Article 3. The national laws enacted by the Reich Cabinet shall be prepared by the Chancellor and published in the official gazette. They come into effect, unless otherwise specified, upon the day following their publication. Articles 68–77 of the Constitution[54] do not apply to the laws enacted by the Reich Cabinet.
Article 4. Treaties of the Reich with foreign states which concern matters of domestic legislation do not require the consent of the bodies participating in

---

[52]The upper house, containing the representatives of the federal states which had now all been coordinated.
[53]These concerned the authority of Parliament over taxation.
[54]These concerned the provisions for enacting new legislation.

legislation. The Reich Cabinet is empowered to issue the necessary provisions for the implementing of these treaties.
Article 5. This law comes into effect on the day of its publication. It ceases to be valid on 1 April 1937: it also ceases to be valid if the present Reich Cabinet is replaced by another.[55]

The demise of the political parties followed. Even the partners in the coalition, the Nationalists, came under increasing pressure, particularly since after the Enabling Law their votes were no longer necessary for legislation. Protests by their leader, Hugenberg, even at Cabinet level were treated with scarcely concealed contempt:

109

7 4 April 1933 (4.0 p.m.): Session of the Reich Cabinet
3. Outside the agenda: information from the Reich Minister of Economics, Food, and Agriculture (Dr Hugenberg):
   The Reich Minister of Economics, Food, and Agriculture pointed out that recently SA men had arrested chairmen and members of Chambers of Commerce who were listed members of the German National People's Party. These persons were removed from their positions in an unlawful way. He would no longer tolerate this state of affairs and urgently requested redress.
   Reich Minister Göring explained that frequently arrests had been made solely at the request of the competent public prosecutor. Moreover, it was urgently necessary to have new elections for the Chambers of Commerce and the Chambers of Farmers as soon as possible. The structure of the Chambers no longer accorded in any way with the present political situation. It was therefore impossible for Reich Minister Göring himself to hold back the SA.
   The Reich Minister of Economics, Food and Agriculture reported that he had already prepared the reorganisation of the provisional Reich Economic Council and that he also wished to order the dissolution of, and new elections for, the Chambers of Commerce and of Farmers. But he had to be allowed a little time to prepare all these things... .

After this Goebbels had good reason to note the following in his diary:

---

[55]In fact the Act was renewed in 1937 for a further four years and the second part of the clause, included to reassure the German Nationalists, was ignored after Hugenberg's resignation on 27 June 1933. This was facilitated by the fact that the pressure for Hugenberg's resignation had come from the Conservatives in the Cabinet led by Neurath, who had objected to his aggressive tactics at the World Economic Conference in London earlier in June.

110

22 April 1933
The Führer's authority is now completely in the ascendant in the Cabinet. There
will be no more voting. the Führer's personality decides. All this has been achieved
much more quickly than we had dared to hope... .

The anti-Nazi activities of SPD *émigrés* in Prague were used as an excuse
to ban the SPD officially on 22 June. By the end of June, the two Liberal
parties and the Nationalists recognised the inevitable and disbanded
themselves. Their membership had by now virtually disappeared, either to
join the Nazis or into what was termed 'inner emigration'.[56] They were
followed on 5 July by the most powerful non-Socialist opposition party, the
Catholic Centre.

The Centre had been still faced with the dilemma of whether or not to
cooperate with the Nazi regime. Many of its members had already been
swept away by the spirit of the 'national uprising' to which Catholics,
traditionally a minority group, could be particularly vulnerable as the
following pronouncement of the Catholic Teachers' Association of the
German Reich, 1 April 1933, indicates:

111

As in the August days of 1914, a feeling of national and German emotion has seized
our people. The *status quo* has been overthrown and new objectives have been set
for a new, developing German nation and a new German state. Regrettably, the
Catholic leadership and Catholic elements have been as little involved in this
change as they were in the foundation of Bismarck's Reich. Thanks to the warning
summons of Adolf Hitler and his movement, and to his work, we have succeeded in
breaking through the un-German spirit which prevailed in the revolution of 1918.

Now the whole German nation in all its various parts, including the Catholics,
has been summoned to cooperate and to build a new order. At this critical moment,
Catholicism must not once again stand aside, adopting a wait-and-see attitude. We
will lend a hand to help with the construction of a new Reich and a new nation,
putting our trust in the leader of the German and *völkisch* movement. If an appeal
is made to the natural and true impulses and groups of our historic nationality in its
totality, the Catholic element cannot be dispensed with. Over the past centuries, it
has become our destiny for the nature of the German character to grow out of
Catholicism and the national characteristics of the German race. After a period of
decline, we now have the duty of participating in the reorientation towards a rise
and a renaissance. We must—and here we agree completely with the leader of the
national movement—we must first become an internally unified nation of German

---

[56]i.e. while refraining from overt opposition to the regime, they witheld from it any
cooperation as far as possible, in an attempt to keep their hands clean.

men and women. We must put aside everthing which divides us and shake hands across the barriers which have hitherto been overemphasised, in order once more to become a nation which believes in honour, cleanliness, and loyalty. The essence of the practising Catholic population, as it has emerged in associations, status groups, and modes of life, is coming to the fore in order to consider what specific Catholic contribution can be made to the national task.

The dilemma facing the Centre was outlined at the time by Karl Bachem. His feeling of impotence in the face of the crisis and his sense of the inevitability of the Nazi take-over since they alone were sufficiently ruthless and determined stand out. Remarkable also is his belief that in the fight against Bolshevism there is 'no point in being fussy about legal subtleties'. The attitude revealed by this statement, made in the context of the Enabling Act and all that had happened since 30 January, helps explain the comparative ease with which the Nazis carried out their policy of 'coordination':

112

So the Centre has been formally dissolved. The Centre has been dissolved by its own resolution! It is said that Brüning was strongly against. But concern for the Catholic civil servants was decisive. Brüning had wanted to wait for the Government to dissolve the Centre, which in that case would not itself have borne any responsibility. The same with the Bavarian People's Party. All political activity in the spirit of the old Centre Party is from now on impossible and 'forbidden'. It has been quite openly declared that any further attempts at such activities will be crushed by brute force.

This is indeed a terrible fate, hardly conceivable for a party with such an honourable record of more than sixty years' achievement. One can do nothing but succumb patiently and meekly to this decision of Divine Providence; even if this time it seems hard, very hard. 'Quam incomprehensibilia sunt judicia ejus, et investigabiles viae ejus', as it says in the Epistle to the Romans.[57] No wonder that particularly the younger, lively members of the Party are terribly upset and use harsh words accusing Brüning, Kaas and all the other leaders of having helped to bring about the downfall of the party through their inactivity and cowardjce. But what in practical terms could Brüning and Kaas have done? Would it have been of any use to call on the Catholic population and the whole Centre Party to offer united resistance? Such resistance would have at once shown up the physical powerlessness of the party and would have been brutally suppressed; the leaders would have immediately been taken into 'protective custody', and thereby have been rendered harmless. The bishops having voted unanimously for the recognition of the new government, such resistance, no longer morally defensible, would have been impossible for us. There is nothing left to do but to follow the example of the

---

[57]Romans 11:33: 'How unsearchable are his judgments, and his ways past finding out!'

bishops and, in spite of everything, continue to try and remain concerned for the protection of our religious interests within the National Socialist Party and in cooperation with it. Nothing else is now possible. All our large organisations have been destroyed. Even the apprentices' associations have been deprived of their independence and coordinated with the 'National Socialist workers' front'. What will happen now no one can say. In the meantime, the future before us remains extremely black. In practice, we can do nothing but continue to try and work for our religious principles within the National Socialist Party and through quiet cooperation in its organisations. National Socialists, particularly Hitler, have often declared that they want 'positive Christianity' as the basis of the State, that they regard the Catholic as well as the Protestant Confessions as 'the most important factors for the preservation of our national character'. That is something, even if it is not yet clear what this 'positive Christianity' will be like and what its effects will be. So our people must now act as 'leaven', as the 'salt of the earth', in order to help the right principles to predominate... .

After describing the chronic state of crisis under the Weimar Republic he concludes:

In short, no more headway could be made with the democratic form of government; there could no longer be any illusions about this. Nor with the Centre's old principle of seeking an improvement in conditions only in a constitutional way, observing the regulations and the existing law. If the nation was not to sink into poverty and the life of the state be completely ruined, a different way had to be found to get out of this appalling situation. It was clear that if this was to be done it would not always be possible to observe the letter of the law... .

So one could only be grateful to the new men who, with determination, took into their hands the task of saving Germany. It really was not possible to go on any further without force, without using the principle of force, and since the Centre, because of its past, could not subscribe to this principle, it could not complain if it was pushed aside. Therefore, it is right to let the new men, particularly the leaders of the National Socialists, go ahead and not put unnecessary obstacles in their way. There are a lot of dubious things in the National Socialist movement, particularly so far as principles are concerned. But that has to be put up with for the time being. Today there is no point in being fussy about legal subtleties. What matters is first to let a strong, efficient government grow and then to support it wholeheartedly in order to suppress Bolshevism. It does seem as if Communism had already become so strong in Germany, so presumptuous, and so self-confident that it was high time to counter it with determination if it was not to result in a new Communist revolution and a terrible civil war.

But despite all this, it is hard for the Centre Party to disappear without trace after such long and honourable activity. In days to come they may say: It had fulfilled its task and could leave the stage of history. But has that task been fulfilled for the future as well? Who from now on will look after the interests of religion, the freedom and welfare of the Church? Are we not now dependent solely on the goodwill of the National Socialist Party? Will the Church keep its rights when no real political power exists to defend them? It is certain that even Catholics loyal to the Church will now join the National Socialist formations in great numbers, just as in Italy. But will their influence there become strong enough to check new animosities against the Catholic Church, especially attacks on our Catholic denominational schools and the schools of our orders etc.? There is to be a concordat with the Vatican. If the Pope concludes it, he will take the vital interests of the Church into account. But will such a Concordat remain permanently valid if there is no political power to support its validity? It is different in Italy. The whole country is Catholic and even the Liberals think of Catholicism as part of the national greatness. In Germany, on the other hand, denominational divisions go deep, and anything that has seemed to favour the Catholic Church has always been offensive to the Protestant section of the people. At the moment there is no evidence of any particularly hostile Protestant agitation against Catholicism. The Protestant Association has obviously lost much of its impetus. But will that remain so? Who knows?...

In fact, the position of the Centre had been further undermined by the negotiations between the Government, the Catholic hierarchy in Germany, and the Vatican over a Concordat. The Catholic authorities proved willing to abandon their political party in return for a Concordat guaranteeing their religious activities. Hitler, however, had no doubt that in the Concordat signed on 8 July 1933 he had a bargain as he told the Cabinet on 14 July 1933:

113

...The Reich Chancellor saw three great advantages in the conclusion of the Reich Concordat:

1. that the Vatican had negotiated at all, considering that they operated, especially in Austria, on the assumption that National Socialism was un-Christian and inimical to the Church;

2. that the Vatican should have been persuaded to bring about good relations with this purely national German State. He, the Reich Chancellor, would even a short time ago have thought it impossible that the Church would be willing to commit the bishops to the support of this State. The fact that this had now been done was certainly an unreserved recognition of the present regime;

3. that, with the Concordat, the Church should have withdrawn from activity in associations and parties, and, for instance, have abandoned even the Christian labour unions. This also he, the Reich Chancellor, would, even a few months ago, have thought impossible. Even the dissolution of the Centre could be termed final only with the conclusion of the Concordat, now that the Vatican had ordered the permanent exclusion of the clergy from party politics.

That the objective which he, the Reich Chancellor, had always been striving for, namely an agreement with the Curia, had been attained so much faster than he had imagined even on 30 January—this was such an indescribable success that, in the face of it, all critical misgivings should be withdrawn.

After all the parties had dissolved themselves, the one-Party State was formally proclaimed by the Law against the Establishment of Parties, 14 July 1933.

114

Art I. The National Socialist German Workers' Party constitutes the only political party in Germany.

Art II. Whoever undertakes to maintain the organisation of another political party or to form a new political party shall be punished with penal servitude of up to three years or with imprisonment of between six months and three years, unless the act is subject to a heavier penalty under other regulations.

(iv) The Revolution Stabilised: Conflict with the SA

Meanwhile, the SA was becoming dissatisfied with the compromises the regime had made with established institutions. It contained a large number of impoverished members of the lower middle class and a number of unemployed. Some were hostile to the Establishment, taking seriously the anti-capitalist aspects of the Party programme. The majority simply felt disgruntled at their failure to turn the Nazi take-over into the kind of concrete material benefits for themselves which they had anticipated. In fact, the Government went some way towards conciliating the Party rank and file by insisting that old Party fighters have priority in employment, a measure which led to some SA men acquiring jobs.

Nevertheless, the leader of the SA, Ernst Röhm, at least was not conciliated and in a newspaper article in June 1933 he expressed disillusionment at the inadequate fruits of the seizure of power and determination to continue the revolution:

115

...A tremendous victory has been won. But not *absolute* victory!

The new State did not have to disown the bearers of the will to revolution as the November men[58] had to with the red hordes who were the followers of their revolution, born of cowardice and high treason. In the new Germany the disciplined brown storm battalions of the German revolution stand side by side with the armed forces.

---

[58]i.e. the Social Democrats.

Not as part of them.

The Reichswehr has its own undisputed task: it is committed to defend the borders of the Reich, so far as its small numbers and completely inadequate armament enables it to do so.

The police have to keep down the law-breakers.

Beside these stand the SA and the SS as the third power factor of the new State with special tasks.

The Leader and Chancellor of the German people needs them for the tremendous work of German revival which still lies before him.

For the SA and the SS are the foundation pillars of the coming National Socialist State—*Their* State for which they have fought and which they will defend. The SA and SS are militant-spiritual [*kämpferisch-geistig*] bearers of the will of the German revolution.

Already here and there philistines and grumblers are daring to ask in astonishment what the SA and SS are still there for, since Hitler is now in power. We are after all, they point out, nationalist again. Swastika flags fly over the streets. There is law and order everywhere. And if it is disturbed, the police will take care that it is restored as quickly as possible. So why the SA and SS?

The philistines and grumblers, whether they stand in the ranks of our eternal and irreconcilable adversaries, or are 'coordinated', or even wear the swastika, have not understood the meaning of the German revolution and never will understand it.

The course of events between 30 January and 21 March 1933 does not represent the sense and meaning of the German National Socialist revolution.

Anyone who wanted to be a fellow-traveller only during shining torchlight processions and impressive parades with rumbling drums and booming kettledrums, with blaring trumpets and under waving flags, and now believes he has 'taken part' in the German revolution—can go home! He has confused the 'national uprising' with the German revolution! He has intoxicated himself with outward appearances; perhaps he has got carried away by the unheard-of mood of 'Potsdam Day', perhaps he was delighted to see millions and millions of workers march for Germany at the Festival of German Labour,[59] and for a few hours felt a breath of our spirit—*but he is not one of us*!! For the coming years of struggle he can creep back to the hearth or the desk or the pub from whence he came. The fighters in the simple brown service shirt of the SA and SS will not miss him on their path forwards to the German revolution, just as they did not meet him when, in long years marked by sacrifices and blood, they fought their passionate fight for a new Germany.

...The SA and SS will not tolerate the German revolution going to sleep or being betrayed at the half-way stage by non-combatants. Not for their own sake, but for Germany's sake. For the brown army is the last levy of the nation, the last bastion against Communism.

If the German revolution is wrecked by reactionary opposition, incompetence, or indolence, the German people will fall into despair and will be an easy prey for the bloodstained frenzy coming from the depths of Asia.

For this reason the fantasy in the minds of some 'coordinated' people and even some low-level dignitaries calling themselves National Socialists, that to keep calm

[59]On 1 May 1933, see below, pp. 423-4.

is the first duty of a citizen, is a betrayal of the German revolution.
The people who are now everywhere 'involved' and murmur—still softly as
yet—their upright-bourgeois little maxim of 'law and order' were nowhere to be
seen during our long pilgrimage in search of the new Germany for which we longed.
At the most they stood aside and looked on as we fought and bled for Germany.
We were too undistinguished for them, too loud, too radical. We still are, as far as
they are concerned. It is enough for them that the black-white-and-red colours of
the Bismarck empire are flying over Germany and, as a concession to the
revolution, the swastika flag. For them the degree of outward power so far
acquired, in which they are allowed a share, is enough. They would have even been
contented with considerably less, because they did not have to struggle; they were
only the beneficiaries of our victory.
    ...If those bourgeois simpletons think it is enough that the State apparatus has
received a new sign, that the 'national' revolution has already lasted too long, for
once we agree with them. It is in fact high time the national revolution stopped and
became the National Socialist one. Whether they like it or not, we will continue our
struggle—if they understand at last what it is about—*with* them; if they are
unwilling—*without* them; and if necessary—*against* them!

The SA were not alone at fault. All sections of the Party were guilty of
arbitrary interference both in the State administration and in the business
community, as the following account by an unusually responsible SA
leader indicates:

116

The authority of the State is in danger through constant unjustified interference by
political officials in the machinery of normal administration.
    Every NSBO[60] functionary, NSBO local branch leader, NSBO district leader...,
every political cell leader, political local branch leader, political district leader is
giving orders which interfere with the exercise of the authority of the ministries at
the lower levels, that is to say, the authority of the regional governments, the
district offices, down to the smallest police station.
    Everyone is arresting everyone else, avoiding the prescribed official channels,
everyone is threatening everyone else with protective custody, everyone is threatening everyone else with Dachau.[61]
    Businesses are being forced to dismiss any number of employees, and businesses
are being compelled to take on employees without checking on their
qualifications... .
    Right down to the smallest police station, the best and most reliable officials have
become uncertain about the hierarchy of authority; this clearly must have a
devastating and destructive effect on the State.

---

[60]*Nationalsozialistische Betriebszellenorganisation*: the National Socialist Factory Cell Organisation.
[61]The notorious concentration camp near Munich.

I really cannot be counted among the pussyfooters, and for that very reason I must see that if the revolution is to be turned into an ordered relationship between State and people, the State apparatus must be made completely safe from all revolutionary interference from the street.

It must be left to the responsibility of the State ministries alone, both in the spheres of policy and of personnel, to embody revolutionary ideas in a form which is suitable to the community... .

Every little street cleaner today feels he is responsible for matters which he has never understood... .

No one can dispute that fact that, at the moment, two-thirds of the daily work in my area, and in all other areas I know, has to be wasted on trifles arising from Party officials' lack of discipline... .

The leadership principle is in grave danger from these conditions.... I do not mind if my giving this warning makes me appear a grumbler. I can only state that these present circumstances must inevitably lead to chaos.

Hitler had little sympathy for the disillusionment of the SA. He was concerned lest constant interference by the Party and the SA at the lower levels might alienate important groups such as the Army, industry, and the Civil Service. It could jeopardise economic recovery and so prevent the regime from gaining the popular support it needed. It could delay his main objective of mobilising the economic resources and will of the nation for diplomatic and strategic purposes. For this a period of stability was essential. On 6 July 1933, therefore, in a speech to the Reich Governors (*Reichsstatthalter*), he formally ended the revolution which, he insisted, must from now on take the form of evolution. This did not mean that there were to be no more fundamental changes but that such changes must in future be initiated from above and not from below, and that tactical compromises would be necessary to ensure the stability of the regime:

117

The political parties have now been finally abolished. This is an historic event, the meaning and significance of which many people have not yet understood. We must now abolish the last remnants of democracy, especially the methods of election and the majority decisions still employed today in local government, in economic organisations and works committees, and the responsibility of the individual must be stressed.

The achievement of outward power must be followed by the inward education of man. We must beware of making doctrinaire decisions from one day to the next and of expecting a final solution from them. People are easily capable of bending outward form to suit their own intellectual stamp. The switch-over must not be made until suitable people have been found to carry out the switching. More revolutions have succeeded in their first assault than, once successful, have been brought to a standstill and held there. Revolution is not a permanent state, it must

not develop into a lasting state. The full spate of revolution must be guided into the
secure bed of evolution. In this the most important part is played by the education
of the people. The present state of affairs must be improved and the people
embodying it must be educated in the National Socialist conception of the State. A
businessman must not therefore be dismissed if he is a good businessman even if he
is not yet a good National Socialist; especially not if the National Socialist put in his
place knows nothing about business. In business, ability alone must be decisive.
The task of National Socialism is the safeguarding of the development of our
people. But we must not keep looking round to see what next to revolutionise;
rather we have the task of securing one position after another in order to hold
them, and occupy them gradually in model fashion. In this we must gear our actions
to a period of many years, and plan in terms of long periods of time. We do not
provide bread for any worker by theoretically coordinating people. History will not
judge us by the number of businessmen we dismissed or locked up, but by whether
we knew how to provide work. Today we have the absolute power to succeed. But
we must be able to replace those we dismiss by their betters. The businessman must
be judged first on his business abilities; we must keep the economic apparatus in
order. We shall not abolish unemployment with economic commissions, or with
theories and blueprints of organisations. The main thing now is not programmes
and ideas but the daily bread of five million people. The economy is a living
organism which cannot be changed at a blow; it is constructed according to
primitive laws bound up with human nature. The carriers of intellectual poison now
seeking to penetrate the economy are a menace to both State and people. Practical
experience must not be rejected simply because it is opposed to a particular idea.
    In confronting the nation with reforms, we must show that we understand things
and can cope with them. Our task is work, work, and again work! Our success in
providing work will be our most powerful source of authority. Our programme is
not a matter of fine gestures, but of maintaining the life of the German people.
    The ideas of the programme do not demand that we act like fools and overturn
everything, but that we realise our concepts wisely and carefully. In the long run,
the more successful the economic underpinning of our programme, the more secure
will be our political power. Reich Governors must ensure, and are responsible for
seeing, that no organisations or party authorities shall claim governmental rights,
dismiss people, or fill offices for which only the Reich Government and, in the field
of economics, only the Reich Minister of Econmics is responsible.
    The Party has now become the State. All power comes under the authority of the
Reich. The emphasis of German life must be prevented from shifting back into
particular areas or even organisations. No longer does authority stem from any part
of the Reich but only from the concept of the Germans as a nation.

This statement, however, had only a limited effect on the Party activists,
and above all, on the SA men, who felt disgruntled at the fact that the Nazi
take-over had made so little difference to their lives, apart from giving
them the satisfaction of revenge on their political opponents. This is clear
from the fact that only three months later on 6 October 1934 Frick felt
obliged to send out the following circular:

118

Despite repeated announcements by the Reich Chancellor and despite my numerous circulars new infringements by subordinate leaders and members of the SA
have been reported again and again during the past weeks. Above all, SA leaders
and SA men have independently carried out police actions either for which they
had no authority whatever or which they carried out in a way that cannot be
reconciled with the existing laws and regulations of the National Socialist Government. In this way even the extra-territorial status of the ambassador of a foreign
power has recently been seriously violated by unauthorised SA men, thereby
involving the foreign policy of the Government.

These infringements and excesses must now cease once and for all. I make it the
duty of Reich Governors, State Governments and all subordinate institutions to
intervene sharply against such infringements or any attempt at unauthorised
interference. Unless members of the SA are employed as auxiliary police officers or
as auxiliary officials in the frontier service by the proper authorities, they have no
police jurisdiction whatsoever. In future, therefore, all police activities of the SA in
all circumstances must cease. Where it becomes necessary in exceptional circumstances to employ members of the SA to assist the police in particular actions, they
must never act independently but only in the *presence* and *under the supervision* of
the police and only in accordance with the orders of the police officer. The leader of
the police force carries full responsibility for the employment and the conduct of
such auxiliary SA men. Furthermore, auxiliary police officers and auxiliary border
customs officers are not to carry out their work except in the company of an *official*.
Only if these orders are minutely observed can *agents provocateurs* be effectively
prevented from damaging the SA and the National Socialist State...

During the autumn and winter of 1933, the SA was becoming more and
more a law unto itself. In addition to the interference of the SA commissars
in the Government offices at various levels, the SA was also intervening in
the judicial process, forcing the prosecuting authorities to drop charges
against SA men and successfully asserting its right to discipline SA men
who broke the law. It had even established its own police force, the
Feldjäger, who claimed sole jurisdiction in matters involving the SA. The
monthly reports prepared by the Gestapo on the political and economic
situation referred to the discontent of the population at the undisciplined
behaviour of the SA and their concern at the obvious inability of the
authorities to do anything about it.

This resentment was not restricted to the State authorities, including the
Gestapo, or the population at large; it was even shared to some extent by
the Party authorities. The SA did not disguise its contempt for the political
leadership at local and district level. According to the Gestapo, the SA
men mocked the local Party officials as 'Christmas tree men' and 'Lametta
stallions' because of their uniforms which the SA felt were undeserved by
these Party bureaucrats. 'Political earthworms' was another current
epithet.

But much more serious from Hitler's point of view were the military ambitions of the SA. Apart from its rather vague social revolutionary aims, the SA under Röhm had a more concrete objective: it aspired to become *the* armed force of the State into which the Regular Army would be integrated. To this plan the Army leadership was totally opposed. Under the new Minister of Defence, General von Blomberg, who was a pro-Nazi, the Army had adopted a benevolent attitude towards the new regime. This was also partly dictated by the belief in the need to win Hitler's support in resisting the ambitions of the SA—a good instance of the way in which Hitler could use the Nazi organisations to put pressure on other bodies so that in effect they 'coordinated' themselves.

But by the beginning of 1934, the Army authorities were becoming increasingly concerned about the military ambitions of the SA, which by absorbing other paramilitary organisations had grown to over 2,500,000 men compared with the 100,000 or slightly more of the Army. Hitler could not afford to antagonise the Army, the one organisation which had the power to remove him from office. An efficient and contented Army was also essential if he was to achieve the aims of his foreign policy. The riff-raff of the SA would be no substitute.

At a conference on 28 February 1934, attended by the Army, SA and SS leaders, Hitler rejected Röhm's idea of a militia. He made Blomberg and Röhm sign an agreement by which the SA would be responsible for pre- and post-military training under the direction of the Army. Two days later, Blomberg drew Hitler's attention to an instance of the growing military activity of the SA, particularly serious as it involved the region demilitarised by the Versailles Treaty. This could cause diplomatic complications which would in turn complicate the process of rearmament:

119

I feel obliged to refer again to the significance of the armed staff guards of the SA. According to an order of the Chief of Staff [of the SA] every *Obergruppe* and group is to set up its own armed staff guards with a heavy machine gun company. This has already begun in certain areas. According to a report by the Commander of Military District VI, leaders of SA brigades are planning the formation of such a staff guard as well and are swearing in SA people for 1–1½ years for that purpose. Selection and training are being carried out with the aim of appearing in public. In terms of numbers this would amount to 6000–8000 men permanently armed with guns and machine guns in that military district alone. It is particularly unfortunate that the formation of these staff guards is taking place in connexion with so-called SA auxiliary labour camps which are mostly situated in the big cities. Today I received a report that a staff guard armed like this is being formed in Höchst am Main, that is to say, in the neutral zone...

Tension between the Army and the SA continued to build up in the early summer. But on 7 June, following a long interview with Hitler, Röhm published the following announcement. Though it showed distinct signs of belligerence, it nevertheless seems to indicate that, despite Hitler's later allegations, Röhm had no plans for a putsch during this period.

120

I have decided to follow the advice of my doctors and take a cure in order to restore my energies which have been severely strained by a painful nervous complaint. My place will be taken by the Chief of the Leadership Office, Obergruppenführer von Krausser.

1934 will require all the energies of every SA fighter. I recommend, therefore, to all SA leaders to begin organising leave already in June.

Therefore, for a limited number of SA leaders and men, June, and for the majority of the SA, July, will be a period of complete relaxation in which they can recover their strength.

I expect the SA to return on 1 August completely rested and refreshed in order to serve in those honourable capacities which nation and fatherland expect of it. If the enemies of the SA live in hope that the SA will not return, or will return only in part, from its leave, we will allow them this brief pleasurable anticipation. They will receive the appropriate reply at the time and in the manner appearing most suitable.

The SA is and remains Germany's destiny.

During June, the crisis was deepened by two further developments. It became clear the Reich President, Hindenburg, had not long to live, which raised the matter of the succession. If Hitler wished to combine the offices of Chancellor and President and avoid a new Conservative President being imposed on him, he would need the approval of the Army.

Secondly, Papen became the spokesman of conservative circles in the bureaucracy and business who were discontented at the excesses of the SA and concerned about talk of a second revolution. On 17 June, Papen articulated this discontent in a speech at the University of Marburg, the reporting of which Goebbels promptly banned:

121

...It is certainly obvious that the bearers of the revolutionary principle should initially occupy also the positions of power. But once the revolution has taken place, the Government must represent the people as a whole, and must on no account be the exponent only of particular groups; otherwise it would fail in its attempt to construct the national community. We must also get away from false romantic notions which are not appropriate to the twentieth century. We cannot, for example, consider dividing the nation after the manner of the ancient Greeks into Spartans and helots. The final outcome of that development was that the Spartans had to concentrate on repressing the helots, thereby weakening the diplomatic strength of Sparta. In a state where there is a true national community, the domestic political war-cries must finally cease. There must certainly be a process of selection. But the natural criterion for the selection of people for appointments cannot be replaced by that of membership of a particular organisation, so long as the motives for such membership cannot be analysed... .

I have defined the problems of the German revolution and my attitude towards them particularly sharply because there appears to be endless talk of a second wave which will complete the revolution. Anyone who irresponsibly toys with such ideas should not deceive himself about the fact that a second wave can easily be followed by a third, that he who threatens the guillotine is the first to come under the knife. Nor is it clear in what direction this second wave is meant to lead. It is true that there is much talk about future socialisation. Have we experienced an anti-Marxist revolution in order to carry out the programme of Marxism? For any attempt to solve the social question by collectivising property is Marxism. Will the German people become richer, will its national income grow bigger, will anybody be better off, except possibly those who smell the possibility of plunder in such a raid? There is certainly a social problem caused by economic and demographic processes. But these can be mastered only if property is once more made aware of its responsibilities, not by raising collective irresponsibility to a principle. A form of economic planning which moves further and further away from personal initiative and responsibility must not be made into a principle. For anyone who has not observed that every form of collectivism leads to ineradicable corruption has been going about the world with his eyes shut.

No nation that would survive before history can afford a permanent uprising from below. At some stage the movement must come to an end; at some point there must emerge a firm social structure held together by a legal system secure against pressure and by a State power that is unchallenged. A ceaseless dynamic creates nothing. Germany cannot be allowed to become a train hurtling into the blue with no one knowing where it will stop. History flows of its own accord, it does not need to be constantly driven forward. If, therefore, a second wave of new life is to sweep through the German revolution, then it must do so not as social revolution, but as the creative completion of work already begun. The statesman is there to create forms, his sole concern is for State and people. The State is the sole power and the final guarantee of that which every citizen can claim—iron justice. In the long run, therefore, the State cannot tolerate any dualism, and the success of the German revolution and the future of our nation will depend on the discovery of a satisfactory solution for the dualism between Party and State.

The Government is well aware of the selfishness, the lack of principle, the insincerity, the unchivalrous behaviour, the arrogance which is on the increase under the guise of the German revolution. Nor has it any illusions as to the threat to that reserve of public confidence on which the Government can draw. If it is desired to achieve an intimate and friendly relationship with the people, then their intelligence must not be underestimated, their trust must be reciprocated and there must be no continual attempt to browbeat them. The German people recognise the gravity of the situation, they feel the economic crisis, they have a keen awareness of the weak points in some of the laws that this crisis has produced, they are acutely sensitive to violence and injustice, clumsy attempts at deceiving them with false optimism merely make them smile. In the long run, no organisation, no propaganda, however good, can alone retain their confidence. My interpretation, therefore, of the propaganda campaign against 'carpers' is different from that of others.[62] Confidence and willingness to cooperate will not be furthered by incitement, particularly incitement of the young, nor by threats against the defenceless classes of the community, but only by discussion based upon mutual confidence. The people know that great sacrifices are expected of them. They will shoulder them and follow the Führer with unshakeable loyalty, provided they are allowed to have a share in the making and carrying out of decisions, provided every word of criticism is not immediately interpreted as malicious, and provided that despairing patriots are not branded as traitors.

It is time to come together in brotherly love and respect for every citizen, to cease obstructing the work of those who are in earnest, and to silence doctrinaire fanatics... .

There was clearly a danger that the Army would combine with the conservative elements in the bureaucracy and business to veto Hitler's succession to Hindenburg, either by persuading Hindenburg before he died to nominate someone else, or by carrying out a *coup* on his death. Hitler might be able to counter such a *coup* with the aid of the SA, but this would make him prisoner of the SA, force him into a revolution, thereby jeopardising all his diplomatic and military objectives, to which the collaboration of business and the professional Army were essential. A period of peace and quiet was needed in order to restore the economic situation dominated by a foreign exchange crisis, and to avoid diplomatic complications in view of the weakness of Germany's diplomatic situation in 1934. All this was threatened by the SA with its demands for a second revolution, its ambition to usurp the role of the Army, and its flagrant contempt for the disarmament provisions of the Versailles Treaty. The SA, which had been very helpful in the acquisition of power, was now a grave embarrassment under the leadership of the ambitious Röhm and his associates.

In the meantime, another organisation had come to play an independent role in the crisis—the SS. During 1933–34, Himmler, the head of the SS, had taken over the political police departments in every state in the Reich, including the Prussian Gestapo. Nominally, the SS was still a part of the SA, and the SA with its huge membership and ambitious leadership was now the main obstacle to the ambitions of the SS. The SS therefore began

---

[62]On 11 May, Goebbels had launched a campaign against 'grumblers and carpers', aimed primarily at Conservatives.

to warn Hitler and the Army of the intentions of the SA. These rumours prompted the Army to take action which antagonised the SA and this in turn gave rise to more suspicion on the part of Hitler and the Army. This encouragement by the SS of mutual suspicion between Army and SA was described after the war by Field-Marshal von Kleist, from whose testimony it appears that General Reichenau, the right-hand man of Blomberg, the Minister of Defence, was also involved:

122

Round about 24 June 1934, I as the army commander in Silesia was warned by the Chief of the General Staff [*Heeresleitung*] that an attack by the SA on the Army was imminent and that I should unobtrusively keep my troops on the alert.

During the tense days following, I received a flood of reports and information which gave a picture of feverish preparations on the part of the SA. This information came from the most varied sources (the troops, the SA, old Stahlhelm types, SS, civilians and government authorities). Despite the very reserved attitude adopted by the troops, a dangerous state of tension developed in the garrisons between them and the local SA. Only a spark was needed to touch off the explosion.

In this situation, I considered that bloodshed could only be avoided by a man-to-man talk.

On the afternoon of 28 June, therefore, I asked SA Obergruppenführer Heines[63] to come and see me; I told him to his face that I knew of his preparations and I gave him a warning.

He replied that he knew all about my measures and had thought that they were preparations for an attack on the SA. He had only put the SA on the alert in order to resist an attack. He gave me his word as an officer and SA leader that he had not planned or prepared any surprise attack upon the Army.

During the night of 28–29 June, he rang me up again. He said more or less that as far as he was concerned the situation had changed. He had just learned that not only the Army in Silesia, but from 28 June the Army throughout the Reich, was on the alert for an SA putsch. He was going to fly to Munich early on the 29th to see Röhm. Whereupon I also flew on 29 June to Berlin and reported to Colonel-General Freiherr von Fritsch and General Beck about my conversation with Heines. I added: 'I have the impression that we—Army and SA—are being egged on against each other by a third party.' By that I meant Himmler and that much of the information came from him. Thereupon, Colonel-General Freiherr von Fritsch summoned General von Reichenau and asked me to repeat to him what I had just said. Reichenau replied, 'That may be true, but it's too late now.'

As tension built, Hitler decided to act. On 29 June he summoned a meeting of SA leaders for the following day at Wiessee in Bavaria. The Army and

---

[63]Police-President of Breslau.

SS were put on the alert and Göring was given the responsibility of carrying out the action in Berlin. Then, on learning that the SA in Munich had been put on the alert, Hitler flew to Munich in the early hours of the 30th. After the war, Kempka, his chauffeur, described the events of 30 June:

123

...It is already dawn when we land at the Munich airport, Oberwiesenfeld. During the flight, there had been a light shower and the grass at the airport is sparkling in the morning light. When Hitler jumps out of the machine, two officers of the Reichswehr report to him. He takes them aside and gives them their orders.

Outside the reception building three cars are waiting which have been ordered by wireless from the garage of the Reich Party headquarters in Munich. Some old friends of Hitler's from the early days of the Party are standing by them. Hitler goes up to the cars and orders the hoods to be raised. I am struck by the harshness of his voice. His face is even more serious than during the flight. I am already at the wheel when he sits down beside me: 'Kempka, we're going to the Ministry of the Interior first.'...

[At the Ministry Hitler arrested the Police-President of Munich, SA Obergruppenführer August Schneidhuber.]

Hitler sits down beside me and gives the order: 'To Wiessee, as fast as possible!' It must have been about 4.30 a.m., the sky has cleared up, it is nearly bright daylight. We meet watering carts and people on their way to work....Hitler sits beside me in silence. From time to time, I hear Goebbels and Lutze talking in the back.

Just before Wiessee, Hitler suddenly breaks his silence: 'Kempka,' he says, 'drive carefully when we come to the Hotel Hanselbauer. You must drive up without making any noise. If you see an SA guard in the front of the hotel, don't wait for them to report to me; drive on and stop at the hotel entrance.' Then, after a moment of deathly silence: 'Röhm wants to carry out a *coup*.'

An icy shiver runs down my back. I could have believed anything, but not a *coup* by Röhm!

I drive up carefully to the hotel entrance as Hitler had ordered. Hitler jumps out of the car, and after him Goebbels, Lutze and the adjutants. Right behind us another car stops with a squad of detectives which had been raised in Munich.

As soon as I have turned the car so that it is ready to leave in a moment, I rush into the hotel with my gun at the ready. In the hall I meet Standartenführer Uhl, the leader of Röhm's staff guard. Hitler's chauffeur, Schreck, is taking him at gunpoint down to the laundry room which for the next hour serves as the first prison for the arrested SA leaders. In passing, Schreck calls out to me: 'Quickly! Run up to the boss! He needs you!'

I run quickly up the stairs to the first floor where Hitler is just coming out of Röhm's bedroom. Two detectives come out of the room opposite. One of them reports to Hitler: 'My Führer...the Police-President of Breslau is refusing to get dressed!'

Taking no notice of me, Hitler enters the room where Obergruppenführer Heines is remaining. I hear him shout: 'Heines, if you are not dressed in five minutes I'll have you shot on the spot!'

I withdraw a few steps and a police officer whispers to me that Heines had been in bed with an 18-year-old SA Obertruppführer. At last Heines comes out of the room with an 18-year-old fair-haired boy mincing in front of him.

'Into the laundry room with them!' cries Schreck.

Meanwhile, Röhm comes out of his room in a blue suit and with a cigar in the corner of his mouth. Hitler glares at him but says nothing. Two detectives take Röhm to the vestibule of the hotel where he throws himself into an armchair and orders coffee from the waiter.

I stay in the corridor a little to one side and a detective tells me about Röhm's arrest.

Hitler entered Röhm's bedroom alone with a whip in his hand. Behind him were two detectives with pistols at the ready. He spat out the words: 'Röhm, you are under arrest.' Röhm looked up sleepily from his pillow: 'Heil, my Führer.' 'You are under arrest' bawled Hitler for the second time, turned on his heel and left the room.

Meanwhile, upstairs in the corridor things are getting quite lively. SA leaders are coming out of their rooms and being arrested. Hitler shouts at each one: 'Have you had anything to do with Röhm's schemes?' naturally, they all deny it, but that doesn't help them in the least. Hitler usually knows about the individual; occasionally, he asks Goebbels or Lutze a question. And then comes the decision: 'Arrested!'

But there are others whom he lets go. Röhm's doctor SA Gruppenführer Ketterer comes out of a room and to our surprise he has his wife with him. I hear Lutze putting in a good word for him with Hitler. Then Hitler walks up to him, greets him, shakes hands with his wife and asks them to leave the hotel; it isn't a pleasant place for them to stay in, that day.

We follow Hitler into the yard and here he tells his chauffeur, Schreck, to charter a bus as quickly as possible to take the SA leaders who are in the laundry room to Munich. How slowly the minutes pass! More and more SA leaders arrive from outside and are brought into the laundry room. I stand at the hotel entrance and hear Röhm order coffee from the hotel manager for the third time.

Suddenly...there is the sound of a car arriving! At first I thought it was the bus chartered by Schreck but instead, to my horror, a lorry full of heavily armed SA men rattles into the yard. Now there'll be some shooting, I think to myself. I can see Brückner negotiating with the Sturmführer of the SA. The man seems to be refusing. Walking backwards, he tries to get to his lorry....At this moment Hitler goes up to him: 'Drive back to Munich immediately!' he tells the puzzled fellow. 'If you are stopped by SS on the way, you must let yourselves be disarmed without resistance.'

The Sturmführer salutes and jumps into the lorry, and the SA men leave again. No shot, no sign of resistance. All this time, Röhm is sitting unsuspectingly drinking his third cup of coffee. Only a single word from him, and the whole thing would have worked out differently...

Now the bus arrives which has been fetched by Schreck. Quickly, the SA leaders are collected from the laundry room and walk past Röhm under police guard. Röhm looks up from his coffee sadly and waves to them in a melancholy way... . At last Röhm too is led from the hotel. He walks past Hitler with his head bowed, completely apathetic. Now Hitler gives the order to leave. I sit at the wheel of the first car with Hitler beside me and our column, which in the meantime has grown to about twenty cars, starts moving...

After the war, the governor of the Stadelheim[64] prison recorded:

124

...Nobody was allowed to leave the prison that night either. Next morning (Sunday 1 July 1934) two SS men asked at the reception desk to be taken to Röhm. Zink, who was at the entrance, in view of the strict instructions he had been given, refused. It was about 9.30 a.m. When the two tried to force their way in, Zink alerted the prison governor and the green police [state police], who at once occupied the corridors and prevented any intrusion. The governor ascertained that neither of the SS men had proper authorisation. It therefore took hours of telephoning to check their papers; even the Reich Chancellery was rung up. When at last it became clear that they had an order from Hitler, the two murderers had to be taken to Röhm in the new building.

There they handed over a Browning to Röhm, who once again asked to speak to Hitler. They ordered him to shoot himself. If he did not comply, they would come back in ten minutes and kill him.... When the time was up, the two SS men re-entered the cell, and found Röhm standing with his chest bared. Immediately one of them from the door shot him in the throat, and Röhm collapsed on the floor. Since he was still alive, he was killed with a shot point-blank through the temple. The bullet not only penetrated his skull, but also the ceiling of the cell below... .

Six of the other SA leaders arrested at Wiessee, were executed by an SS firing squad at Stadelheim Prison. The rest of the executions were carried out in the Berlin barracks of Hitler's bodyguard. In Berlin the purge was under Göring's direction. The following description by a police official gives a sense of the atmosphere of the occasion:

125

...Suddenly there are loud shouts in the large room next door. It is Göring's study, where the executive committee is meeting. From time to time Gestapo messengers come rushing in bringing small white pieces of paper. Through the door one can see

---

[64]The prison in Munich.

Göring, Himmler, Heydrich and little Pilli Körner, Göring's State Secretary in the Minister-Presidency, putting their heads together. Of course it is impossible to hear what they are talking about. But things are happening devilish fast. Occasionally we hear an inarticulate sound like 'Off!' or 'Aha!' or 'Shoot!' or simply raucous laughter. In any case they don't seem in a bad mood.

Göring even exudes an air of well-fed comfort. He gives the impression of being in his element. He strides round his room. He struts to and fro, an unforgettable picture: with his flowing head of hair, his white tunic, his grey-blue military trousers, his white boots with their high flaps reaching up over the knees of this unwieldy pot-belly. A comparison springs to my mind: there goes Puss in Boots!...

But, as I said, things suddenly begin to get very noisy within. Police Major Jakobi rushes out of the room in great haste with his helmet on and his chinstrap under his red face. Göring's hoarse voice booms after him: 'Shoot them down...Fetch a whole company...Shoot them down...Shoot...Shoot at once...Just shoot them down...Shoot...!' One can't begin to describe the blatant bloodthirstiness, the savage fury, the hideous vindictiveness, and yet at the same time the terror, the craven terror shown in this scene. Everyone senses, Someone has escaped who must not be allowed to escape, someone whose escape will undo the whole day's work... .

The man thought to have got away was Gregor Strasser, Hitler's old colleague and rival. The rumour was untrue; Strasser was murdered all right. The purge was used by the Nazis to pay off a number of old scores. The former Bavarian State Commissioner, Gustav von Kahr, who had thwarted Hitler at the 1923 putsch, was murdered; so was General von Schleicher, who had tried to split the Nazi Party with the help of Strasser in 1932. Hitler also struck at his conservative and Catholic opponents. Papen himself was only placed under house arrest, but the author of his Marburg speech, the writer Edgar Jung, was murdered and so was his press officer, von Bose. The exact number of those murdered was probably not less than a hundred, and may have run into hundreds. It included Wilhelm Schmidt, the music critic of the Munich paper, *Münchener Neueste Nachrichten*, mistaken by the SS assassins for someone else.

The Army played a significant role in the affair. Not content to look on benevolently, it had actually provided arms and transport for the SS squads and had made preparations to counter any SA resistance. When it was all over, Blomberg, the Defence Minister, on 1 July publicly thanked Hitler in the name of the Army:

126

The Führer with soldierly decision and exemplary courage has himself attacked and crushed the traitors and murderers. The Army, as the bearer of arms of the entire people, far removed from the conflicts of domestic politics, will show its gratitude through devotion and loyalty. The good relationship towards the new SA demanded by the Führer will be gladly fostered by the Army in the consciousness that the ideals of both are held in common. The state of emergency has come to an end everywhere.

The President also sent his good wishes by telegram on 2 July with a similar telegram to Göring. He was no longer capable of making an independent assessment of the situation. That he was prepared to lend his prestige to the purge was of considerable help to Hitler who had the task or persuading public opinion that it had been essential for the security of the State:

127

I note from the reports I have received that through your decisive intervention and your courageous personal commitment you have nipped all the treasonable intrigues in the bud. You have saved the German nation from serious danger and for this I express to you my deeply felt gratitude and my sincere appreciation.

The Cabinet then retroactively legalised the purge:

128

At the meeting of the Reich Cabinet on Tuesday 3 July, the Reich Chancellor, Adolf Hitler, began by giving a detailed account of the origin and suppression of the high treason plot. The Reich Chancellor stressed that lightning action had been necessary, otherwise many thousands of people would have been in danger of being wiped out.

Defence Minister General von Blomberg thanked the Führer in the name of the Reich Cabinet and the army for his determined and courageous action, by which he had saved the German people from civil war. The Führer had shown greatness as a statesman and soldier. This had aroused in the hearts of the members of the Cabinet and of the whole German people a vow of service, devotion, and loyalty in this grave hour.

The Reich Cabinet then approved a law on measures for the self-defence of the State. Its single paragraph reads:
'The measures taken on 30 June and 1 and 2 July to suppress the acts of high treason are legal, being necessary for the self-defence of the State.'

Reich Minister of Justice Dr Gürtner commented that measures of self-defence taken before the imminent occurrence of a treasonable action should be considered not only legal but the duty of a statesman.

On 13 July 1934 Hitler justified his action in the Reichstag with a fictitious story of a plot:

129

...Without once informing me and at a moment when I had no thought of any such action, Chief of Staff Röhm entered into relations with General Schleicher through an utterly corrupt and dishonest go-between, a certain Herr von A.[65] It was General Schleicher who spelt out the secret aims of Chief of Staff Röhm. It was he who gave concrete form to the ideas of the latter and maintained that:

1. The present regime in Germany is not to be tolerated.
2. Above all, the Army and all national associations must be united in a single band.
3. The only man to be considered for such a position is Chief of Staff Röhm.
4. Herr von Papen must be removed and he himself would be ready to take the position of Vice-Chancellor; moreover, further important changes must be made in the Cabinet of the Reich.

As usual in such cases, there began then the search for the men to form the new Government, always with the understanding that I myself should, at least for the time being, be left in the position which I now hold.

The carrying out of these proposals of General von Schleicher was bound, as soon as Point 2 was reached, to come up against my unalterable opposition. Considering either the facts or his personal character, I could never have consented to a change in the Reich Ministry of War or to the appointment of Chief of Staff Röhm to that Ministry.

Firstly: consider the facts. For fourteen years I have stated consistently that the fighting organisations of the Party are political institutions and have nothing to do with the Army. On the facts of the case I should consider it a disavowal of my own convictions and of my fourteen years of political life if I were now to summon the leader of the SA to the command of the Army. In November 1923 I proposed as the head of the Army not the man who was then leader of my SA, Captain Göring, but an officer.

Secondly: consider the question of human character. On this matter I could never have concurred in General von Schleicher's proposal. When these plans became known to me my view of Chief of Staff Röhm's personal worth was already such that as a man of conscience and for the sake of the Army I could then under no circumstances even think of admitting him to that post: the supreme head of the Army is none other than the Field-Marshal and President of the Reich. As Chancellor I have given my oath into his keeping. For all of us his person is inviolate. The promise I gave him that I would preserve the Army as a non-political instrument of the Reich I hold as binding, both from my innermost conviction and also from my pledged word. Furthermore, considering my personal relations with the Defence Minister of the Reich, any such act would have been impossible. Not only I myself but all of us are happy to recognise in him a man of honour from the crown of his head to the soles of his feet. He reconciled the Army with those who were once revolutionaries and has linked it up with their Government today and he has done this from his own deepest convictions. In the most genuine loyalty he has made his own the principle for which I myself will stand to my last breath.

---

[65] Werner von Alvensleben, an associate of Schleicher's.

In the State there is only one bearer of arms—the Army; there is only one bearer of the political will—the National Socialist Party... .

In the meantime, Frick, the Reich Minister of the Interior, had seized his opportunity to eliminate the influence of the SA on the administration. This had been exercised officially through the special SA delegates (*Sonderbevollmächtigte*) appointed to supervise the various levels of administration under an order issued by Röhm on 12 May 1933. On 4 July 1934 Frick wrote to the new SA Chief of Staff, Viktor Lutze:

130

Some time ago, the previous Chief of Staff ordered the appointment of special SA delegates and representatives to the State Governments and their subordinate offices. This institution has not proved in the least beneficial. The delegates and representatives have in many cases claimed powers to which they were not entitled and have interfered with and impeded the orderly conduct of business by the State apparatus. I therefore request that you recall the special delegates and representatives at once.
The State Governments have received a copy of this letter.

Less than a week later, on 10 July, Lutze abolished the institution of SA delegates to the State administration.
However, this victory of the State authorities in their battle to retain their authority and independence was to prove only temporary. A far greater threat to their power had emerged out of the Röhm 'putsch'—the SS. On 20 July 1934 Hitler repaid his debt to the SS for their role in the affair by separating them from the now emasculated SA and granting them the status of an independent organisation. The SS were to provide the regime with a much more effective weapon for social control. Whereas the SA terror had been spontaneous, arbitrary, crude and disruptive, the SS were to make use of techniques which were far more coordinated, systematic and sophisticated; in the service of the regime they were to make terror a bureaucratic weapon. Furthermore, whereas the SA had embarked on a fruitless attempt to control the State administration (from a position outside the bureaucracy) through the SA delegates, the SS had from the start adopted a policy of infiltrating the bureaucracy and taking over segments of the State apparatus, beginning with the political police. This tactic was to prove itself infinitely more successful:

131

In view of highly meritorious service on the part of the SS, especially in connexion with the events of 30 June 1934, I elevate it to the status of an independent organisation within the NSDAP. The Reichsführer SS is therefore, like the Chief of Staff [of the SA], directly subordinate to the Supreme SS Führer. The Chief of Staff and the Reichsführer SS are both invested with the Party rank of Reichsleiter.

On 2 August 1934 President Hindenburg died. Immediately, the following law dated 1 August was promulgated. The Army and the Conservatives had repaid their debt to Hitler, who had saved them from the SA. Hitler had sacrificed the 'old fighters' to his major objective—internal mobilisation, to which political stability and economic recovery were essential. He was now officially Führer not only of the Party but also of the German people.

132

The Reich Government has enacted the following law which is hereby promulgated.
Section 1. The office of Reich President will be combined with that of Reich Chancellor. The existing authority of the Reich President will consequently be transferred to the Führer and Reich Chancellor, Adolf Hitler. He will select his deputy.
Section 2. This law is effective as of the time of the death of Reich President von Hindeburg.

The absolute control which Hitler now exercised over the State was reflected in the following oaths, introduced on 20 August. Significantly, they were taken to Hitler not as Head of the State, but as 'Führer of the German Reich and people', a totally new form of authority. The first stage in the 'seizure of power' was complete.

133

Article 1. The public officials and the soldiers of the armed forces must take an oath of loyalty on entering service.
Article 2.
1. The oath of loyalty of public officials will be:
   'I swear: I shall be loyal and obedient to Adolf Hitler, the Führer of the German Reich and people, respect the laws, and fulfil my official duties conscientiously, so help me God.'

2. The oath of loyalty of the soldiers of the armed forces will be:
'I swear by God this sacred oath: I will render unconditional obedience to Adolf Hitler, the Führer of the German nation and people, Supreme Commander of the Armed Forces, and will be ready as a brave soldier to risk my life at any time for this oath.'
Article 3. Officials already in service must swear the oath without delay according to Art. 2, number 1.

Hitler sent von Blomberg a message of thanks dated 20 August 1934:

134

Now, after the confirmation of the Law of 2 August by the German people, I wish to express my gratitude to you and through you to the Wehrmacht for your oath of loyalty to me as your leader and Commander-in-Chief. Just as the officers and men of the Wehrmacht pledge themselves to the new State in my person, so shall I always regard it as my highest duty to support the continued existence and inviolability of the armed forces in compliance with the testament of the late Field-Marshal [Hindenburg] and faithful to my own will to establish the Army firmly as the sole bearer of arms in the nation.

The attitude of the population to the Röhm affair varied. Some of the more educated people, particularly those with foreign sources of information, were horrified at what had happened. The propaganda of the Left in exile also made capital out of the crushing of the 'revolutionary' wing of the Nazi movement, though Nazi propaganda cleverly emphasised the involvement of 'reactionary elements' and made it appear as if it was these which had been crushed. The majority of people seem to have been relieved by what they saw as a timely lesson to the most undisciplined section of the Nazi movement. Hitherto they had comforted themselves with the belief that the Führer was not aware of the actions of these local Nazis and would not have approved if he had been. Now Hitler's measures over the Röhm affair seemed to confirm this judgement and they hoped that he would continue the purge through other Party organisations.

The following report of the Harburg-Wilhelmsburg Gestapo office of 5 July 1934 throws light on the attitude of the population to the purge:

135

In the month covered by this report the 30th of June naturally has pride of place. The measures proceeded smoothly in this area....Among the population at large, confidence in the Führer has been consolidated by his energetic action. There are, however, increasing requests for further energetic measures to be taken in the various Party organisations right down to the lowest levels, and in particular there are demands for liberation from 'the local Mussolinis'. If all the [Party] formations restricted themselves to the tasks delegated to them by the Führer instead of giving orders to the governmental authorities, the whole population could long ago have been filled with the spirit of National Socialism—in particular, with a sense of responsibility, cleanliness and discipline. It is essential that the Führer's announcement regarding the purging of the SA[66] should be acted upon by all Party organisations... .

One hard core SA man later reflected on his post-January 1933 experience of the events as follows:

136

That was not an SA any more. All those with money or a degree went into the SS and all the rest came into the SA on the basis of the motto: I must join otherwise...This dilution ws terrible. Ernst Röhm was stupid in thinking after 1933 that he now had a tremendous power base. The SA had swollen enormously and he relied on that—but it could not be effective...

We were only waiting for Röhm to carry on the revolution, the social revolution...We thought: *we* created that, *we* prepared the way, why shouldn't we carry on with it. We were strong enough in those days to influence the party. We simply laughed at the party members running around in their uniforms after 1933. The 'officials' or whatever they called themselves—we didn't take them seriously. The politicians, these party functionaries were not at all popular with us. Party politics were suspect. And they made such a big thing of themselves: 'We define the political objectives'. We couldn't take that. A twit running around in a brown uniform and he is to define our political objectives and we are to carry out *his* political will!

We were the *fighting troop*. And we didn't want anyone to take over from us. In May, six weeks before the 'Röhm putsch' Röhm was here in Hamburg—there was a big parade—he made a very clever speech: 'They shouldn't imagine they will escape the night of the long knives', he said.

After the disgusting events at Wiessee that was the end of it for me. And not only for me. It had become pointless. Earlier on we had the Strassers, in Berlin we had Stennes and at the end we put our faith in Röhm...

What I can't understand is that after the murders in Wiessee the SA let itself be stripped of power so easily. Simply fizzled out. But by then most of the SA had got jobs. The hunt for jobs was on: an SA man could becomes a gas man, a state employee. One got a job with the Welfare Office, another with the Job Centre. Many had been unemployed and now they had work...Most of them lost much of their revolutionary elan. The real revolutionaries drew the consequences and got out. Resigned to it...

---

[66] This announcement of 2 July 1934 consisted of twelve points laid down by Hitler for the reorganisation of the SA.

List of Sources

1. Ernst Deuerlein (ed.), *Der Aufstieg der NSDAP 1919–1933 in Augenzeugenberichten* (Düsseldorf 1968), p. 60.
2. Ernst Deuerlein, 'Hitlers Eintritt in die Politik und die Reichswehr' In *Vierteljahrshefte für Zeitgeschichte* 7 (1959), pp.203ff.
3. E. Deuerlein, *Aufstieg* pp.108–112.
4. *Ibid.* pp.100–1.
5. R.G. Phelps, 'Hitler als Parteiredner: Dokument Nr. 17'. In *Vierteljahrshefte für Zeitgeschichte* 11 (1963), p.325.
6. Kurt Ludecke, *I Knew Hitler* (London 1938), pp.699–702.
7. Georg Franz-Willing, *Die Hitlerbewegung. Bd. I: Der Ursprung 1919 bis 1922* (Hamburg and Berlin 1962), pp.110ff.
8. Deuerlein, *Aufstieg*, p.144.
9. Albrecht Tyrell (ed.), *Führer befiehl...Selbstzeugnisse aus der'Kampfzeit' der NSDAP. Dokumentation und Analyse* (Düsseldorf 1969), pp.33–4.
10. Werner Jochmann (ed.), *Nationalsozialismus und Revolution: Dokumente* (Frankfurt 1963), pp.88–9.
11. Deuerlein, *Aufstieg*, p.144.
12. Tyrell, *Führer befiehl*, p.58.
13. Deuerlein, *Aufstieg*, pp.145–6.
14. ibid., pp.164–6.
15. ibid., p.192.
16. ibid., p.192–3.
17. Ernst Deuerlein, *Der Hitler-Putsch: Bayerische Dokumente zum 8/9 November 1923* (Stuttgart 1962), p.496.
18. Deuerlein, *Aufstieg*, pp.193–5.
19. Deuerlein, *Der Hitler-Putsch*, p.497.
20. Deuerlein, *Aufstieg*, pp.195–6.
21. Deuerlein, *Der Hitler-Putsch*, pp.511–12.
22. Tyrell, *Führer befiehl*, pp.65ff.
23. Ludecke, *I Knew Hitler*, pp.217–18.
24. *Völkischer Beobachter*, 26.ii.1925.
25. ibid.
26. Tyrell, *Führer befiehl*, pp.281–3.

27. Jochmann, *Nationalsozialismus und Revolution* pp.207ff.
28. ibid., pp.212–13.
29. *Nationalsozialistische Briefe* 15.x.1925.
30. *The Early Goebbels Diaries: 1925–1926* (London 1962), pp.66–7.
31. 'Geschichte der Ortsgruppe Affinghausen/Diepholz', Niedersächsisches Hauptstaatsarchiv, Hanover, Hann.Des. 310 I A Nr. 60.
32. Albert Krebs, *Tendenzen und Gestalten der NSDAP: Erinnerungen an die Frühzeit der Partei* (Stuttgart 1959), pp.42–3.
33. Geschichte der Ortsgruppe Harlingerode/Bad Harzburg, Niedersächsisches Hauptstaatsarchiv, Hann. Des. 310 I A Nr.69.
34. Ludolf Haase, *Aufstand in Niedersachsen: Der Kampf der NSDAP 1921–1924* (mimeo 1942) pp.192–3.
35. Hoover Institution Microfilms. NSDAP Hauptarchiv Reel 6 Folder 17.
36. Martin Broszat, 'Die Anfänge der Berliner NSDAP 1926–7' in *Vierteljahrshefte für Zeitgeschichte* 8 (1960), pp.102–3.
37. ibid.
38. Jochmann, *Nationalsozialismus und Revolution*, pp.241–2.
39. Tyrell, *Führer befiehl*, pp.235–6.
40. ibid., pp.163–4.
41. Niedersächsisches Hauptstaatsarchiv Hanover Hann. Des. 310 I A Nr.17.
42. Niedersächsisches Staatsarchiv Oldenburg 136 Nr.2860.
43. *Das Programm der NSDAP und seine weltanschaulichen Grundgedanken von Dipl. Ing. Gottfried Feder* (Munich 1932), pp.4–6.
44. *Völkischer Beobachter*, 31.v.1928.
45. W. Michalka and Gottfried Niedhart, *Die Ungeliebte Republik. Dokumente zur Innen-und Aussenpolitik Weimars 1918–1933* (Munich 1980), p.262.
46. Otto Strasser, *Hitler and I* (London 1940), pp.114ff.
47. Michalka and Niedhart, *Die Ungeliebte Republik*, p.62.
48. Deuerlein, *Aufstieg*, pp.306–7.
49. Michalka and Niedhart, *Die ungeliebte Republik*, pp.283–5.
50. a) Niedersächsisches Hauptstaatsarchiv, Hann. Des. 310 I B Nr.1.
    b) ibid.
    c) ibid.
51. Jochmann, Nationalsozialismus und Revolution pp.404–5.
52. Bayerisches Hauptstaatsarchiv, Munich, MA 101238.
53. Niederšachsisches Hauptstaatsarchiv Hanover, Hann. Des. 310 I A, Nr.35.
54. ibid.
55. ibid.
56. Hans Christian Brandenburg, *Die Geschichte der HJ* (Cologne 1968), p.100.
57. Niedersächsisches Staatsarchiv, Oldenburg 131 Nr.1207.
58. Bayerisches Staatsarchiv (Neuburg a.d. Donau), Bezirksamt Nördlingen, 1315.
59. Jochmann, *Nationalsozialismus und Revolution*, p.405.
60. E. Matthias and R. Morsey, (eds.), *Das Ende der Parteien 1933* (Düsseldorf 1960), p.782.
61. *Partei-Statistik 1 January 1935*. Herausgeber: Der Reichsorganisationsleiter der NSDAP (Munich 1935) Bd. I. p.162.
62. Ibid., p.70.
63. Nuremberg Document (ND) 2512-PS.
64. Hans-Adolf Jacobsen and Werner Jochmann (eds), *Ausgewählte Dokumente zur Geschichte des Nationalsozialismus 1933–1945* (Bielefeld 1961) Bd.I.
65. *Documents on British Foreign Policy, 1919–1939*, Second Series, vol.II, pp.296–8.
66. N.H. Baynes (ed.), *The Speeches of Adolf Hitler 1922–1939* (Oxford 1942), Vol.I, pp.826–9.

67. Deuerlein, *Aufstieg*, pp.353–4.
68. Gordon A. Craig, 'Briefe Schleichers an Groener', *Die Welt als Geschichte* II (1951), pp.130ff.
69. R.G. Phelps, 'Aus den Groener Dokumenten', *Deutsche Rundschau* 76 (1950), pp.1019ff.
70. R.G. Phelps, 'Aus den Groener Dokumenten', *Deutsche Rundschau* 77 (1951), pp.23ff.
71. ibid.
72. Joseph Goebbels, *My Part in Germany's Fight* (London 1938), pp.77ff
73. Niedersächsisches Hauptstaatsarchiv, Hanover, Hann.Des.310 I A Nr.37.
74. Walther Hubatsch, *Hindenburg und der Staat* (Göttingen 1966), p.388.
75. Goebbels, *My Part*, p.122. (modified translation).
76. Niedersächsisches Hauptstaatsarchiv, Hanover Hann.Des.310 I B Nr.15.
77. National Archives, T-81, roll 1, frames 11427–11432.
78. Niedersächsisches Hauptstaatsarchiv, Hanover, Hann.Des.310 I A Nr.37.
79. Jochmann, *Nationalsozialismus und Revolution*, pp.407ff.
80. Hinrich Lohse, 'Der Fall Strasser', Forschungsstelle für die Geschichte des Nationalsozialismus in Hamburg.
81. ibid.
82. Deuerlein, *Aufstieg*, pp.411–14.
83. ND 3309-PS.
84. *The Ribbentrop Memoirs* (London 1954) pp.23–26.
85. *Documents on German Foreign Policy (DGFP)*, series C, vol.I, pp.5–8 (modified translation).
86. Jochmann, *Nationalsozialismus und Revolution*, p.421.
87. Jacobsen and Jochmann, *Ausgewählte Dokumente*, Bd II.
88. Jochmann, *Nationalsozialismus und Revolution*, pp.424ff.
89. ND 203-D.
90. *The Times* 21.ii.1933.
91. Hagen Schulze, ed., *Anpassung oder Widerstand? Aus den Akten des Parteivorstandes der deutschen Sozialdemokratie 1932/33* (Bonn 1975) pp.161–65.
92. Matthias and Morsey, *Das Ende der Parteien*, pp.234.
93. ibid., p.239.
94. Rudolf Diels, *Lucifer ante portas* (Stuttgart 1950), pp.142–4.
95. Reichsgesetzblatt (RGBL), Jg.1933, Teil I, Nr.17, p.83.
96. Jochmann, *Nationalsozialismus und Revolution*, p.427.
97. Henning Timpke ed. *Dokumente zur Gleichschaltung des Landes Hamburg* (Frankfurt 1964), pp.56–61.
98. Diels, *Lucifer ante portas*, p.200.
99. *Braunschweig unter dem Hakenkreuz* (Zurich 1933).
100. Walther Hofer, *Der Nationalsozialismus: Dokumente 1933–1945* (Frankfurt 1957), p.55.
101. Diels, *Lucifer ante portas*, pp.192–4, 199.
102. Erich Ebermayer, *Denn heute gehört uns Deutschland...Persönliches und politisches Von der Machtergreifung bis zum 31. December 1935* (Hamburg–Vienna 1959) p.47.
103. DGFP, Series C, Vol.I, pp.113–16.
104. Max Domarus, *Hitler: Reden und Proklamationen, 1932–1945*, Bd.I (Würzburg 1962), pp.232–3.
105. Matthias and Morsey, *Das Ende der Parteien 1933*, pp.431–2.
106. Hans Müller, *Katholische Kirche und Nationalsozialismus* (Munich 1963), pp.73–4.
107. Wilhelm Hoegner, *Der Schwierige Aussenseiter* (Munich 1963), pp. 92–3.
108. RGBl., Jg.1933, Teil I Nr.25, p.141.
109. Matthias and Morsey, *Das Ende der Parteien 1933*, p.643.
110. Goebbels, *My Part in Germany's Fight*, p.248.

111. Müller, *Katholische Kirche*, p.86.
112. Matthias and Morsey, *Das Ende der Parteien*, pp.443–4, 451–2.
113. DGFP, series C, vol.I, pp.652–3.
114. RGBl., Jg.1933, Teil I, Nr.81, p.479.
115. Jacobsen and Jochmann, *Ausgewählte Dokumente*, Bd.II.
116. Quoted in Peter Diehl-Thiele, *Partei und Staat im Dritten Reich* (Munich 1969), p.95.
117. Jacobsen and Jochmann, *Ausgewählte Dokumente*, Bd.II.
118. Timpke, *Dokumente zur Gleichschaltung des Landes Hamburg*, pp.217–18.
119. ND 951–D.
120. Heinrich Bennecke, *Hitler und die SA* (Munich 1962), p.82.
121. Jacobsen and Jochmann, *Ausgewählte Dokumente*, Bd.II.
122. Bennecke, *Hitler und die SA*, p.85.
123. *Ursachen und Folgen: Vom deutschen Zusammenbruch 1918 und 1945 bis zur staatlichen Neuordnung Deutschlands in der Gegenwart*, ed. H. Michaelis et al. (Berlin, undated), Bd. X, pp.168–72.
124. E. von Aretin, *Krone und Ketten: Erinnerungen eines bayerischen Edelmannes*, eds. Karl Buchheim and Karl Otmar von Aretin (Munich 1955), pp.365–6.
125. H.B. Gisevius, *Bis zum bittern Ende* (Zurich 1954), pp.142ff.
126. *Deutsche Allgemeine Zeitung*, Nr.302, 2.vii.34.
127. *Völkischer Beobachter* 3.vii.1934.
128. *Völkischer Beobachter* 5.vii.1934.
129. Baynes, *The Speeches of Adolf Hitler* vol.I, pp.311–13.
130. Staatsarchiv Bremen, N7 ia, No.1149.
131. *Völkischer Beobachter*, 26.vii.1934.
132. RGBl., Jg.1934, Teil I Nr.89, p.747.
133. RGBl., Jg.1934, Teil I Nr.98.
134. *Völkischer Beobachter*, 21.viii.1934.
135. Niedersächsisches Hauptstaatsarchiv, Hanover, Hann.Des., Lüneburg III XXV, Nr.5.
136. *Terror und Hoffnung in Deutschland 1933–1945. Leben im Faschismus*, Herausgegeben von Johannes Beck et.al. (Hamburg 1980), pp.63–65.

A Selective Bibliography

T. Abel, *Why Hitler Came into Power*, 2nd edition (Cambridge, Mass. 1986).

D. Abraham, *The Collapse of the Weimar Republic. Political Economy and Crisis*, 2nd rev. edition (New York 1986).

W.S. Allen, *The Nazi Seizure of Power: the Experience of a Single German Town 1922–1945*, 2nd rev. edition (London 1984).

P. Aycoberry, *The Nazi Question. An Essay on the Interpretation of National Socialism* (New York 1981).

P. Baldwin, 'Social Interpretations of Nazism: Renewing a Tradition', *Journal of Contemporary History* 1990, vol. 25, pp. 5–37.

R. Bessel, *Political Violence and the Rise of Nazism. The Stormtroopers in Eastern Germany 1925–1934* (London 1984).

R. Bessel, *Germany after the First World War* (Oxford 1995).

R. Bessel & E.J. Feuchtwanger, *Social Change and Political Development in Weimar Germany* (London 1981).

K. Borchardt, *Perspectives on Modern German Economic History and Policy* (Cambridge 1991).

K.D. Bracher, *The German Dictatorship: the Origins, Structure and Effects of National Socialism* (London 1971).

M. Broszat, *The Hitler State* (London 1981).

M. Broszat, *Hitler and the Collapse of Weimar Germany* (Leamington 1987).

A. Bullock, *Hitler. A Study in Tyranny* (London 1962).

J. Caplan, 'The Rise of National Socialism in Germany' in G. Martel *Modern Germany Reconsidered* (London 1991).

W. Carr, *Hitler. A Study in Personality and Politics* (London 1978).

F.L. Carsten, *The Reichswehr and German Politics* (Oxford 1966).

T. Childers, *The Nazi Voter. The Social Foundations of Fascism in Germany* (Chapel Hill 1983).

T. Childers, ed., *The Formation of the Nazi Constituency* (Beckenham 1986).

T. Childers, 'The Social Language of Politics in Germany: The Sociology of Political Discourse in Weimar Germany', *American History Review* 1990, 95.2.

J.M. Diehl, *Parliamentary Politics in Weimar Germany* (Bloomington, Ind. 1977).

G. Eley, *The Reshaping of the German Right* (New Haven 1980).

T. Eschenburg, ed., *The Road to Dictatorship 1918–1933* (London 1974).

R.J. Evans and R. Geary, eds, *German Unemployed 1918–36* (Beckenham 1986).

J. Fest, *Hitler* (London 1974).

C. Fischer, *Stormtroopers: A Social Economic and Ideological Analysis 1929–35* (London 1983).

C. Fischer, *The Rise of the Nazis* (London 1995).
P. Fritzsche, *Rehearsals for Fascism: Populism and Political Mobilization in Weimar Germany* (Oxford 1990).
D. Gessner, 'Agrarian Protectionism in the Weimar Republic', *Journal of Contemporary History* 1977 12.4.
J. Goebbels, *The Early Goebbels Diaries* ed. H. Heiber (London 1962).
J.H. Grill, *The Nazi Movement in Baden 1920–1945* (Chapel Hill 1983).
R.H. Hamilton, *Who Voted Nazi?* (Princeton 1982).
R. Heberle, *From Democracy to Nazism. A Regional Case Study on Political Parties in Germany* (New York 1970).
A. Hitler, *Mein Kampf* (London 1969).
H. Holborn, ed., *From Republic to Reich* (New York 1972).
E. Jaeckel, *Hitler's Weltanschauung* (Middletown, Conn. 1972).
E. Jaeckel, *Hitler in History* (London 1984).
H. James, *The German Slump. Politics and Economics 1924–36* (Oxford 1986).
L.E. Jones, 'The Dying Middle. Weimar Germany and the Fragmentation of Bourgeois Politics', *Central European History* 1972 5.
L.E. Jones, *German Liberalism and the Dissolution of the Weimar Party System 1918–1933* (Chapel Hill 1988).
M. Kater, *The Nazi Party. A Social Profile of Members and Leaders 1919–1945* (Oxford 1983).
I. Kershaw, ed., *Weimar: Why did German Democracy Fail?* (London 1990).
R. Koshar, *Social Life, Local Politics and Nazism* (Chapel Hill 1986).
E. Kolb, *The Weimar Republic* (London 1988).
A. Krebs, *The Infancy of Nazism: The Memoirs of ex-Gauleiter Albert Krebs 1923–1933* ed. W.S. Allen (London 1978).
H. Lebovics, *Social Conservatism and the Middle Classes in Germany 1914–1933* (Princeton 1969).
M.R. Lepsius, 'From Fragmented Party Democracy to Government by Emergency Decree and National Socialist Takeover' in J.J. Linz and A. Stephan, eds, *The Breakdown of Democratic Regimes. Europe* (Baltimore 1980).
P.H. Merkl, *Political Violence Under the Swastika* (Princeton 1975).
H. Mommsen, 'National Socialism: Continuity and Change' in *Fascism. A Reader's Guide* ed. W. Laqueur (London 1976).
D. Mühlberger, *Hitler's Followers* (London 1991).
A.J. Nicholls, *Weimar and the Rise of Hitler* (London 1980).
A.J. Nicholls & E. Matthias, eds, *German Democracy and the Triumph of Hitler* (London 1971).
J. Noakes, *The Nazi Party in Lower Saxony 1921–1933* (Oxford 1971).
E. Nolte, *Three Faces of Fascism* (New York 1965).
J. Nyomarkay, *Charisma and Factionalism in the Nazi Party* (Minneapolis 1967).
D. Orlow, *A History of the Nazi Party Vol. 1 1918–1933* (Newton Abbot 1969).
D. Petzina, 'Germany and the Great Depression', *Journal of Contemporary History* 1969.
D.J.K. Peukert, *The Weimar Republic* (London 1991).
G. Pridham, *Hitler's Rise to Power. The Nazi Party in Bavaria 1925–1933* (London 1973).
B. Smith, *Adolf Hitler. His Family, Childhood and Youth* (Stanford 1967).
P. Stachura, ed., *The Nazi Machtergreifung* (London 1983).
P. Stachura, ed., *Unemployment and the Great Depression in Weimar Germany* (London 1986).
W. Struve, *Elites against Democracy* (Princeton 1973).
K. Theweleit, *Male Fantasies* (Minneapolis 1987).
T.A. Tilton, *Nazism, Neo-Nazism and the Peasantry* (Bloomington, Ind. 1975).
H.A. Turner, *Germany Big Business and the Rise of Hitler* (Oxford 1985).
R. Waite, *Vanguard of Nazism. The Free Corps Movement in Post-War Germany 1919–1923* (Cambridge, Mass. 1952).

B. Weisbrod, 'Economic Power and Political Stability Reconsidered', *Social History* 1979.

J. Wheeler-Bennett, *Nemesis of Power. The German Army in Politics 1918–1945* (London 1967).

H.A. Winkler, 'The Social Conditions of Hitler's Rise to Power', *Journal of Contemporary History* 1976.

The despatches of the British Ambassador in Berlin, Sir Horace Rumbold, provide an illuminating account of developments in Germany in 1930–33. Cf. *Documents on British Foreign Policy 1919–1939* Second Series Vols II–IV.